EUROPE DIDN'T WORK

Why We Left and How to Get the Best from Brexit

LARRY ELLIOTT AND DAN ATKINSON

YALE UNIVERSITY PRESS
NEW HAVEN AND LONDON

Page 29, 'Rat Trap', written by Bob Geldof, lyrics reproduced by kind permission of Mute Song Limited. Page 115, Dennis O'Driscoll, 'The Celtic Tiger', *Weather Permitting*, Carcanet Press Ltd, 1999, is used with permission.

For information about this and other Yale University Press publications, please contact:
U.S. Office: sales.press@yale.edu   yalebooks.com
Europe Office: sales@yaleup.co.uk   yalebooks.co.uk

Typeset in Minion Pro by IDSUK (DataConnection) Ltd
Printed in Great Britain by Hobbs the Printers, Totton, Hampshire

Library of Congress Control Number: 2017948022

ISBN 978-0-300-22879-3

A catalogue record for this book is available from the British Library.

10 9 8 7 6 5 4 3 2 1

CONTENTS

PREFACE

Actors have parts they secretly want to play. Rock musicians have records that for some reason remain unmade. Authors have ideas that gnaw away at them but take years to find their way onto the page. Our equivalent is this book.

It is the fifth we have jointly written since 1998, but it is the one we have always wanted to write since we first worked together as reporters at the Press Association in 1986. It was a different world back then: filing copy on typewriters rather than computers (the latter still, then, a few months in the future); financial news from the rest of the world arriving by means of wire machines; reporters needing to find a public telephone box to speak to the news desk.

Europe, too, looked different three decades ago. Berlin was still a divided city in a disunited Germany; attempts to create a single European market were just underway; the notion of a single currency was in its infancy. There were twelve members of the European Community against the twenty-eight members of today's European Union.

On the surface, the issue of 'Europe' had been off the boil in the UK for some time. The country had voted eleven years earlier to remain a member and had declined the offer of withdrawal (this time without a referendum) from Michael Foot's Labour Party in the

1983 election. The big issue on the continent in the first half of the 1980s had been defence, specifically nuclear confrontation with the Soviet bloc, a matter in which the European Community had no real standing.

But beneath the surface, British attitudes towards Europe were in a state of flux. Under Margaret Thatcher, the Conservative Party, which had traditionally been the more pro-European of the UK's two main parties, was becoming sceptical. The Labour Party, until then more cautious about the benefits of closer ties with the European Economic Community, was moving in the other direction.

In reality, both parties were split over Europe. The Conservatives had enthusiasts such as Michael Heseltine and Kenneth Clarke. Nigel Lawson, who has been prominent in the recent campaign for Britain to leave the European Union, was then, as chancellor of the exchequer, prepared to peg the value of the pound to that of the West German mark in the hope that it would help to control inflation.

The Labour leader Neil Kinnock was warming to the idea of Europe, as were a number of prominent trade union general secretaries. But many on the left remained suspicious, either because of what they saw as an inbuilt bias towards deflationary economic policies, or because they thought creating a single European economic space complete with its own money and its own central bank offered more to the owners of multinational corporations than to the people who worked for them.

Then, as now, we were in the second camp. We were with the Bryan Goulds, the Peter Shores, the Tony Benns and the Jeremy Corbyns, who doubted whether the claims made for ever closer integration were all they cracked up to be. We were working together on the *Guardian* by the time Britain formally tied itself to the German mark in 1990 through the Exchange Rate Mechanism (ERM), and were pretty much alone in thinking it a rotten idea. Similarly, when the rest of the paper's staff saw departure from the ERM as a day of disaster, we saw Black Wednesday as a moment of liberation.

It was curious to us that, in Britain, most of the running against the Maastricht Treaty that paved the way for the single currency was made by Conservative Eurosceptics.

When we came to write our first book together in 1998, the birth of the single currency was little more than a year away. In retrospect, it might have been better had we written *The Euro Won't Work* rather than *The Age of Insecurity*, in which we devoted a chapter of the book to the problems we foresaw for monetary union.

Still, better late than never. There are those on the left who feel uneasy about voicing their concerns about the euro, in the main because of the political company they have to keep. This book explains why those misgivings are unnecessary. The single currency was not, is not, and never will be a progressive project.

Over the following ten chapters, we trace the origins of monetary union to the gold standard, track its development during the design stage in the late 1980s and 1990s, and then compare the euro in theory against the euro in practice. Some commentators have been surprised by the failure of the single currency to live up to its advanced billing. We are not. We always thought it would end this way.

For this paperback edition, we have written an epilogue that encompasses the seismic events that have occurred since the first edition went to press in May 2016. The most obvious is the 23 June vote in Britain to leave the EU. Then there was the defeat of the Italian government in a referendum later in the year, and tightly fought electoral contests in the Netherlands, France and parts of Germany.

In what is a fast-moving political and economic scene in Europe, it is not easy to stay abreast of history as it unfolds, but we hope we have covered the major developments to date.

We could begin our story in any one of the nineteen countries that currently use the single currency but have chosen not to do so. Our tale starts not in Europe at all, but in Atlanta, Georgia.

Larry Elliott and Dan Atkinson
London, August 2017

CHAPTER 1

THE REAL THING

A tale of two product launches

All wonder is the effect of novelty on ignorance.

Samuel Johnson

23 April 1985 was a momentous day in the life of the Coca-Cola Company. It had been ninety-nine years since the first glass of Coke was poured in a drugstore in Atlanta, Georgia, and they had been good ones for a company that in its first year sold an average of just nine drinks a day at five cents each. Sixty years later, Coca-Cola was the world leader in soft drinks. For almost two decades after the former Confederate colonel John Pemberton first marketed the drink, Coke was laced with a kick: cocaine extracted from coca leaves. In 1903 the hard drug was removed from the formula, but over the course of the first half of the twentieth century Americans became more and more addicted to Coke and it established itself as the market leader – so much so that by the end of the Second World War it had cornered three-fifths of the US market.

In its way, Coke's rise to its zenith mirrored that of the US in the late nineteenth and early twentieth centuries, when it first challenged and then comfortably overtook Great Britain to become the world's biggest and richest economy. By the early 1980s, there was a darker mood. The 1970s had been a chastening decade. It had begun with Washington's admission that the dollar was no longer strong enough to act as the anchor for the post-war fixed exchange-rate system; it had seen defeat in Vietnam, and the resignation of Richard Nixon; and it had ended with the humiliation of US embassy staff being imprisoned by revolutionary guards in Tehran. By the close of the decade, the US was suffering from high inflation and its economic supremacy was under threat from Japan and West Germany.

While Paul Volcker, the chairman of the Federal Reserve Board appointed by Jimmy Carter, was ratcheting up interest rates to expunge inflation from the US economy, the executives running the Coca-Cola Company decided it was time to confront reality. Coke's market share had declined to 24 per cent and its lead over its main rival in the soft drinks market, PepsiCo, had been declining for more than a decade. Under chief executive Roberto Goizueta, Coke planned to see off the competition from Pepsi by changing the secret century-old formula to something a bit sweeter. There was no expense spared for the development of the new drink, code-named Project Kansas, and it went down well in blind tastings and focus groups. By the spring of 1985, 200,000 people had sampled the new drink, and, judging by the response, the Coca-Cola board members assumed they had a winner on their hands.

They were wrong. It took just seventy-nine days before Coca-Cola caved in to pressure from customers and brought back the old drink. Coke's rapid volte-face was good news for Ford, because ever since the late 1950s when it had produced the short-lived Ford Edsel, the Michigan-based car company had been saddled with the reputation of being responsible for the biggest marketing disaster of all time. In 1985, it handed that badge of dishonour over to the Coca-Cola Company.

Yet, the speed with which Coca-Cola acted meant that a marketing disaster did not become a corporate disaster. The company didn't presume to say that consumers were wrong, even though some executives thought that they were. It didn't pretend that New Coke had been a cunning marketing ploy governed by Oscar Wilde's dictum that the only thing worse than being talked about is not being talked about. It didn't say that, given time, the new drink would be a success. It didn't plough on simply because it had invested heavily in Project Kansas and couldn't stand the loss of face. Instead, it recognized that there was only one option: to go back to the traditional formula. On 11 July 1985, Coke Classic was back on the shelves.

The long wait is over

16 December 1995 was a big day for the European Union. As the winter solstice neared, the name for the new single currency that would be created as a result of monetary union was announced. It was to be called the euro, and, just as with New Coke, there was a delay of several years in bringing the product to market. The euro was first used as an accounting currency on 1 January 1999, but consumers in the eleven countries that adopted the new currency from its inception had to wait three more years before they could handle and use the new notes and coins.

The single currency had a wider geopolitical purpose: it was the weapon with which European countries intended to do battle for global economic hegemony. Europe had America squarely in its sights.

When the Second World War ended, the US accounted for half of global gross domestic product and its economic dominance was absolute. America was rich enough to finance the Marshall Plan, a four-year programme during which Congress allocated an average of 2 per cent of US GDP annually to the reconstruction of Western Europe. The motivation was threefold: a humanitarian desire to rescue economies threatened by malnutrition and unemployment; a political desire to prevent countries turning to communism; and a commercial incentive to ensure that there were thriving markets to which American companies, such as Coca-Cola, could export.

It was shrewd of the Truman administration to bet on Europe's potential for recovery. Once the Second World War was over, there was scope for a period of rapid growth; indeed, it was occurring even before the Treaty of Rome, creating the Common Market, was signed in 1957. As the economist Barry Eichengreen has noted, economic blunders and political instability meant Europe had failed to exploit the new products and new methods of industrial organization that had been developed in the US in the interwar period, and could now do so provided that things did not go wrong as they had in the 1920s and 1930s: 'That they did not go wrong now reflected the fact that Europe possessed a set of institutions singularly well suited to the task at hand. Catch-up was facilitated by solidaristic trade unions, cohesive employers associations, and growth-minded governments working together to mobilize savings, finance investment, and stabilize wages at levels consistent with full employment.'[1]

As in Japan, post-war reconstruction was a vital factor in generating strong growth in Europe, pre-dating the Common Market. Over the next five decades, the gap between the US and Western Europe narrowed, although it did not close completely, and in the period after 1980 progress was much slower than in the 1950s and 1960s. There were many claims made for monetary union during its gestation period between the demolition of the Berlin Wall in late 1989 and the launch of the euro in virtual form a little less than a decade later – such as, that monetary union would accelerate Europe's growth rate and that it would raise living standards. But the intention also was that the euro would complete the catch-up process. Monetary union would make the European single market work more efficiently and enable a challenge to be mounted to the United States. To be sure, it was hoped that millions of jobs would be created, but it was also fondly believed that the single currency would safeguard Europe's social model and see off the threat of Anglo-Saxon capitalism. In the 1990s, there were plenty of paeans to Rhenish capitalism which, it was said, ensured that capital went towards inventing new products rather than wasteful speculation. As it happened, this analysis was wrong: US universities and Silicon Valley proved to be the driving force behind the new wave of digital technologies appearing in the last decade of the twentieth century.

It took some time, however, for Europe to realize that it did not have a Bill Gates, Steve Jobs or Larry Page, and in the mid-1990s, the mood was still bullish. There was talk of a new model of managed stakeholder capitalism that would be the counterpoint to a winner-takes-all US model. The euro, it was said, would raise investment levels by making capital flows across borders friction-less; it would complete the construction of the single market; it would stimulate innovation; and, last but certainly not least, it would bind a reunified Germany into Europe, just as the first tenta-tive steps towards European integration adumbrated by Robert Schuman and Jean Monnet in 1950 had ensured that Germany's economic strength would be harnessed for peaceful ends.

Here is one of the encomiums to the new currency, penned in 1997 as speculation grew about whether Britain under Tony Blair's newly elected Labour government would be one of the founder members of the euro:

> In an era of sweeping globalization, European monetary union will provide an essential foundation for stable and sustainable growth that generates jobs. A single European currency will weaken the power of those who thrive on monetary chaos and financial speculation. It can also help ensure that the over-weaning [sic] power of the global market place is better balanced and constrained by democratically decided economic and social priorities.[2]

Even the most cursory rereading of this paragraph shows that none of these claims came to fruition. Growth has been slower, not faster; unemployment has been higher, not lower; financial speculation has at times threatened to blow the euro apart; democratically elected governments have been subject to diktats forcing them to impose austerity measures that their voters have rejected. Indeed, the prediction would be almost comical in its wrong-headedness, were it not for the fact that millions of people have suffered in Europe as a result.

And continue to suffer, since the failings of the euro continue to be excused by its apologists, just as the brutality and inefficiency of the Soviet Union were excused by its supporters, even when it had become apparent that the idealism that generated the Russian Revolution of 1917 had been corrupted. It took five decades for the pooling of coal and steel resources under the Schuman Plan to become the pooling of currencies under European economic and monetary union, and another ten years before it became obvious that the only way that the euro could be considered a success was that it was still there. As far as meeting its original prospectus was concerned, it was a complete flop. Had the euro been launched by one of Europe's big firms, by BMW for example, it would have bankrupted the company.

Investment rates have fallen, not risen. The gap between Europe and the US has widened, not narrowed. Germany has felt less and less constrained by post-war guilt and has shown a willingness to use the political leverage provided by its economic strength. Far from being killed off, the Anglo-Saxon model is thriving, in Europe as much as in the US. It is the European social model that appears to be on its last legs, and the failure to offer voters rudimentary economic security – a job, a living wage, a pension providing dignity in old age – has had predictable consequences. Right-wing political extremism, supposed to have been banished by the move towards ever closer union, is stronger than at any time since 1945.

New dawn or false dawn?

The euro was particularly admired by those on the centre-left, who bought heavily into what they fondly assumed would be the advent of a kinder, gentler capitalism in which the power of multinational corporations would be matched by the transnational organization of labour that would recreate the shared prosperity of the post-war Golden Age. Tony Judt took it as read that the American century was over and that the global centre of gravity was shifting eastwards across the Atlantic from the New World, celebrating 'Europe's emergence in the dawn of the twenty-first century as a paragon of the international virtues: a community of values and a system of interstate relations held up by Europeans and non-Europeans alike as an exemplar for all to emulate'.[3] Mark Leonard riffed on the John

Lennon song: 'Imagine a world of peace, prosperity and democracy ... What I am asking you to imagine is the "New European Century".'[4] These two tributes to this imagined workers' paradise were penned in 2005, by which time the problems of the euro were already evident. A decade later, in light of what actually happened, it all seemed a bit naïve.

We were very much in the minority when we sketched out a left-wing critique of the euro in our first book together, published the year before the single currency came into being. Our view was the opposite of Judt's and Leonard's: we predicted that monetary union would prove to be the economics of the madhouse in which all the adjustment costs of adverse economic shocks would be borne by the weak in the form of wage restraint and public spending cuts.[5] Our view was shaped, partly, by our belief that the euro was flawed in concept; partly because we were suspicious of handing control of monetary policy to unelected and unaccountable technocrats; and partly because politics was moving in a new direction.

Even in the late 1990s, it was evident that the end of the Cold War, the reunification of Germany and the spread of the market economy to parts of the global economy where it had previously been out of bounds had put the mixed-economy model under threat. The existence until 1989 of the Soviet bloc had acted as a constraint on policymakers in Europe, even those of a free-market bent. The fear that disaffected working-class voters might turn to communism limited the attacks on real wages and welfare states.

This was no longer a risk after the Berlin Wall came down, with the result that parties of the centre-left, such as Bill Clinton's Democrats and Blair's Labour Party, were bolder in their 'reforms' of welfare than Margaret Thatcher and Ronald Reagan had been in the 1980s. We expected the single currency to accelerate this process, and predicted that it would be working people who would suffer from the euro's failure. Sadly, we have not been proved wrong. When Angela Merkel notes that Europe comprises 7 per cent of the world's population, 25 per cent of its output and 50 per cent of its welfare spending, she comes to bury the European social model, not to praise it.

Gloating is not the point here – although those of us who warned from the start that the euro would end badly could be forgiven a little smugness. Nor is failure the issue, since the story of human progress has been the story of trial and error. Many of the ideas that were cooked up in the garages of Silicon Valley were duds, but a few were not. As the economist Paul Ormerod noted in the title of his book, most things fail.[6] It isn't necessarily a problem, because lessons are learned from such failures; progress is made through a process of trial and error in which, in a Darwinian sense, good ideas survive and bad ideas fall by the wayside. This has been the case ever since the first stirrings of modern capitalism emerged from Reformation England.

The early Anglo-Saxon variant of capitalism was built on two distinct traditions: empiricism and dissent. It was a bottom-up process, sceptical of centralized authority, and based on the principle of experimenting until something worked. New Coke is an example of this way of thinking: the new formula seemed like a good solution to a particular problem – namely, that Pepsi tasted sweeter – but was rejected by the only people that mattered: the customers. As a result, Coke acknowledged the failure and went back to a tried-and-tested formula.

Lessons were also learned when companies deviated from this principle. Steven Bach's *Final Cut*, one of the best books about Hollywood, is an account of how United Artists was bankrupted by its decision to allow Michael Cimino, director of the film *Heaven's Gate*, to spend nearly five times his budget.[7] UA adopted the opposite approach to Coke: rather than cutting its losses, the film company indulged Cimino's ego, allowing him to continue wasting money while the film fell further and further behind schedule. UA wanted Diane Keaton or Jane Fonda to play the female lead; instead they got the French actor Isabelle Huppert, who could barely speak English. The studio thought they were getting a box office smash and an Oscar contender. What they got was critical derision and the flop of all time. The movie moguls in their Beverley Hills mansions took notice. For a while, there was a marked shortage of self-indulgent five-hour Westerns with the leading parts played by

Gallic relative unknowns. Cimino, courted by UA after the critical success of *The Deer Hunter*, was never able to resuscitate his career. What has turned the euro from a failure into a social and economic tragedy has been that, faced with the choice between cutting their losses like Coca-Cola or ploughing on regardless like United Artists, those in charge of running the single currency have thrown their weight behind *Heaven's Gate*.

There is a reason for this. Europe's industrial revolution came later than England's and, particularly in France, developed in accordance with two different traditions: that of the Catholic Church and the Enlightenment. Both lent themselves to a top-down centralized approach and the drawing up of grand designs for human happiness. The French model has dominated the creation and development of European institutions and policy-making ever since the 1950s. In this sense, Europe's response to the US's early lead in information technology is instructive: it held a summit in Lisbon and announced a ten-year plan. If voters objected to it, then the answer was to re-educate the people, not to change the plan. The Soviet Union is one example of Enlightenment thinking gone wrong; the euro is another. In both cases there was a refusal to admit that the concept was flawed even when all the available evidence pointed to the contrary. Almost up until the point when it collapsed, the assumption was that the Soviet Union would continue to exist, although perhaps in a reformed state. The same blindness applies to the euro, which is similarly perceived by its creators to be just a couple of tweaks away from perfection.

Thus, there has been the 'socialism hasn't really been tried' line of argument trotted out by those who say that monetary union will not really work until it is buttressed by full political union. There has been the 'workers are suffering from false consciousness' argument. This plays down growing hostility to the harsh disciplines of the single currency by stating that voters don't appreciate what is in their own best interests.

Then there has been the 'it will all work out well in the end' argument, a thesis put forward by Kathleen McNamara, who said that all the talk about whether the euro was good economics was immaterial; all that really mattered was that there was sufficient political will, as there had been in the US, to create a single currency:

> European leaders weren't stupid or self indulgent when they decided to move ahead with the euro, without fiscal union or strong Europe-level democracy. They just cared more about politics and international security than economics. They wanted to build a Europe that had transcended the divisions of the Cold War, and bind together Germany, which was reunited and much more powerful, with the rest of Europe.[8]

McNamara's argument is questionable on a number of levels. It ignores the fact that monetary union in the US was a gradual process that began with Alexander Hamilton laying the foundations of fiscal union in the 1790s and culminated more than a century later with the creation of the Federal Reserve Board in 1913. It was an organic process: there were many competing currencies circulating in the US in the nineteenth century before the supremacy of the dollar was established. It wasn't imposed; it beat off the competition.

What's more, the prospectus for the euro did not mention that the citizens of Europe might have to make sacrifices in terms of jobs, pay, welfare benefits and pensions in order to 'transcend the divisions of the Cold War', whatever that might mean. Indeed, all the evidence suggests that questionable economic decisions taken for political reasons end up being both bad economics and bad politics. Nowhere has this been proved truer than in the idea that the euro would bind a reunited Germany together with the rest of Europe and loosen the stranglehold of its central bank, the Bundesbank.

The original aims of Robert Schuman and Jean Monnet's 1950 blueprint for European integration were, for many decades after the Second World War, fulfilled. As Monnet outlined in his memoirs, previous attempts 'to keep Germany in check . . . mainly at French instigation, had come to nothing, because they had been based on conquest and temporary superiority':

> But if the problem of sovereignty were approached with no desire to dominate or take revenge – if, on the contrary, the victors and the vanquished agreed to exercise joint sovereignty over part of their joint resources – then a solid link would be forged between them, the way would be wide open for further collective action, and a great example would be set to the other nations of Europe.[9]

In other words, Germany was Europeanised. France, supported by the US, wanted Germany to be tightly bound into a more integrated Europe, and Germany was more than willing to be restrained.

Even before the creation of the euro, this relationship was changing as a result of Germany's clear economic dominance in Europe. The period since the financial crisis had clarified the new terms of trade. Germany's attitude towards balanced budgets, its preference for what its finance minister, Wolfgang Schäuble, called expansionary fiscal contraction over Keynesian deficit finance, governed Europe's response to the crisis from 2009 onwards and became even more evident when five Eurozone countries required bailouts. The price for Germany paying Europe's bills was that Europe had to be Germanised. Not only in Greece, but also in France and Italy, founder members of the European project, anti-austerity demonstration placards depicting Merkel and Schäuble in Nazi uniforms tell their own story.

One final argument has been used to explain away the euro's abysmal performance: namely, that failure is all part of the plan. This takes as its starting point Monnet's dictum, 'Europe will be forged in crises and will be the sum of the solutions adopted for these crises.' Monnet believed that Europeans would be so delighted with the transfer of powers from national governments to supra-national bodies that they would demand more integration. But just in case, he thought The Project should be constructed in such a way as to make reversing the integration process difficult as well as costly. It has been left to two Italians to explain how Monnet's theory applies to the euro, ensuring that failure is merely an opportunity to press ahead with fresh vigour. As one of the founders of the euro,

Tommaso Padoa-Schioppa, put it in 2004, 'the road toward the single currency looks like a chain reaction in which each step resolved a preexisting contradiction and generated a new one that in turn required a further step forward.'[10] Romano Prodi, then president of the European Commission, was equally frank when interviewed by the *Financial Times* shortly before the launch of euro notes and coins: 'I am sure the euro will oblige us to introduce a new set of economic of economic policy instruments. It is politically impossible to propose that now. But some day there will be a crisis and new instruments will be created.'[11]

Padoa-Schioppa and Prodi have been proved half-right. The years after 2010 have seen the euro in an existential crisis that has provided the opening for further moves towards integration.

Ultimately, however, this approach has its limitations. In the short term, the schemes of politicians can often be inured from the pressures that bear down on companies, but governments too can be put out of business if the failures are big enough. If a company gets it wrong, the impact is swift: sales suffer, profitability falls, market share is lost. In the most extreme cases, companies go out of business, so the tendency is for boards to admit they were wrong, cut their losses and move on. Politics sometimes works in a similar fashion, as when it became obvious to the Conservative Party in 1990 that Margaret Thatcher's poll tax was an epic vote-loser, and both the policy and the prime minister were ditched. Yet, there are many more examples of politicians persisting with ideas even when they are not working, and eventually having to admit defeat. The idea that military force can pacify Afghanistan is one such belief that a century of failure has failed to shake.

Five men, one vision

In the summer of 2015, when Greece rejected austerity in a referendum and appeared to be on the brink of leaving the single currency, a report was published in Brussels. It was signed by the leaders of five European institutions: Jean-Claude Juncker, president of the European Commission; Mario Draghi, president of the

European Central Bank; Donald Tusk, president of the European Council; Jeroen Dijsselbloem, president of the Eurogroup; and Martin Schulz, president of the European Parliament.[12]

The theme of what became known as the Five Presidents' Report was that any supposed defects of the single currency – mass unemployment, for example – were mere teething troubles that could be cured by further integration. 'The euro is a successful and stable currency,' the report began. 'It is shared by 19 EU Member States and more than 330 million citizens. It has provided its members with price stability and shielded them against external instability.' Apart from the obvious point that any member of the Politburo could have claimed the same for the rouble between 1917 and 1991, continued existence does not necessarily equate with success. Nor is it really correct to say that the citizens of Europe have been protected from external instability, since the value of the single currency has gyrated against the dollar and the yen.

Even so, it is not hard to see why Juncker et al. feel a strong emotional attachment to the single currency. They came of political age when the pre-euro European Union was popular. The EU was seen as a symbol of peace and prosperity following a period when the continent had been beset by mass unemployment, poverty, dictatorship and war. More than that, the move towards 'ever closer union' was seen as a crucial factor in generating the spectacularly high growth rates and full employment of the 1950s and 1960s. In truth, European economic recovery had been underway, courtesy of Marshall Aid, for more than half a decade before the Treaty of Rome was signed in 1957, while the equally rapid growth during the same period by Japan suggests that postwar reconstruction was a factor in generating rates of expansion not seen before or since. The role of closer integration in preventing European nations going to war has also been overstated. The explanation for the expansionist policy pursued by Germany in 1914 and 1945 is not that there was no European Union to keep the kaiser or Hitler in check. Rather, it was that the nineteenth-century balance of power, which meant no nation could hope to extend control over the continent, broke down and was not reconstituted until 1945, when for both the United States and the Soviet Union the costs of going to war with each other outweighed any benefits.

Yet, in one sense it is irrelevant whether the importance of these early moves towards closer integration have been exaggerated or not. It is certainly true that during this period when Europe was at peace, Germany, France and Italy were closing the gap with the US in terms of living standards, and that countries not in the 'club of six' were losing out on the dynamism that Europe could provide. Britain's two rebuffed attempts to join the Common Market in the early and late 1960s, and its eventual decision to join what was then the European Economic Community in 1973, stemmed from the belief that the secret of economic success was to be found on the other side of the English Channel.

Other countries felt the same. They believed that access to a bigger market would improve their economic prospects. In the last quarter of the twentieth century, output per head in Greece, Portugal, Spain and – most spectacularly – Ireland rose more rapidly than it did in core countries such as Germany and France. The gap in incomes per head did not entirely disappear but it certainly narrowed. It was therefore no surprise that countries in Eastern Europe wanted to join the EU after the collapse of communism: Europe was associated with democracy and prosperity, a winning combination.

The golden age of European growth ended with the first oil shock of 1973 – long before the birth of the single currency, but a time when there were already attempts, following the break-up of the post-war fixed exchange-rate system, to find a European alternative to freely floating currencies. Europe's economic performance worsened steadily as countries struggled to maintain their currencies inside the Exchange Rate Mechanism, but it has deteriorated further since the creation of the euro.

Does this mean that it would have been better had the euro been strangled at birth? The Five Presidents' Report has a short answer to any such suggestion: absolutely not. What's happened so far is not even remotely a failure; rather, it is an opportunity to finish the job:

Europe's Economic and Monetary Union (EMU) today is like a house that was built over decades but only partially finished. When the storm hit, its walls and roof had to be stabilised quickly. It is now high time to reinforce its foundations and turn it into what EMU was meant to be: a place of prosperity based on balanced economic growth and price stability, a competitive social market economy, aiming at full employment and social progress. To achieve this, we will need to take further steps to complete EMU.[13]

The report spells out what this means. It requires moves towards a financial union, including the completion of a banking union, a fiscal union and 'finally towards a political union that provides the foundation for all of the above through genuine democratic accountability, legitimacy and institutional strengthening'. What it means, in other words, is New New Coke, with extra ingredients to give an even stronger taste.

But the sovereign debt crisis that has led to bailouts for five countries has taken its toll, as have the doubling of unemployment and falling living standards. The countries that have joined the single currency have retained some sovereign powers and they are understandably reluctant to give them up. They are like the diehard Coke devotees who stored thousands of cans of the traditional formula in their cellars in 1985.

As a result, progress towards financial union, let alone full political union, will be glacially slow, if it happens at all. For that reason, Padoa-Schioppa and Prodi were only half-right in their belief in a chain reaction; for that reason, also, Monnet's formula that crisis will lead to further integration no longer holds true. The abject failure of the euro to deliver its promised benefits has meant that voters in Europe no longer feel warmth towards the euro; they merely fear that the disruption caused by its demise would make their lives even more miserable. In these circumstances, it is no longer possible to complete The Project surreptitiously.

As Enrico Spolaore, professor of economics at Tufts University, wrote in Vox, the CEPR's policy portal, in July 2015:

Heterogeneity stemming from different preferences, values, beliefs, and behaviours among Europeans cannot be systematically ignored or sidestepped by stealth, forcing governments and voters to accept further integration in order to reduce the high costs associated with incomplete and flawed institutions. Europe can no longer be built on the idea that a series of gradual steps can lead to an irreversible path towards an 'ever closer union' in the absence of extensive democratic support for the whole project. If Europeans really want a political union, they must go for it directly and explicitly. And if they don't, the solution is not a gradual chain reaction strategy that underestimates heterogeneity costs and overestimates convergence. Going back to the metaphor of the incomplete house, if a political union is truly a necessary 'foundation' for a complete and effective economic and monetary union, as stated in the Five Presidents' Report, it cannot be a 'roof' placed on top of a ramshackle construction at a late stage, out of necessity. Instead, it should be built right away, at the base of the building, but only if solidly grounded in democratic consensus.[14]

That consensus does not exist. It has been some decades since a left-wing case against the euro was articulated, but the way in which Greece was forced to accept austerity measures that were both economically illiterate and democratically illegitimate generated the first signs of a progressive backlash. Excuses for the single currency's woeful performance were no longer considered good enough. The new, more sceptical mood has been noted. For the time being at least, the integrationist rhetoric has been toned down while the true believers in the Monnet doctrine regroup.

This is not the first time this has happened. Tony Benn's diaries for the period leading up to Britain's 1975 referendum on whether to remain in what was then the European Economic Community illustrate how easily politicians have mistaken tactical retreat for strategic failure. Labour had gone into the 1974 elections pledging to leave the EEC unless it could secure better terms – something that Prime Minister Harold Wilson and Foreign Secretary James

Callaghan said had been achieved when they reported back to cabinet. 'Jim made a few general points. There had been a substantial change in the Community since we first examined it, the Commission was under tighter political control, the Economic and Monetary Union was now no more than a twinkle in the eyes of its advocates, and the federal idea was dead.'[15] Benn was not convinced, as the entry for the following day, when the debate continued in cabinet, shows:

> We are at the moment on a federal escalator, moving as we talk, going towards a federal objective we do not wish to reach.
>
> In practice, Britain will be governed by a European coalition government that we cannot change dedicated to a capitalist or market economy theology.[16]

We leave it to our readers to decide whether Callaghan or Benn was better at futurology. It is worth noting also that perhaps the only crisis that could spur the Eurozone, or some of its members, towards deeper integration would be a British vote to leave the EU.

Out, but not down

It should perhaps come as little surprise that the European Commission and the European Central Bank retain their faith in ever closer union, because neither the commissioners in Brussels nor the central bankers in Frankfurt can be held to account for their decisions by voters. Even so, the limitations of Monnet's strategy have been exposed, with, as one study puts it, no desire to move forward, but too much fear to move backward. The paper describes how Monnet's strategy has come tantalizingly close to achieving success, with integration moving forward to the point where it is 'almost' irreversible. It has done so, however, by jeopardizing future sustainability. 'The key word is "almost". Europe and the euro are not irreversible; they are simply very costly to revert.' It adds: 'As long as the political dissension is not large enough, Monnet's chain reaction theory delivered the desired outcome, albeit in a very non-democratic way. The risk of a dramatic reversal, however, is real.'[17] Chain reactions, in other words, can go in more than one direction. A collapse of the euro could end with a meltdown.

There were three examples of Europe's political impasse in the summer of 2015. The first was the threat of Greece leaving the euro; the second was the suspension of the Schengen Agreement that permits free movement of people across the internal borders of countries party to the agreement; and the third was the UK government's insistence that it wanted to remain in a reformed European Union but had no intention of ever joining the euro even it was strengthened by a banking union and a common budget. We shall explore all three events later in the book, but our aim in this opening chapter is to examine whether the countries that joined the Eurozone would have been better off had they kept their own currencies and maintained a degree of control over their own macroeconomic policies. It could be argued (indeed, it is argued) by the euro's supporters that life would have been just as tough, if not tougher, had the single currency never been founded. This counterfactual argument does not stand up to scrutiny.

Let's start, as the US economist Paul Krugman has done, by comparing the performance of two pairs of Scandinavian countries – Sweden and Finland, and Sweden and Denmark – since the global recession of 2008. All countries have their own character, but Sweden, Finland and Denmark share certain cultural traits and have tended to develop their economies along similar lines. Sweden and Finland, for example, were both pioneers of mobile telephony in the 1990s, a period that followed a severe banking crisis that affected both countries. Finland's recession in the early 1990s was deeper than Sweden's but it rapidly caught up, and over the period from 1989 to 2008, incomes per head adjusted for inflation rose by 45 per cent in both countries. Subsequently, both countries suffered a marked fall in living standards, from which Sweden has recovered but Finland has not. The gap in living standards is now more than 10 percentage points. Denmark, too, has seen living standards stagnate while those of Sweden have increased. Finland is a member of the euro. Denmark, while not a member, has been shadowing the euro and imposed austerity on itself. Sweden is not a member of the euro and has been running its own monetary policy.

This might be seen as prima facie evidence that a one-size-fits-all interest-rate policy coupled with budgetary policies that penalize rather than support countries that are struggling is a flawed idea. Although it could be argued that the recent poor performance of Finland and Denmark vis-à-vis Sweden is the result of the financial crisis and its aftermath rather than any design flaw in the euro, this argument does not stack up either, as the European Commission's own analysis shows.

Europe is blessed with timely and reliable economic data. There are regular updates on the performance of both the Eurozone and the wider twenty-eight-nation European Union, which includes countries such as Sweden, Britain and Poland that are not members of the single currency. Sometimes there is a blurring of the line between academic rigour and comment, as in a particularly ill-timed 2009 paper that chose the moment when the euro sovereign debt crisis was about to erupt to castigate US economists for their pre-launch doubts about the single currency.[18] But, for the most part, the reports and studies play it straight. That was the case with the quarterly report on the Eurozone, published in 2013, in which Marco Buti, director-general of the division of the Commission responsible for the study, said that 'medium-term projections for the euro area do not give grounds for excessive optimism'.[19] Displaying a penchant for understatement, Buti said that potential output in the Eurozone was expected to grow by 1 per cent a year over the coming decade, half the rate experienced in the ten years leading up to the financial crisis. Over the same period, living standards as measured by gross domestic product per head of population were expected to decline by more than half a percentage point to less than 1 per cent.

It is an article of faith in Brussels that the answer to Europe's growth problems is a willingness to embrace structural reforms, and Buti did not deviate from the mantra, expressing the belief that this was the way to boost productivity and raise living standards.

Interestingly, in the light of the discrepancy between Sweden and its two Nordic neighbours detailed above, he said structural reforms made countries more resilient, noting this was of 'particular importance in EMU, since countries cannot use monetary policy to react to idiosyncratic shocks'.

Buti's analysis is hard to square with the facts. By the time the global economy was starting to pull out of its deep slump in the spring of 2009, unemployment in the United States and the Eurozone was almost the same at just under 10 per cent of the workforce. Since then the Eurozone's jobless total has risen while that of the US has fallen. American unemployment is back to its pre-recession levels of 5 per cent while Eurozone unemployment stands at just under 11 per cent. There has been no sudden introduction of rules and regulations in Europe during this period. Politicians and their officials have not been dreaming up fiendish new ways to impede market forces. On the contrary, they have been promoting moves that would make welfare systems less generous, drawing up plans to privatize state-owned companies and increase competition, and to make it easier for companies to hire and fire. So, it is not feasible to argue that it has been a lack of structural reform that has prevented the Eurozone from seeing the improvement in unemployment witnessed in the US. A much more plausible explanation is that the Eurozone has suffered from a dearth of demand stemming both from the original concept of the single currency and the way macro-economic policy has been mismanaged.

Close examination of the Commission's study puts paid to the idea that incomes per head in the US and the Eurozone started to diverge only after the financial and economic crisis of 2008–09. It makes the point that without reform the Eurozone will continue to fall further behind the US in terms of living standards, but makes clear that the break with the post-war trend came in 1995 rather than in 2008. Repeatedly, the study returns to the mid-1990s as the moment when things started to go wrong for Europe, not just in terms of losing ground to the US but also when countries inside the monetary union started to grow apart rather than grow closer together.

Whilst the growth patterns for the euro area as a whole are expected to evolve along the path just described, the respective paths for the individual euro area countries are forecast to diverge significantly from the euro area average. This divergence pattern will represent a continuation of the trends seen since the mid-1990s and exacerbated by the crisis, where existing imbalances and differences with respect to the need for, and consequently the speed of, deleveraging have strongly influenced relative actual growth patterns in the euro area as a whole. Regarding potential growth, this deleveraging process is showing up in particular in a drop in investment rates and persistently high unemployment rates, with knock-on effects on per capita income developments.[20]

One way of judging the performance of an economy is through total factor productivity (TFP). This measures not just how much labour and capital it takes to produce a given quantity of output, but how effectively these factors of production are deployed. High levels of TFP indicate that a country is dynamic and operating at the cutting edge of technology.

The euro area had strong growth in total factor productivity during a period of catch up that lasted until the mid-1990s. There was, however, a divergence among individual countries from the early 1980s onwards and a 'significant break in the TFP series around 1995'. What was happening in 1995 and thereafter which might explain why the US and Europe have been on such different economic journeys? The Commission paper hazards a guess that the US had the upper hand when it came to 'absorbing and developing' new technology but draws a veil over alternative explanations, such as design flaws in monetary union and the determination to throw weak countries into debtors' prisons.

A similar inability to spot the blindingly obvious is evident in the Commission's account of the financial crisis and its aftermath. It notes that the average 0.5 per cent a year shrinkage of the Eurozone economy from 2009 to 2013 shows that the impact of the financial crisis on activity is 'already resoundingly evident' and that the US will continue to exhibit a stronger recovery even when the near-collapse of the global banking system in the wake of Lehman Brothers' September 2008 bankruptcy becomes a distant memory. In the decade between 2014 and 2023, the US will return to the sort of growth in living standards that it enjoyed before the crisis; the citizens of the Eurozone can expect to have increases in real per capita incomes only half as big as they were before 2008.

The Eurozone has committed some egregious economic blunders since the crisis. It was slower to cut interest rates, lagged behind the US in recapitalizing its banks, and imposed austerity measures far too soon. But crisis management during and immediately after the Great Recession cannot explain why the Eurozone will continue to underperform. 'Why does the US come out faster?' the paper asks, rhetorically. 'Were there fewer imbalances, fewer structural rigidities?'[21]

Well, yes, perhaps it is the case that the US's single market is more efficient than Europe's. Given the US shares a common language that Europe does not, that might be expected. But, just possibly, the disparity between the West's two largest economies might have something to do with the fact that one of them created what one critic dubbed an economic doomsday machine and the other did not. It might be explicable in two words: New Coke.

The cost of failure will be considerable, as the paper candidly admits. 'On the assumption that the euro area and US forecasts underpinning this scenario prove accurate, the euro area is forecast to end up in 2023 with living standards relative to the US which would be lower than in the mid-1960s.'[22] In reality, Europe would always struggle to close the gap with the US in terms of incomes per head because Americans tend to work longer hours than Europeans; but over the years Europe has gradually closed the productivity gap with the US. By 1995, productivity levels in the Eurozone were 90 per cent of those in the US, and since productivity is the key driver of living standards, the gap in per capita incomes also narrowed. There was a period of strong convergence in the 1960s and 1970s, followed by broadly similar per capita income trends in the 1980s and 1990s, when countries were submitting themselves to the disciplines of the Exchange Rate Mechanism, the forerunner to the single currency. Then, from 1995 the process went into reverse – a trend that cannot be explained by Stakhanovite Americans staying later at the office and lotus-eating Europeans spending more time sunning themselves on the French Riviera. Between 1995 and 2013, relative productivity levels in the Eurozone deteriorated by a full ten percentage points, so that they were down to 80 per cent of US levels. On unchanged policies, the Commission expects a further six-point decline, so that by 2023, productivity in the Eurozone will be 73 per cent of US levels.

All in all, in less than three decades the Eurozone will have seen its productivity shortfall compared with the US increase by 16 percentage points, and the gap in living standards widen to the same levels as when Lyndon Johnson was in the White House and Charles de Gaulle was in the Élysée Palace. And this is all due to Europe's lack of a Bill Gates generation? It would appear so, according to the Commission, which says this growing divide is 'undoubtedly linked to relative ICT [information and communication technology] developments, with the US enjoying a much stronger burst of TFP growth in a range of industries producing ICT equipment and with the falling relative prices of ICT boosting the rate of ICT capital deepening to a greater extent in the US than in Europe'.[23]

But this brings us back full circle. If the reason for this catastrophic performance is due to trends in ICT, then why has Finland been doing so badly? Finland is one of the most tech-savvy countries in Europe. It spawned Nokia, for a while the most successful mobile phone company in the world.

Another way to test the counterfactual argument is to look at the performance of countries that did not join the euro, Britain being the obvious example. As noted above, the UK had lagged behind Germany, France and the Netherlands in the immediate post-war decades, and this was why both Conservative and Labour governments became convinced of the benefits of joining the Common Market in the 1960s. In the period between the signing of the Treaty of Rome in 1957 and the oil shock of 1973 that brought the post-war boom to an end, German growth averaged 4.7 per cent a year, slightly slower than the 5.2 per cent a year recorded by France and the 5.3 per cent a year notched up by the Netherlands. Over the same period, Britain's growth averaged 2.8 per cent a year.

As Roger Bootle has noted,[24] Britain had been less damaged by the war and so had less scope for catch-up than Germany, France or the Netherlands. Moreover, its performance had been better in the 1930s, when it was faster to pick up on the developments in light engineering and consumer products happening in the US. The idea that it was exclusion from the Common Market alone that caused Britain's lower growth rate is called into question by the strong performance of Sweden and Switzerland, which did not join either. Both grew by 4.3 per cent a year between 1957 and 1973.

The two oil shocks of 1973 and 1979 were a watershed, and growth rates were lower for all developed countries from 1980 onwards than they had been previously. Yet, the relative economic performance of Britain improved: between 1980 and 2012 the original six members of the Common Market grew by 1.6 per cent a year on average while the UK grew by 2 per cent a year.

This in itself proves nothing about the euro. It could be argued, indeed was argued, that years of relative decline ended with Margaret Thatcher's shock treatment following her election in 1979. An alternative explanation is that from the mid-1970s, Britain was the beneficiary of North Sea oil, giving a significant boost to economic growth at its peak in the 1980s and 1990s, whereas continental European countries were not.

But, over the past fifteen years, it has become clear that the UK has serious and deep-seated problems. It has been over-reliant on the City of London and the housing market for its growth. The oil and gas reserves in the North Sea have been dwindling. Large trade deficits have become endemic. So, if anything, Britain's relative economic performance should have deteriorated markedly during this period. However, a study by Stephen King of HSBC shows that this has not occurred.[25] While there has been a slight deterioration relative to Germany, the UK's decline has been far less marked than that of Italy and France, both of which joined the euro as founder members. King's analysis is similar to that of the Commission, with the difference that he brings things down to the level of individual countries. And the outlook does not appear promising for the Eurozone's second, third and fourth biggest economies.

When the single currency was launched in 1999, France – for all its angst about the influence of the Bundesbank – could boast per capita incomes that were 99 per cent of those in Germany. Italy's were a respectable 91 per cent of Germany's, while Spain – starting from a much lower base after its return to democracy in the 1970s – had per capita incomes that were 72.4 per cent of Germany's. Move the clock forward fourteen years, and French per capita incomes had fallen ten points to 89 per cent of Germany's, those in Italy had dropped by seventeen points to 74 per cent and Spain – after the bursting of its real-estate bubble – had seen its living standards relative to Germany drop by more than eight points to 64.2 per cent. King estimates that on current trends, French living standards will be 80 per cent of Germany's by 2029, while in Italy and Spain they will be 60 per cent and 56.9 per cent respectively. To amend slightly the words of a Coke commercial from a different age, things don't go better with the euro.

The UK's GDP per capita was slightly higher than Germany's in 1999 (103.2 per cent), and has lost ground since – but not nearly as much as those countries that joined the euro. In 2013, after its deepest and longest recession of modern times, the UK's GDP per capita was 99 per cent of Germany's and on existing trends would be 95 per cent of German levels in 2029.

In pre-euro times, France, Italy and Spain had the option to make their goods and services more competitive on international markets through devaluation. As King observes, there was a cost to this, because the price of imported goods went up, reducing disposable incomes. But costs were also incurred by those countries on the other side of the devaluation, whose currencies increased in value. The revaluing nations found that their exports became more expensive and the assets they held in the countries that had devalued were less valuable. The burden of adjustment was shared by the strong and the weak – but that hasn't happened since the creation of the euro. Instead, all the burden of adjustment has fallen on the weak nations, who have been left with no alternative but to make themselves more competitive through wage cuts. Old-fashioned currency devaluation has been replaced by so-called 'internal devaluation', which has become the modern manifestation of the beggar-thy-neighbour policies of the 1930s. A country such as Spain, for example, has made itself more competitive by squeezing labour costs, but in the process has put pressure on Italy and France to do the same. It is a mathematical impossibility for all Eurozone countries to improve their relative competitiveness at the same time, even though Germany appears to think that they can.

King notes that Germany's relative economic performance was unimpressive in the 1980s and 1990s. Although comfortably Europe's biggest economy, Germany ranked fourth for per capita income growth among the big five economies, with Spain and the UK vying for first place, Italy third and France bringing up the rear. Post-1999, the pecking order has been Germany, the UK, Spain, France and Italy. 'Since the euro's inception, Germany has been the big winner. Italy, at the opposite end of the spectrum, has floundered: Italians are no better off today than they were in 1999. It appears that the single currency has unintentionally become a mechanism to create winners and losers, an outcome which may ultimately prove to be unsustainable.'

We draw three conclusions from sixteen years of the single currency. The first is that its economic performance has been woeful. Not one of the claims made for the euro, other than that it would be a bulwark against inflation, has proved correct. Productivity is down, investment is down, living standards are down, and unemployment is up. Debt levels have been rising sharply, five countries have required bailouts, and each crisis has brought monetary union closer to outright collapse. There has been divergence, not convergence, both between the Eurozone and the US, and between the member states of the Eurozone themselves.

The second conclusion is that it would have been better had the single currency never been created. Even when allowance is made for the impact of the financial crisis, trends in productivity and per capita incomes have markedly deteriorated in comparison to the pre-euro era. On unchanged policy, the future seems to offer more of the same.

There is little dispute about the first of these conclusions, and many of those who originally supported the idea of monetary union would agree with the second. There has been a welcome period of silence from those who said in the early 2000s that it was Britain's ineluctable destiny to join the single currency.

Our final conclusion will, though, prove more contentious. There are those who, while accepting that the euro has so far been a machine for destroying rather than creating jobs, believe that The Project is redeemable provided the teething troubles can be sorted out. By this, they mean following the advice of Rahm Emanuel, adviser to Barack Obama, who, in the spirit of Jean Monnet, said 'You should never let a serious crisis go to waste.' What needs to happen, according to the euro reformers, is that progress towards a banking union should be accelerated and a common fiscal policy created that would transfer money from German taxpayers to the poorer parts of the Eurozone. Debts of the struggling countries should be written off; expansionary macroeconomic policies should be accompanied by burden-sharing across the Eurozone.

The chances of this coming to pass over the next decade are zero, or as close to zero as is statistically relevant. The Germans are not going to stand behind the banks of other Eurozone countries, and they are certainly not going to write cheques for the Greeks and the Portuguese. Conversely, the Greeks, the Italians and the French do not want to have their budgets set in Berlin.

So, the choice is not between the euro as it currently exists and the perfect, but illusory, euro that its creators envisaged in the mid-1990s. It is between continuing with something that is not working and trying something different. We shall explore what that might be later in this book, although it would include a core euro centred on Germany, returning to the more flexible ERM, or returning to full national economic autonomy. There would, of course, be costs involved, but the costs involved in sticking to the status quo will almost certainly be higher. Monetary union was an experiment that has failed, and, as one critic put it, 'the costs of dismantling the single currency cannot survive much longer as an argument in favour of its continuation.'[26]

The following chapters will look in turn at the deliberately claustrophobic and constricting design of the single currency; at its resemblance to the pre-war gold standard; at the deep division as to how the Eurozone ought to operate between Germany and other 'northern' members and the Mediterranean nations; and at the contrasting experiences of near neighbours Ireland and Iceland, one in the Eurozone and one outside it.

We then look at the history and implications of Britain's ultimate refusal to join the single currency; at the travails first of Greece and then of Italy; at the fact that this is a crisis that never ends; and finally at the growing disillusion on the left with what was supposed to have been a progressive social-democratic project.

Our message throughout this book is simple: the euro was a bad idea. Getting rid of it and reverting to a more sensible way of running the European economy is not as easy as taking a product off the shelves. But the single currency is New Coke, and the sooner Europe realizes that the better.

The following chapter opens with someone who, as we shall see, used a different metaphor from American popular culture to describe the euro.

CHAPTER 2

'A BURNING BUILDING WITH NO EXITS'

Designing a euro inferno

You'd better find a way out, hey! Kick down the door.
The Boomtown Rats, 'Rat Trap'

For a man facing the prospect of a charge of high treason, Yanis Varoufakis, the former Greek finance minister, seemed remarkably relaxed as he gave an interview to London's *Observer* newspaper in 2015. Hosting lunch in his holiday home overlooking the sea, the motor-cycling maverick and self-styled 'erratic Marxist' told the paper's Andrew Anthony that he paid little attention to the criminal investigation launched into what Varoufakis himself admitted was an attempt earlier in the year to hack into the computer files of his own finance ministry in order to gain access to the tax-account numbers of Greek citizens. His political opponents, unsurprisingly, were making hay. 'I think it's going to fizzle out,' he said. 'However, if I'm prosecuted and convicted of high treason, it would be interesting.'[1]

Indeed it would. The first point of interest is why the finance minister would need or wish to obtain surreptitious entry to his own ministry's computer files. In terms of 'need', the answer is quite straightforward: Greece's electronic tax files were under the control of the European Commission, the European Central Bank and the International Monetary Fund – the 'troika' of creditors that had bailed Greece out of its initial debt crisis. Greece's patchy (to say the least) record of tax collection was a key issue in the bailout discussions and an improved revenue system was one of the main reforms being demanded by the troika. Put simply, Varoufakis would have needed to ask permission to access the computers.

As to why he would wish to, the minister was in the position unusual for a hacker of proposing to put money into the hacked accounts rather than taking it out. Some time after the left-wing party Syriza's victory in the January elections, running on a platform of opposition to the troika's austerity programme, a small cell began work in the finance ministry under Varoufakis's direction on a scheme to inject 'parallel liquidity' into the economy in the event that Greece's creditors turned off the taps.

Accounts would have been credited with electronic IOUs that would initially have been denominated in the euro, but could have been transformed into the drachma, Greece's previous national currency, almost instantly. This could have allowed the government to pay its domestic bills, such as public servants' salaries, in local currency while still allowing Greece to pay off its debt.

According to the *Daily Telegraph* on 26 July 2015, 'Mr Varoufakis said any request for permission would have tipped off the troika immediately that he was planning a counter-attack. He was ready to activate the mechanism the moment he received a "green light" from the prime minister, but the permission never came.'

Varoufakis's hacking expedition has been portrayed, understandably, as an attempt to break into somewhere, namely the public revenue office at the finance ministry. But in a sense he was trying also to break out of something, namely the constraints of the single-currency bloc, which denied Greece an ability enjoyed by almost every sovereign state in the world, not to mention some subnational territories: the ability to issue legal tender in the interests of the people for whose welfare the leaders are responsible.

Varoufakis wanted an 'out' in a system designed to have none. He was looking for the door in a monetary regime that was all walls. We shall never know whether his parallel liquidity would have proved acceptable or whether individuals, companies and markets would have reacted in horror to the appearance of what could be characterized as electronic funny money.

Since the early days of the euro, there has been speculation that the single currency contains a secret mechanism to allow national currencies to emerge in one or more member countries in the event of severe crisis. Given Germany was felt to be the most disgruntled at having to give up its beloved currency for what it saw as an inferior model, fanciful tales were told of stashes of fresh Deutschmark notes being held in caves under the Bavarian Alps, ready to be put back into circulation.

Such obvious conspiracy theories were fuelled by occasional remarks from those much closer to the action in terms of the euro's launch. In response to the authors' point at a public debate that the single currency had no emergency exit, a former Europe minister at the British Foreign Office riposted: 'If I showed you an escape hatch, would you change your minds about joining?' He did not elaborate.

The travails of Portugal, Ireland, Spain and, notably, Greece in the first half of the 2010s gave new impetus to the hunt for this emergency hatch, with journalists and others alighting on the most likely candidate – the national serial numbers printed on each and every euro-denominated banknote. This was the *Mail on Sunday* on 26 June 2011:

> Should you be holding euros, you may wish to exchange those whose serial numbers begin with Y, M or T for those whose numbers start with an X.
>
> Why? Well in doing so you will swap euros issued by, respectively, Greece, Portugal and Ireland – the three most troubled members of the Eurozone – and get in return euros issued by the Continent's economic powerhouse, Germany.

The paper went on to state that in theory there should be no difference in the value of one euro banknote and another, regardless of the country of issue.

At the time of writing, neither the serial numbers nor any other monetary ejector seat has emerged during the turmoil in the

Eurozone. The architects of the euro, it seems, were not bluffing. Joining the single currency was supposed to be for keeps. There really were no emergency doors. Once in, you were in for good. Or, as Varoufakis put it to Bloomberg Radio in May 2012: 'The last line in "Hotel California" [by The Eagles] explains where we are: you can check out any time you like, but you can never leave.'

In this chapter, we examine why anyone thought it a good idea to create a restrictive currency system with no escape hatches, what motivated them and why, in particular, the left was attracted rather than repelled by this project.

Like a house on fire: A prophecy in the forest

William Hague, leader of Britain's Conservative Party and of the official opposition in Parliament, had tried his hand at single-currency phrase-making before. In November 1997, in the run-up to the annual conference of the Confederation of British Industry in Birmingham, he had urged business leaders not to act like 'lemmings' by joining an unthinking rush to get Britain to join the euro. 'I'm just here to find out what lemmings eat for breakfast,' quipped a very grand figure, addressing one of the conference's early-morning meetings. The attendees chortled knowingly. Hague and his much-diminished Euro- (and euro-) sceptic Tory Party were on the wrong side of history. Business-friendly New Labour was firmly in the saddle, leading the charge into a bright European future. Not to put too fine a point on it, the Conservatives were a bunch of losers.

They were certainly in a tight spot. Tony Blair's election victory earlier that year left the number of Tory MPs smaller than the size of Labour's majority. Hague was thought to be failing to connect with the public and was widely expected both to be the first Conservative leader since Austen Chamberlain to fail to reach Number 10 and to be discarded in favour of one or other of two more charismatic rivals, the former defence secretary Michael Portillo or the ex-chancellor Kenneth Clarke.

The first expectation was borne out, the second was not.

In May the following year, Hague returned to his alma mater, the INSEAD business school in Fontainebleau, the district of Paris renowned for its great forest. Hague made a speech in which he warned that countries in the Eurozone could find themselves 'trapped in a burning building with no exits'.

This time, his imagery hit home. Seventeen years later, he recalled: 'Chirac [the then French president] and many others were appalled . . . [the] phrase brought me a fair amount of controversy and abuse.' He added: 'I was regarded around the EU as a rather eccentric figure, almost pitiable in being unable to see where the great sweep of history and prosperity was heading.' All that time later, Hague, while admitting his fair share of mistakes as party leader, said it was time for the Eurozone leaders to put their hands up to the fact that the single currency's critics had been proved right.[2]

Hague's 'burning building' remarks were certainly prescient. Indeed, they may well have represented his most successful policy intervention. In a broader sense, the staunch opposition to swapping sterling for the euro displayed by both Hague and his successor Iain Duncan Smith (Conservative Party leader from 2001 to 2003) – thereby denying Tony Blair the chance to boast that all the parties' leaders were signed up to The Project – played a major part in keeping Britain out of the single currency.

But so resonant have Hague's words become that it is easy to forget how odd is the thing being described. Who on earth would design a building with no exits? How did they entice its unfortunate residents to allow themselves to be walled in? Why did they ignore the evidence that such a structure would be dangerously flammable?

It's not as if there were no historical precedents to guide the architects of this bizarre construction. The euro's predecessor, the European Exchange Rate Mechanism, had caught fire in 1992–93 and burned to the ground. Hague had a ringside seat at the conflagration, being parliamentary private secretary to Norman Lamont, chancellor of the exchequer at the time of sterling's ejection from the ERM in September 1992.

The ERM debacle incinerated the career of Hague's then boss. Its legacy helped to bring down the 1992–97 Conservative government. That is hardly surprising, given how much political capital had been invested in British membership of the system. Until the moment the roof fell in, John Major, the prime minister, was insisting that leaving the ERM or staging a devaluation within it would be 'fool's gold' and a soft option.

So, the immolation of the ERM was a disaster for the Tories, helping to lock them out of power for thirteen years under three unsuccessful leaders and to deny them a parliamentary majority for eighteen. But for the country, it was a very much happier story. Interest rates were cut and cut again, economic growth picked up and unemployment started to fall. This was possible because, unlike the Eurozone, the ERM did have an emergency exit, in that its members retained fully functioning currencies (Luxembourg sharing with Belgium) that could, in extremis, be cut loose to float on foreign exchanges. Use of that exit could prove politically fatal – that was the British experience. But it was at least available.

Speculative attacks on the ERM had mounted in the summer of 1992, with currency traders betting that political resolve to remain within the system at the high interest rates brought about by German reunification had been fatally weakened by the No vote to the Maastricht Treaty recorded in Denmark in June. They were to be proved correct. On 13 September, Italy staged a 7 per cent devaluation of the lira, far outside the permitted trading bands. On the 16th, an uncontrollable wave of speculation blasted sterling clean out of the ERM.

The proximate cause of sterling's departure had been speculation, not least by financier George Soros. The fateful day, 16 September, was instantly dubbed Black Wednesday. But as the economy responded positively to devaluation, it was suggested that White Wednesday or even Golden Wednesday might be more fitting. The majority of commentators in the financial pages drummed home the message that the speculators had done Britain a huge favour, ushering sterling towards the exit that politicians were determined not to use. Without the speculators, so the argument went, Britain would still be enduring the misery of high interest rates in a doomed attempt to hold sterling steady at 2.95 against the Deutschmark. Not just doomed, but, as it turned out, pointless, because the inflationary surge that had been widely predicted to follow the pound's exit from the ERM simply never happened.

In short, those excitable young currency dealers and their Soros-type clients were our friends, just as the free-market think tanks had always argued. They tended to be pretty well rewarded, so there was no need to get carried away in our gratitude, but a quiet vote of thanks may have been in order.

The view being taken across the Channel, however, was very different.

A sea of tranquillity: Banishing the speculators for good

That the ERM had proved to be a building with exits was, from the point of view of the euro's inventors, the whole problem, the essential weakness in the system. In Britain, the exits were seen as good, because they allowed people to escape. In Brussels and other capitals, they were seen as bad, because they let the arsonists – in the form of the speculators – in. Keep them out, and there would be no fire, hence no burning building.

The single currency would seal up these entrances. With no exchange rates within the Eurozone, there would be nothing at which speculators could take aim. In this regard, the euro's architects were in unlikely agreement with the post-1992 conventional wisdom in Britain, which was that it was crazy to announce a fixed exchange rate because this would inevitably attract speculative attacks just as surely as a magnet will attract iron filings. But the conclusions to be drawn were diametrically opposed.

The British believed the answer was to embrace the joys of floating, allowing currencies to find their own level on foreign exchanges. The euro's architects believed the answer was to abolish the foreign exchanges.

In the spring of 1996, perhaps the most important of those architects was in Washington to collect an honorary doctorate from

Georgetown University. His remarks at a lunch left little doubt as to where he stood. One report said that, for Jacques Delors, the single currency 'is but a first step in a counter-attack against foreign currency speculators', adding that the former Commission president 'has been harshly critical of foreign exchange traders' ever since they drove sterling and the Italian lira from the Exchange Rate Mechanism in 1992 'and forced a major realignment of the system in 1993'.[3]

Rare victories, such as that of the French government in 1993 against market pressure to devalue the franc, merely strengthened the case for the euro. In late 1992, Jean-Claude Trichet, then director of the French treasury, later president of the European Central Bank, battled market pressure on the French currency at a time when, it was later suggested, he believed there was an 'Anglo-Saxon' conspiracy to 'get the franc': the monetary symbol of resistance to the untrammelled rule of the market and of 'Anglo-Saxon economics'.[4]

Much later, Trichet recalled the episode in slightly more moderate terms – reminiscent of one of those exercises in 'burning the speculators' fingers' that in years gone by had been engaged in even by that most 'Anglo-Saxon' of institutions, the Bank of England. Remembering sleepless nights, however, he ended on a combative note: 'we showed market participants that attacking the franc was a losing battle. It was difficult, but we beat the speculators.'[5]

The key word in all this is 'stability'. The 'Anglo-Saxon' view was that, more often than not, speculation aided the stability of markets, because it provided someone prepared, for a price, to stand on the other side of each deal, smoothing the process of exchange. The view from Brussels held that speculation generated market instability. Remove the opportunities for speculation and the cause of instability is likewise eliminated. This latter take on events led naturally to the conception of the Eurozone as a sea of monetary tranquillity in which no bad things – such as currency crises and speculative attacks – would be able to take place.

Looked at one way, this made perfect sense. Intra-European currency crises could be avoided by the simple expedient of having no intra-European currency markets. That this remedy may be seen as akin to curing diarrhoea by swallowing quick-setting cement is an opinion that would have found little support in the new Eurozone in January 1999, when the currency was launched, to be followed by the issuing of banknotes and coins in January 2002.

One need not be fully convinced of the beneficence of speculators (we certainly are not) to grasp that there may be more to the creation of stability than closing down one marketplace, in this case the foreign-exchange market. Yet there can be no doubt that the implicit and explicit assault on financial speculation was one aspect of the 'building without exits' exerting a powerful appeal on the left, in Britain and elsewhere. In leftist demonology, speculators were the epitome of the parasitical money interest, the enemies of the real economy. Bretton Woods had banished them to Tangier and Macao, two jurisdictions outside the system. But since the 1970s, they had crept back onto the economic world's centre stage, able to ply their disreputable trade with the full approval of a new breed of politicians who had cravenly bought into the notion that 'you cannot buck the market'. Worse, they shamelessly appeared in the media, demanding that elected politicians pursue 'credible' policies, i.e. those policies likely to prove most profitable for the speculators.

They were particularly detested on the British left, where they were blamed for having humiliated a Labour government during the 1976 sterling crisis, forcing it (per this not very accurate reading of events) to abandon 'expansionary' policies and implement the nostrum of monetarism. European currency policy held out the prospect of stymying the speculators, which helps to explain Labour's conversion to the joys of ERM membership. Bryan Gould, then a Labour high-flyer, later recalled Gordon Brown addressing Labour MPs on the great advantages of joining the ERM, which Brown suggested would involve applying 'socialist planning to the economy' rather than leaving an important issue to market forces. Added Gould: 'The party responded warmly to the notion that speculators would be disarmed.'[6]

In this view, speculation is either the expression of a malignant plot to force socialist or social democrat politicians off course, or it is a deliberate attempt to foment the sort of instability from which profits can be made. Debunking this latter view is made no easier by the attitude of some financial practitioners. In an off-the-record talk with us in the mid-2000s, a senior economist at a major British bank, quizzed as to the fact that the London money market had been consistently wrong for more than a year about the direction of British interest rates, initially accused his interlocutors of being 'judgmental', then added that the inaccuracy of the market's forecasts did not really matter because 'you need some sort of view to trade on'. Furthermore, as Doug Henwood has pointed out,[7] one oft-quoted justification for speculation, especially in commodities – that it gives price certainty to producers such as farmers – is a little suspect. Having 'certain' prices for something whose supply is uncertain may create more instability than would otherwise have been the case.

The thinking that informed the launch of the euro stressed the need to make the currency speculator-proof – indeed, market-proof. A counterweight to the chaos of the currency markets would be the power of the European Central Bank. Far more than a mere reserve institution, the ECB would embody the supremacy of European Union politics over finance. 'Technocrats have long been fascinated by the power of banks,' wrote author, journalist and academic John Laughland at this time. He cited Jacques Attali (adviser to President François Mitterrand and first president of the European Bank for Reconstruction and Development) and Jacques Delors in this regard, the former wanting his career to end with a triumphant presidency of a 'European bank', while Delors, having begun his career as an official in the Bank of France, 'finished it with the single currency project'.[8]

This conception of banks as essentially political rather than commercial institutions has deep roots in France, stretching back as least as far as John Law's hugely ambitious Banque Générale in 1716, later the Banque Royale, later still insolvent. In the renowned French novelist Émile Zola's *L'Argent* (1891), anti-hero Aristide Saccard establishes his Universal Bank, the vaulting aims of which include the installation of the pope in Jerusalem. Obsessed by hatred for 'the Jew Gundermann' (Baron James de Rothschild in real life, as Zola's footnote points out), Saccard is determined to build a 'Christian bank'. Sad to say, his interpretation of Christianity includes the raiding of shareholders' funds and the rigging of the stock market.

The prospect of immensely potent supranational institutions that would bring generally unruly markets to heel had wide appeal, not merely in France and not solely on the left. Nor was it confined to the ECB, although increasingly the bank was the source of such attraction. On 11 February 1991, we wrote:

> Fifty years ago, George Orwell warned of the intellectual stratum that is fatally prone to bully-worship and to love of huge, powerful organizations ... today's power-ideology is Europe. Since January 1989, 71 per cent of all articles in the British press concerning the European Community had also contained at least one use of one or more of these words – power, powers, powerful, tough, action, strong and strength.[9]

We were, perhaps, being a little harsh. There was nothing in principle wrong with wishing to banish the sort of turbulence that had routinely produced violent movements in the value of the pound: most recently in 1976 (violently downwards), 1979–80 (violently upwards) and 1985 (sharply downwards again), with another precipitate plunge just around the corner, in 1992. However, there was no reason to believe that the abolition of 'internal' exchange rates would achieve the desired result. The only justification for taking such a view would be the sincere belief that it is the existence of national currencies that creates the differences between different economies and that the abolition of these currencies will similarly do away with the differences.

The contrary view would be that the currencies exist because the differences exist. If this were true, then market movements – and speculation – would be expressed in a manner different from the movements of currencies, but they would continue to be expressed even after the disappearance of those currencies. The most obvious channel for such expression would the government bond markets, these offering the most immediate connection between the markets and national governments given the individual currencies had vanished. If, as eventually happened in August 2012, the ECB calms turbulence and divergence in these markets by offering to act as buyer of last resort, the expression of these differences simply moves on: to municipal and other subnational debt, to the equity market, to real-estate prices, corporate bond markets, the market in credit and elsewhere.

Don't fence me in: The euro as a unifier

If the prospect of being able to 'stymy the speculators' was one major attraction to the left of an Economic and Monetary Union without exits, another was its role as a powerful solvent, erasing frontiers within the EU. Such erasure was, of course, not confined to EMU. It was at the heart of the 1985 single-market programme and dated back to the foundation of the European Community in 1957.

The notion that frontiers create rather than describe differences between nations was also implicit in the structure of the Community, later the EU. But the single currency was the best opportunity to date to demonstrate this belief under battle conditions. Freer trade and free movement of labour – in place since the 1950s – could not compare with the huge psychological and practical impact of one money for Europe, circulating from the Atlantic to the Finnish–Russian border, from the Aegean to the Baltic.

The left, internationalist to varying degrees across the continent, could, for the most part, only cheer. Borders were barriers between people, and one of the most obvious expressions of those barriers, now that the EU had removed frontier posts and customs sheds, was the existence of different national currencies. Nobody, so the thinking went, really wanted these different denominations. Their continued existence was testimony to vain, stick-in-the-mud national politicians who had failed to give a lead but who now were being swept along by the powerful currents of the post-Cold War world.

Indeed, the overriding lesson that was drawn from the extraordinary events following 'Europe's 9/11', the fall of the Berlin Wall on 9 November 1989, was that barriers, borders, frontiers – all were artificial constructs imposed by the powerful and swept away with contempt once the masses had the chance. At the first chance to break down barriers the people seized it with both hands, reaching out to their fellow humans on the other side of these redundant obstacles to international friendship.

In this excitable spirit of unification, the breaching of the Berlin Wall and the more general dismantlement of the 'Iron Curtain' separating Soviet-dominated Eastern Europe from the west was taken as the key inspiration, the practical demonstration, of the irrelevance – indeed, the malignancy – of national frontiers in the new Europe, and of the contempt the great majority of people held them in. This was an inspiration with powerful resonances on the left.

It was also misleading and wrong-headed.

Most national frontiers do not resemble the Berlin Wall or the Iron Curtain. That between the United States and Canada does not, nor that between Austria and Switzerland. These frontiers exist because Americans and Austrians live on one side of the respective borders and Canadians and Swiss people on the other. The east–west European divide was imposed from outside, by the Soviet Union and its lieutenants in the eastern-bloc countries. Once they were gone, so was it.

As John Laughland noted, 'the acuteness of this division naturally encouraged Germans to want to overcome', and also 'fixed in the German mind the idea that all borders were barriers like the Berlin Wall, rather than domains of jurisdiction'. Convinced, Laughland said, that the Franco-German border was comparable to Germany's internal border, the Germans logically went on to demand that frontiers across Europe be lowered. 'This desire chimed in neatly with a very German yearning for synthesis and harmony, and a fear of conflict.'[10]

In basing their thinking on this misinterpretation of recent events, the euro's architects were building on shaky ground, to say the least. Buying into this rationale was to put the left in an awkward position when it emerged that opposition to single-currency membership was not, as was constantly suggested in the UK, a stance inspired by 'Euro-phobia', a hatred of foreigners, a desire to turn back the clock, a clinging to past glories, or (in a play on the campaign to 'save the pound') a laughably nostalgic attitude caricatured as an urge to 'save the groat'.

By declaring that the post-1989 collapse of communism in Eastern Europe demonstrated the redundancy of national frontiers and national currencies, the designers of the euro drew quite the wrong lesson from the events of 1989–90. It may have been more fruitful to ponder the fate of grand political schemes whose architects refuse to abandon their *idée fixe* regardless of the human cost and who consequently lose the trust and consent of the people.

Nor is it necessary to highlight the bitter irony that an economic and monetary union inspired in part by the breaking down of the world's most notorious wall between people of the same country should have ended up bricking in tens of millions of Europeans of different nationalities in a single-currency cell from which there was no obvious means of escape.

Up the workers: The 'social dimension'

If the banishment of speculators and the sweeping away of 'obsolete' national frontiers commended the exit-free euro structure to those on the left, the prospect of its bringing about a 'single social space' in Europe stoked their enthusiasm to new heights. That this prospect coincided in Britain with what turned out to be the second half of an eighteen-year period of Conservative rule, one in which various workplace entitlements had been curtailed and trade union laws tightened, made it seem sweeter still.

On 8 September 1988, addressing the Trades Union Congress in Bournemouth, Commission president Jacques Delors highlighted three key points of the 'social dimension', the most important of which was the first: 'The establishment of a platform of guaranteed social rights, containing general principles, such as every worker's right to be covered by a collective agreement, and more specific measures concerning, for example, the status of temporary work.' The other two points were the creation of a statute for European companies, which would include the participation of workers or their representatives, and the extension to all workers of the right to lifelong education. One of Britain's most senior trade unionists, Ron Todd, general secretary of the Transport and General Workers' Union, spoke for many when he told the TUC that 'the only card game in town is in a town called Brussels'.

This, of course, was before the official adoption of the goal of a single currency as put forward in the Delors Report of the following year. As recalled many years later by Notre Europe (the institute founded by Delors), afterwards, the pace quickened considerably. In December 1991 the Social Protocol of the Maastricht Treaty was adopted (by eleven member states, with Britain opting out), which gave the 'social partners' – unions and businesses – the right be consulted on regulations and legislation proposed by the Commission, and which was supposed to entrench the rights of workers to be consulted by their employers. The paper adds that, from the perspective of 2015, it is clear that the social agreements were not as watertight as had been expected, because 'the transposition of these independent agreements into national law reveals an uneven and occasionally disappointing outcome'. The answer, as always, was to block up any remaining exits, with the paper demanding that 'the value of negotiations and of their results ... be recognised ... in order to avoid undermining this form of social regulation', concluding: 'It seems obvious that independent agreements must result in compulsory implementation, whether their transposition is effected by legislative or contractual means.'[11]

Back in the early 1990s, the fact that Britain had opted out of both the euro and the social chapter was, from a left-wing perspective, deeply significant. Delors had made it clear that the two went hand-in-hand. Britain was joining neither. It was more than enough to give escape hatches a bad name. Thus, when the incoming Labour government signed the social chapter in 1997, it seemed only logical that it would eventually also abandon its opt-out (strictly speaking, an opt-in) regarding the single currency.

So, in the new Europe, there was to be no room for currency speculation, no room for outmoded barriers between countries and no room for 'social dumping'. Nor, incidentally, would there be any potential for the beggar-thy-neighbour devaluations that too often involved beggaring one's own workers, who were left with less spending power for each unit of output, once again bearing the burden of 'adjusting' the economic mistakes made by corporate and national management.

From a leftist perspective, these were all powerful recommendations for taking up residence in the building without exits that had been brought into existence by the Maastricht Treaty. Not only would any exits prove in fact to be entrances through which speculators could enter the 'common European home' (to use the phrase employed by both the former West German chancellor Willy Brandt and Soviet president Mikhail Gorbachev) but they would also create ratholes through which unscrupulous employers supported by right-wing governments would be able to slip out of their obligations to their employees and to society in general.

The unified Europe of the single market and the single currency also offered scope for another activity of keen interest to leftists, and furthermore one that, yet again, individual national governments and national businesses would find hard to avoid given that it, too, would take place in an exit-free forum: industrial policy.

They are the champions: Picking Europe's winners

Progressive liberals and leftists had long been enthusiasts for industrial strategy. The Great Depression of the 1930s had shown, in their eyes, that unplanned free-market capitalism wasted human and natural resources on an epic scale. John Maynard Keynes had demonstrated that market economies could equilibrate at high levels of unemployment and low levels of output, in defiance of classical economic theory. Left to their own devices, capitalist managers would fail to take the long-term view and fritter away the energies of the economy on wasteful competition.

What was more, modern economies needed government direction and financial support if they were to exploit the potential of the jet age, the space age, the era of science and the power of the atom, and the possibilities of the new computer technologies. Storming these frontiers of knowledge and productivity could not possibly be left to inefficient private firms with their short-sighted shareholders and amateurish managers.

For the first thirty or so years after the war, this was the view held across the political spectrum. It had been Charles de Gaulle who had set up the Commissariat général du Plan in 1946, and Harold Macmillan who steered the Rootes car group to Linwood in Scotland in 1961, his Tory colleagues having already helpfully presided over the construction of the nearby Ravenscraig steelworks in 1954, which supplied the new vehicle plant.

But by the late 1980s, the intellectual tide was turning against economic planning and industrial strategy. To an extent, this reflected the changed priorities of a new generation of politicians, notably Margaret Thatcher in Britain, who believed government had no business being in business. Just as industrial strategy had been embraced in the post-war period by centre-right politicians, now deregulation and market-based economic solutions attracted centre-left leaders, notably in New Zealand, Australia and Sweden.

Partly, also, it reflected the dynamics of the move towards much freer international trade. As within the EU, although to a less detailed and prescriptive extent, the liberalization of cross-frontier trade brought with it rules designed to ensure, in the favoured phrase, a level playing field. The General Agreement on Tariffs and Trade and its successor, the World Trade Organization, took a keen interest in state aid and general government assistance to domestic industries.

In all, the climate for industrial policy was turning distinctly chilly.

To an extent, this withdrawal of the state from industry was less pronounced than it appeared. Just as planning in post-war Europe took place in large part within the confines of a recognizably market-based economy, so the supposed revival of *laissez-faire* capitalism in the '80s and beyond did not preclude state intervention when circumstances were deemed to require it.

In Britain – one of the countries most closely associated with the new thinking – it was taken as read that 'Thatcherism' did not apply to Northern Ireland; the troubled province continued to soak up industrial subsidies on a large scale. Scotland was spared the full rigours of the doctrine associated with Britain's prime minister, as was Wales, where Peter Walker, secretary of state from 1987 to 1990, was known as 'Peter the Plaque' in recognition of his ability to steer new industrial and business units to the principality, which would then be opened with due ribbon-cutting ceremony. Even in free-market England, the Nissan plant in Sunderland was announced in 1986 on the back of extensive government assistance.

But these were designed to be the exception to a rule that equated industrial strategy with 'government interference', a tampering with the natural order and consequently a tilting of the playing field unfairly towards the politically connected and those with sharp elbows. Even inside the European Commission, there were supporters of the new hands-off approach, notably the UK's Sir Leon (later Lord) Brittan, who served as competition commissioner from 1989 to 1995 and who formulated the doctrine that states ought normally to make investments (including wholesale nationalization) only on the same basis as would a private-sector investor. His boss during those years, Commission president Jacques Delors, took a very different view.

An enthusiast for industrial policy, Delors believed European political autonomy could be guaranteed only by having a core group of European champion-companies, and regarded the Airbus consortium as the model to follow. Furthermore, Delors promoted his view with a brio bordering on abrasiveness that mirrored the blunt certainties of Margaret Thatcher. Asked why he wanted to impose special tariffs on Japanese photocopiers, Delors retorted that if everybody bought the cheapest product on offer, then Europe would have a trade deficit.[12] He rejected the notion of the 'consumer as king' and actually tried to remove the consumer-protection passages from the 1991 Maastricht Treaty. This was music to the ears of those on the left who had long suspected that 'consumerism' was essentially a right-wing notion, set up to cancel out the power of the trade unions. Indeed, future Tory cabinet minister Douglas Hurd had stated as much.[13]

High on the Delors industrial agenda was the creation of a 'technological community', the centrepiece of which was a plan for a distinctly European model of the high-definition television (HDTV), the next-generation consumer visual broadcast receiver that would deliver cinema-quality pictures and would bring into existence a whole new broadcasting system. Delors wanted a European presence in HDTV, not merely on competition grounds but 'in the name of cultural defence . . . The Community refuses to leave the monopoly of audio-visual techniques to the Japanese and that of programmes to the Americans.'[14]

The Cato Institute takes up the tale: 'With industry assistance, government bureaucrats in both regions [Japan and Europe] tried to coordinate all the actors and variables in the HDTV transmission chain so that an attractive product would be available to entice consumers into the market.'[15] But this was to be a vast undertaking, going far beyond simply co-ordinating research and development across the public and private sectors, but rather creating and testing a transmission system, subsidizing purchases of production equipment and also paying towards programme production, launching and operating an HDTV satellite to deliver the programmes, getting the TV sets into the shops and organizing public demonstrations to whet the appetite of consumers. However: 'The industrial planners in Japan and Europe underestimated the complexity of the high-tech food chain and overestimated their ability to co-ordinate producers and to play the role of consumers.'[16]

Europe's HDTV scheme failed, and was effectively buried in 1993. Delors was bitter, according to Charles Grant, although not everybody was sympathetic. John Gillingham, expert in European industry, commented scathingly that 'The EC's HDTV policy was an exercise in pure protectionism.'[17]

But as the 1990s progressed, European industrial policy was far from dead and buried. On the contrary, it was on course to unveil its

most visible and distinctive product, the A3XX superjumbo passenger
jet, announced in June 1994 and entering service as the Airbus A380
in October 2007, the largest civil airliner in the world. Parallel to this
were pan-European projects in the field of strike aircraft and military
transporters, and as the millennium approached there was excited
talk of a giant 'Euroco' corporation that would unite the EU's activities in defence, aviation and space.

For enthusiasts for industrial strategy, the euro promised to
formalize and strengthen such policy at the European level, cutting
out the naysayers in Britain and elsewhere – numbering amongst
whom was even the generally pro-European Kenneth Clarke, then
trade and industry minister and later chancellor of the exchequer,
who famously explained his refusal to participate in a space
programme thus: 'We have declined to spend £200 million a year
on a project to put Europeans – probably Frenchmen – into orbit
by the year 2000. That does not have adequate advantages. We are
now examining what other projects might be of industrial advantage to us, and what participation the private sector is prepared to
contemplate to obtain commercial advantages for itself.'[18]

Again, the lack of exits in the euro 'building' could only appeal
to leftists. A single industrial strategy was set to become the hand-
maiden of the single currency. Both would take place at the
European level, with national governments playing a secondary
role (if that).

As a footnote to the story of the A380 airliner, in an interview
with the *Daily Telegraph* on 20 February 2016, Tom Williams, chief
operating officer at Airbus and second-in-command at the group,
said of the superjumbo that the programme as a whole would never
be profitable, and suggested it had been, in essence, a vanity project.
It was, perhaps, a metaphor for so much that had happened in the
EU in the 1990s and beyond.

The 'Big Four' benefits of the exit-free single currency – an end
to speculation, the diminishment of national frontiers, the
entrenchment of employment and social rights, and the promotion
of activist industrial policy – more than compensated many on the
left for any uneasiness about the absence of escape routes. In terms

of blocking up these apertures, there was really very little to which the left could object. Moreover, once snug inside the common home – or perhaps 'common European fortress' would be a better description – there were plenty of fittings and furnishings practically guaranteed to delight those of a leftist frame of mind. It is to two of the most important of these – the concepts of 'cohesion' and 'convergence' – that we now turn.

Munichs for everybody: Creating Europe's 'social space'

Strictly speaking, cohesion and convergence were distinct notions to emerge from the excitements of the late 1980s. The former had its roots in the idea that moving money round the EC/EU from richer areas to poorer ones would act to buttress a sense of European identity by, in effect, compensating people in the poorer regions for their economic underperformance. The latter notion, as the name suggests, was based on the idea of trying to lift the poorer regions to the self-sustaining economic level of the wealthier ones, thus attempting to ensure that, over time, the affluence of communities in such places as Munich or Amsterdam would be matched in the Italian south or the Iberian peninsula.

In fact, the distinction was more apparent than real. Both notions were key pillars of the 'single social space' that enthused the architects of EMU. They were, in fact, intimately linked, as was made clear by Bruce Millan, a British member of the European Commission. He said: 'Cohesion cannot take place without a long-term and consistent effort on the part of the Structural Funds. Without an agreement to strengthen further cohesion there would have been no decision at Maastricht on the Union Treaty.' Millan added that there was 'a clear link' between the cohesion proposals and the possibility of achieving real convergence, adding: 'Without cohesion and convergence, EMU will not work.'[19]

Seven years earlier, Commission president Jacques Delors had called for policy towards the regions to be more ambitious, claiming that during the previous years, 'regional disparities within the Community have widened', with the traditionally deprived areas in the rural periphery being joined by decaying industrial rust-belt areas 'whose traditional economic base is in structural decline'. The Community's structural funds, he said, ought to support structural conversion and adjustment projects in the troubled areas, rather than being used in a palliative manner. 'The Commission aims to reverse the trend toward treating these funds as a mere redistribution mechanism.'[20]

This was music to the ears of the British left, whose heartlands were indeed in 'structural decline' and for whom assisted adjustment to new industries would be most welcome. Furthermore, British leftists had long suspected that regional imbalances within the UK resulted from structural unfairness, in that the wealthier regions, such as the south-east, were essentially parasitic upon the poorer ones, and that the poverty of the latter was directly traceable to the greed of the former. One expression had it that the roots of the economic tree were in the north of the country but the fruit was picked in the south. If this were true, then redirecting money from richer to poorer regions, whether for the purposes of convergence or cohesion, would be only right and proper. Anyway, glaring inequality between one region and another was no more acceptable than between one person and another. To leftists, chance plays as big a role as hard work, innate genius or grit and determination in the achievement of economic prosperity, both at the individual and the regional level. Redistribution is thus a moral imperative.

There was a further recommendation of the policy for the left: the stout opposition of Margaret Thatcher, Britain's Conservative Party leader, who had no time whatsoever for the whole idea, as seen in this outburst: 'Social space is the latest one [in European political circles]. "Social space," I said, "what do you mean, you want an extension to your house because you have not got enough living room, what sort is social space?" . . . Social cohesion? It is not a phrase I ever use!'[21] Less than two months later, in an exchange in the House of Commons, Dafydd Elis-Thomas (Plaid Cymru MP for Meirionnydd Nant Conwy) asked the prime minister whether she understood that the Community's 'social dimension' and 'social space' were so called because they referred to the 'inequalities created spatially by a free-market system'? He asked her to commit herself anew to more regional spending to offset inequalities likely to be created by the completion of the European single market in 1992. It seemed unlikely, and indeed the prime minister replied, first, that structural funds were already being increased and, second, that her interpretation of the social dimension did not see 'two sides to industry; we believe in every earner and owner pulling together for the prosperity of all'.[22]

According to a Commission paper, 1988 was the watershed year for regional policy, and Delors was leading the way. He had, it seems, 'one bold objective in mind', which was to transform the policy from 'an essentially intergovernmental budgetary transfer to that of a genuine regional development tool' that could provide real solutions for the poorer regions of the Community.[23]

Marjorie Jouen, writing for Notre Europe, noted that the cohesion policy was based on the notion that everyone would be a winner, because sums distributed to the poorest regions would have 'indirect feedback effects' for the economies of the wealthier parts of the Community. This had been borne out, she wrote: 'This catching-up mechanism led to a second-tier movement of capital, with 30%–40% in favour of contributing countries.'[24]

For the left, there were few if any aspects of cohesion or convergence to which to object.

Europe united: The wider picture

The liberal left was not, of course, the sole 'target audience' for European Economic and Monetary Union, a project of which the euro is, today, the most visible manifestation. Many of the key impulses behind EMU either spanned the political spectrum or were of no specific interest to many on the left. Indeed, EMU was, in many ways, a coming together of various strands of the intellectual legacy of recent decades.

The first strand can perhaps be discerned in the lingering Cold War politics of the 1950s, which continued to inform decision-making right up until the collapse of the Soviet Union in 1991. The

European Community had never enjoyed the same status in that conflict as had the North Atlantic Treaty Organization – an ill-fated attempt to found a European Defence Community had foundered in 1952. The obvious way for the EEC (as was) to up its game would have been to go for full political union, thus becoming the joint largest 'state' in NATO, alongside the United States.

But this was fraught with difficulties, even after the departure in April 1969 of the EEC's arch-antifederalist, Charles de Gaulle. With six members (nine after 1973), there was no clear agreement as to what political union could mean, and thus no obvious way forward. To Americans or the Japanese, for example, political union is self-defining: there is a central authority – however circumscribed its powers – from which subsidiary bodies draw their authority. Europe seemed to be edging towards a confederal model in which the constituent leaders formed a sort of cabinet, the European Council, which took decisions by majority vote.

In parallel, the institutions of the European Community/European Union were emerging not as common-service agencies that worked on behalf of the Council but as equal partners. In this unusual, not to say bizarre, system, it is perhaps unsurprising that by 2015 the EU boasted no fewer than five 'presidents' – of the ECB, the Council, the European Commission, and the European Parliament, along with the head of government of the country holding the rotating six-monthly EU presidency.

At the time of the Delors Report, presidential inflation had yet to reach such heights: the total was holding steady at a modest two (Commission and Parliament). But the urge to press ahead with the unification of (firstly) Western Europe was running strong, not least because the Single European Act of 1986, establishing the single market, was seen as ending the period of stagnation brought about by the economic turmoil of the 1970s.

The December 1990 Rome Conference was, in theory, two conferences – one on economic and monetary union and the other covering political union. But there was little doubt that it was to the first of these conferences that most attention was directed. Monetary union had long been identified as a 'quick win' in the integration of Europe. According to the Delors Report: 'In 1969 the Heads of State or Government, meeting in The Hague, agreed that a plan should be drawn up with a view to the creation, in stages, of an economic and monetary union within the Community.' It added that the report in 1970 of Pierre Werner, Luxembourg's prime minister and finance minister, presented a plan for economic and monetary union, and in March 1971, following the Werner Report, member states expressed 'their political will to establish an economic and monetary union'.[25]

But the beauty of EMU is that it could be presented as an essentially technical matter, a successor – as suggested by Delors – to Bretton Woods, to the short-lived 'snake' system of the early 1970s, and to the EMS/ERM, while at the same time involving an enormous shift of authority to the European level. The circle is squared thus: 'the need for a *transfer of decision-making power* from Member States to the Community as a whole would arise primarily in the fields of monetary policy and macro-economic management [our emphasis].'[26]

If this impetus to use a single currency and single economic policy to create what was to become known as a European superstate had some roots in the Cold War atmosphere of the '50s, it also owed a debt to the 'big is beautiful' thinking of the '60s, an era of huge (by the standards of the time) corporate takeovers, new global institutions (the UN Conference on Trade and Development, the UN Industrial Development Organization), a general rise across the West in the size and scope of government and a feeling that the amalgamation of operating units of all types, from schools and hospitals to businesses and even countries, was inevitable.

In a world of 'big players', according to this argument, none of the individual members of the EU could stand up to them alone. This kind of thinking was explicit in French support for the 1985 single-market legislation, which took effect in 1992. One advertisement depicted a plucky young boxer in tricolour shorts explaining that he was always being knocked about by the Americans and the Japanese. 'But now,' he added, 'I have my buddies to help me' – at which point eleven other plucky little fellows piled into the ring, each of whose shorts were decorated with his national flag. It was not very subtle and showed scant regard for the rules of boxing. But the message could not be clearer: together we are not only strong but we are as big as the big guys.

Economic and monetary union would help to create a new bloc capable of standing up to competitors from within the capitalist world. What was more, in this age where size mattered, the three powers would be able to collaborate and make the world safer and more prosperous. This thinking was alive and well as recently as 2003, expressed here by former Conservative MP and national journalist Robert Harvey:

> The real hope lies in deals between the three main economic groupings – the three world superstates ... the American super-state [NAFTA joins 250 million Americans with 87 million Mexicans and 25 million Canadians with combined GDP of $7 trillion a year] ... The European superstate of some 350 million people produces a combined GDP of more than $6 trillion a year. The Japanese superstate ... has a population of 126 million and an output of $3.5 trillion.[27]

If this was to be a new global directorate, Europe would be a one-third shareholder, and the most visible immediate manifestation of this power would be a single European currency, a mighty reserve asset to sit alongside the dollar and the yen. A single Eurozone seat on institutions such as the International Monetary Fund would further enhance and magnify the clout of the single-currency bloc.

By the mid-1970s it has become clear that there was nothing especially inevitable about this process: not only had nationalist movements dismembered the European colonial empires, but, more recently, centrifugal forces were threatening to pull apart some of the post-colonial states (in Biafra and Bangladesh) as well as menacing the unity of long-established nations, in Flanders, the Basque Country, Scotland and elsewhere.

But the questioning mood seemed to have passed European officialdom by. Bigger was better because 'Europe' needed to stand up to other large entities, because the day of the nation state was past, because the resource base needed to fund commercial, scientific, technical and infrastructural development needed to be on a European scale, and because the age of mass air travel, high-speed trains and instant communication rendered internal frontiers obsolete – especially those that were represented by the need to exchange currency when moving from one part of the European Community to another.

From the 1960s to the 1970s, where we find another inspiration for the euro in the Bundesbank's much-praised handling of the inflationary aftershock of the 1973 energy crisis. In this it was helped by both its constitutional position and the German public's historic aversion to inflation (the two are, of course, linked). As Bernard Connolly described: 'The Bundesbank reigned supreme: its freedom to set interest rates, free from electoral or other forms of political accountability, allowed it to crack the whip at the government and unions.'[28] The EMS was an attempt by other members of the European Community to tap into the Bundesbank's rock-hard credibility and to benefit not only from the stability of using the Deutschmark as an anchor currency but also from the lower interest rates this was expected to bring. This admiration for the German way of doing things was cemented in May 1983, when the two-year-old socialist government of President Mitterrand was forced to abandon its reflationary policies and negotiate an 8 per cent devaluation of the franc against the mark. The quid pro quo for agreeing to the devaluation was for France to adopt German-like policies on wages, government budgeting and targets for the current account.[29]

By the end of the 1980s, looking up to the Bundesbank was the conventional attitude in Britain, continental Europe and elsewhere. In, let us say, 1980, the notion of freeing the UK's reserve bank from political control was an eccentric viewpoint, little discussed. Even by the middle of the decade, it was seen as a far-fetched idea usually described as 'privatizing the Bank of England' and regarded by many as making little more sense than the satirical 'politician' Screaming Lord Sutch's demand for a second Monopolies and Mergers Commission, on the grounds that having just one constituted . . . a monopoly.

And by 1990, the positions were reversed, the defenders of the status quo being required to explain why anyone in their right mind would wish to reject the huge benefits of having a Bundesbank-type institution take charge of the nation's monetary policy. The Bundesbank was to be the inevitable template for the ECB. They were even to be based in the same city, Frankfurt am Main. It was to be granted both operational independence and 'target' independence.

Was the Bundesbank's record oversold? Perhaps so from the point of view of its stewardship of the Deutschmark, which may have been a hard currency in relation to other major European Community denominations such as the franc, the pound and the lira, but fared rather less well against the (then gold-backed) Swiss franc. As John Laughland noted, writing in 1995, 'the allegedly perfect D-Mark has depreciated by one-third of its value against the Swiss franc since 1972', and 'has also lost 75 per cent of its value against gold since the Bundesbank was created in 1957'.[30]

Misplaced or not, if admiration for the Bundesbank's record in the '70s was a prompt for the creation of the single currency, so too was the monetarist thinking of the '80s. The 'prominent role for money' written into the constitution of the monetary union was a clear statement of intent that no other objectives set for the central bank would be allowed to elbow aside consideration of the money supply.

The eventual structure of the bank was said to rest on two pillars – money-supply growth, and other economic and financial conditions – with price stability to be achieved by analysis of both. There is a double irony in Margaret Thatcher's vociferous opposition to the establishment of the ECB. Not only was she the politician most closely associated with the doctrines of monetarism in the earlier part of her premiership, but by the time she left office she and her Treasury colleagues had long given up any pretence of taking seriously the once all-important 'money numbers', monthly statistics for the various measures of the quantity of money in the system.

Beyond these historically rooted impulses, there were more immediate motivations for the creation of the euro. Perhaps the most important was the alleged need to 'restrain' Germany as its unification neared in 1990 following the spectacular collapse of the epically misnamed German Democratic Republic at the end of 1989. This enfolding of Germany into a larger political unit would be accompanied by extending a welcome into a greatly expanded European family to the newly orphaned countries of the disintegrating eastern bloc. A grand European settlement, including the unified Germany, was at hand. The single currency would be its most visible manifestation. But by the time the euro was founded at the end of the 1990s, the world had moved on.

Alongside this post-Cold War political architecture, the euro was credited in advance with all sorts of other wondrous secondary properties. It was going to lift EU growth by eliminating cross-border transaction costs, a key element of what Brussels insiders called 'non-Europe'. It was going to facilitate a wave of mergers that would create European corporate 'champions'. It would promote price transparency, bringing down costs for consumers; low inflation and interest rates would be benignly exported from Germany. It would tackle a long-standing beef of enthusiasts for a united Europe, that of people travelling round the continent having to endure the time, trouble and expense of purchasing foreign currency. This last aspect prompted an amusing intervention from the former British chancellor Lord Lawson in July 1995, during a debate on monetary union at which he was sharing a platform with Karl von Wogau, chairman of the European Parliament's Committee on Economic and Monetary Affairs. Mr Wogau told of a recent harrowing experience in which he had seen a third of his 1,000 Belgian francs (set aside, but not needed, for cab fares during a visit to Madrid) swallowed up in transaction charges. Find some different moneychangers, advised Lawson – those rates are totally uncompetitive.

Above all, the biggest permanent source of uncertainty – the exchange rate – would be removed for those doing business within the EU. Exporters would trade across a stable currency platform.

No tool does every job, and the sheer range of benefits being ascribed to single-currency membership ought to have aroused scepticism, as should the unspoken theme running through all the above-mentioned sources of inspiration: the bringing into existence of a huge new political unit.

The euro planners' fundamental mistake was to assume that the creation of a 'United States of Europe' would be facilitated by a currency akin to the dollar and a central bank akin to the Federal Reserve Board. This, though, misunderstood the lessons of the US, namely that the dollar and the Fed emerged only after more than a century of economic and political development, and that the US had the preconditions in place to make a single currency work: a large federal budget, a flexible labour market and – most importantly – a single language. Many American economists, including Paul Krugman, Joseph Stiglitz and Rudi Dornbusch, warned that the euro would not work. They were right. This attempt to reverse-engineer a political federation was woefully misconceived.

As with those features of special interest to the left, the appeal of these wider aspects of the EMU project was not despite the absence of escape hatches but because of it. In a superpower Europe based on big-is-beautiful thinking, there could be no room for opt-outs or exits. The lack of any side doors into which recalcitrant governments could duck if the going got tough, or if they – or, more likely, their electorates – objected to a development of policy or a major decision, was what would distinguish a truly united Europe from just another international club.

Next, we turn to the monetary philosophy underlying the single currency, one that has much in common with that which underpinned the gold standard. Like the euro, the gold standard was supposed to last for ever, more or less. If anything, the gold standard, unmourned by the left since its demise in the Great Depression, was more flexible.

A common factor, we believe, links the two systems: France.

CHAPTER 3

THE FRENCH VICE

Gold, the euro and a peculiar taste for monetary discipline

. . . they told her that her hands would be untied, but merely so that they could be fastened anew, a short while later.

Pauline Réage, *The Story of O*

The International Bureau of Weights and Measures is situated in an historic French building, the Pavillon de Breteuil, built in 1672, in a public park in Sèvres on the outskirts of Paris. In a secured vault within the building sits a small metal cylinder about the size of a saltcellar and made of an alloy of platinum and iridium. This is the kilogram. Not a kilogram, but *the* kilogram, the one against which every other kilogram in the world is measured.

The French National Assembly launched the kilo along with the metre in 1799, dedicating these measures 'to all nations' and 'to all times', neatly encapsulating post-Revolutionary France's search for universality and permanence, alongside a yearning for precise and objective measurement. Other manifestations of this have included the attempt to metricate the calendar (with its ten-day week and 144-minute hour) and the rather more successful legacy of the 1789 'Declaration of the Rights of Man and of the Citizen'.

Then there is French officialdom's long love affair with gold bullion. President Charles de Gaulle weighed in on the subject in 1965, speaking of the need for 'an indisputable monetary base which bears the mark of no country in particular'. What base? he asked. 'In truth, there can in this regard be no other criterion or standard than gold.' Why? Gold, said the president, 'does not change its nature' and 'can be cast indifferently into bars, ingots or coins'; furthermore, it 'has no nationality' and is held 'eternally and universally as the inalterable fiduciary value par excellence'.[1] De Gaulle's remarks, made in front of a thousand journalists, were praised by his economic adviser Jacques Rueff as showing the president to be 'the statesman *who will restore true money*'.[2]

Again, the same search for permanence, for a standard that does not change, for rules, a search that may be taken as demonstrating the Janus face of French society, the side looking in the opposite direction to that countenance more familiar to outsiders, that of the freewheeling café-frequenting gourmand for whom a spot of late-afternoon *cinq-à-sept* adultery is (supposedly) no big deal.

Official France's fondness for gold may seem to contradict the aforementioned search for rational, rigorous standards. But that is to see bullion through British Keynesian eyes as being, barbarous or not, a 'yellow relic', a hangover from a superstitious, premodern era. From the French viewpoint, by contrast, gold resembles rather more one of those precious, scientific measurements, less a romantic, irrational fetish, more a monetary version of the distinctly prosaic definition of the standard unit of length, the metre: the length of the path travelled by light in a vacuum during a time interval of $1/299{,}792{,}458$ of a second.

France has long been a 'goldbug nation', partly for historical reasons. Notes Peter L. Bernstein: 'The French have changed their monetary system on many occasions over the centuries, which is probably why French peasants have earned the reputation of being congenital hoarders of gold.'[3] In a sense, the worthless paper *assignats* issued by the crumbling French monarchy between 1790 and 1795 – which sparked the riots whence sprang the French Revolution – may be seen as France's Weimar moment.

As we shall see, France was the last major country to leave the gold-exchange standard in the 1930s, and de Gaulle's insistence on exercising his right to swap dollar bills for bullion helped to break the post-war Bretton Woods fixed exchange-rate system in the late 1960s. France today holds the fifth largest stock of official gold reserves in the world, and the four higher-ranking gold-holders include the International Monetary Fund itself.[4] France's 2,535.5 tonnes of gold compares with just 310.3 tonnes in the vaults of the Bank of England (the UK is in eighteenth place). More than 65 per cent of France's official reserves are held in gold, against just 11.2 per cent in the UK. Until 1999, under the Warsaw Convention, compensation for passengers injured in the course of international air travel was calculated in the delightfully antiquated currency of the gold franc.

And France, of course, was the prime architect of the euro. The report that called it into existence was compiled by a committee chaired by former French finance minister Jacques Delors, the same Jacques Delors who in 1983 had ushered in the 'franc fort' policy under which the French currency was lashed to the Deutschmark and German rigour imported into French economic management.

Our contention is that there is a streak of gold that runs right through the middle of the single-currency project: that it is, in effect, a modern-day version of the gold standard, and that it will fail, just as the gold standard failed, and for similar reasons. This chapter is about the parallels between the euro and the nineteenth-century gold standard. The comparisons are marked, as we show.

The gold standard involved countries giving up control over their own currencies (albeit most currencies would have been backed by some kind of metallic standard at that time).

So does euro membership.

It involved a commitment to total free movement of capital.

So does euro membership.

It insisted on deflation for countries that were running balance of payments deficits.

So does euro membership.

And it put no pressure on creditor countries to help weaker countries.

Neither does euro membership.

A key similarity between the gold standard and the euro is that both systems ensured that the burden of 'adjustment' to each shock that buffeted the economy would fall largely on working people and the poor, in contrast to the option of letting the purchasing power of the currency take the hit, either internally, through inflation, or externally, through a fall in the exchange rate.

The euro has all these features plus a few extra, including countries being prepared to abandon their own national currency and to cede control over monetary policy to a central bank run by technocrats. In extremis, as seen in 1931, a country could take its currency off the gold standard. No such option exists within the euro system, although the international law principle of *lex monetae* safeguards the right of countries to change their currency without consulting anyone else.

But if, as we say, there is a streak of gold running through the euro like the word 'Brighton' through a stick of seaside rock, so France will be a constant reference point throughout this chapter. France was a devoted member of the gold standard and its post-First World War successor, the gold-exchange standard. It valued the Bretton Woods system for its ultimate link to bullion but disliked the intermediating role of a paper currency, the dollar, and sought to end its use. It was a key architect of the 1978 European Monetary System and from 1983 onwards helped turn the system's Exchange Rate Mechanism into a rigid hard-money regime.

Finally, it was the prime mover behind Economic and Monetary Union, the creation of *la monnaie unique*, one currency for the whole of Europe, one indivisible and permanent means of accounting, of storing value and of exchange. One unit that would brook no alternatives because, in truth, how could there be alternatives to the sole denomination? In terms of absurdity that would be akin to having an 'alternative kilogram'. Britain's Margaret Thatcher, in what was to prove the latter stages of her premiership, tried to head off the euro by promoting, variously, 'competing currencies' (with all European Community – as was – currencies enjoying legal tender status in every national territory), and a common currency, which would circulate alongside the national currencies. Her chancellor, John Major, suggested this could be a 'hard' version of the ECU, or Ecu – the European Currency Unit that served as the numeraire for Community accounting purposes.

It was to no avail. EMU was not about a common currency. It was about a single currency.

It could be argued that the euro represents the last great French European project, rounding off the sequence that began with the European Iron and Steel Community and taking in the ERM and the huge programme of harmonization of regulations and majority-voting concomitant upon the 1985 single market. As authors, we tend to avoid expressions such as 'the first' or 'the last' because events have a way of springing surprises. But it is inarguable that France's position within the EU has weakened in the twenty-four years since the signing of the Maastricht Treaty, the document that paved the way for the euro. Whether a less powerful France in the final decade of the twentieth century would have created the conditions for a substantially different form of EMU, shorn of the French-led insistence on a monetary monolith whose unchallengeable status was remarkably close to that of gold itself in times gone by, is impossible to judge.

We shall look first at the gold standard and gold-exchange standard, examining ways in which it pre-echoed the single currency. Then we shall look at the Bretton Woods system, one based on gold but designed to achieve very different outcomes – namely, to deal with unemployment and impoverishment – from those ascribed by critics to the gold-exchange standard and, by implication, its pre-First World War predecessor. After this comes the period between the breakdown of Bretton Woods in 1971 and the launch of the euro in January 1999, a period marked by two attempts to 'anchor' European currencies rather than cast them adrift on the white waters of the foreign-exchange markets: the 1972–74 'snake in the tunnel' and the EMS/ERM, the heyday of which lasted from 1978 to 1992/93, although officially it remains in existence. Finally, we look at the euro, and will argue that, it many ways, the wheel has come full circle: the Eurozone countries are, in effect, back on the gold standard – one of their own devising.

Before going further, we would like to explain the chapter title. For more than a century, the notion of *le vice anglais* has been a standing accusation against the British (especially British men), the vice in question being an alleged fondness for reliving childhood punishments, perhaps with the assistance of a cane-wielding 'dominatrix'. But it is the French rather than the British who seem to have developed a taste for 'strict discipline' in the economic and monetary sphere, who demand to be 'bound tightly' to 'hard' monetary measures – gold, the Deutschmark, the euro – and who insist on stringent penalties for those who break the rules, though they become a little squeamish when, as in 2003, it is their turn for a taste of the lash.

We ought not to tease our French friends too much. From the British or American perspective, France's repeated attempts to define a 'real' value for money, in much the same way as the country pioneered attempts to define units of weight or distance, may seem a misbegotten Enlightenment-era enterprise, conjuring up visions of top-hatted 'men of reason' sitting round a huge table in a baroque hall. But it could be argued that France's attempts, however misguided, to anchor its currency at a fixed value are more honourable than the attitude of the Anglo-Saxon nations, who allow the dollar or the pound to slide up and down the exchange-rate tables with little thought as to the quite unfair damage being inflicted on investors, consumers and businesses, especially export businesses.

It is in that spirit that we examine these different monetary regimes and France's key place in each of them.

An olden goldie: The bullion argument

Surprising as it may seem, to the dedicated goldbug, the gold standard, even in its late nineteenth- and very early twentieth-century prime, is very much a second-best system. In the eyes of gold aficionados, a paper-money system backed by gold, even when the paper can freely be exchanged for the underlying bullion, can never stand shoulder to shoulder with one in which 'the commodity which serves as a means of exchange has, or should have, value in its own right, independently of its function of money'.[5] This is the 'bullionist' argument, that money is not really money unless its physical representation carries its own embedded worth. Anything else comprises worthless bits of cupronickel and crinkly paper, backed by nothing other than the dubious pledge of transient political figures.

In recent times, there have been suggestions that the bullionists may ultimately be proved right, should paper money cease to exist on paper and be dematerialized into the electronic ether. Then, the only valuable physical money would be that which contains valuable metals, gold in particular.[6] Bill Bonner and Addison Wiggin put the bullionist argument at its starkest. 'Do you know what the long-term mean value of paper currency is?' they ask. As with fellow goldbug de Gaulle, they have a ready answer: 'Well, it is zero. That is what the average paper currency is worth most of the time . . . the dollar is almost certain to revert to its real value – which is as empty as deep space.'[7]

In October 2015, it seemed that bullionism might have been about to sign up an unlikely recruit – President Barack Obama and Secretary of the Treasury Jack Lew. With Congress refusing to raise the federal government's borrowing limit, the prospect arose that the US government would start to default on 3 November. Loopholes in the constitutional bar on any organ of the federal government other than Congress borrowing money led to suggestions that the Treasury could mint high-value coins made of platinum, which would retail at very high prices (thus bringing cash in the door) but would technically be legal tender, the issue of which is a Treasury responsibility. Fortunately for all concerned, perhaps, Congress and the White House agreed a deal at the end of October.

All that said, most goldbugs (we use the expression in a neutral, not a pejorative sense – 'gold fans' or 'gold lovers' sounding twee, or worse) are happy – or would be, were it on offer – with a system in which the money issue is backed by bullion but in which the denominations themselves can be in the form of base metal, paper – or electronic book-entries. They are more interested in the bedrock justification for the use of gold as a monetary asset to back a currency issue, which is that it represents an objective, almost absolute, form of value. The argument for gold's intrinsic, unchanging worth is bolstered by the assertion that it is the only monetary asset that is nobody else's liability, that it does not rely on anyone's 'promise to pay', and that for this reason it is universally acceptable. There is, in truth, no other store of value with which it can be compared.

In his remarks in 1965 quoted above, Charles de Gaulle was not suggesting the replacement of the paper franc with gold coins, but rather the establishment of a monetary system based on gold reserves. The pre-1914 gold-standard system, in fact. After all, were de Gaulle's assertion that gold's value is 'eternal and universal' to be accurate, one would need a very strong argument against putting it at the foundation of the monetary order. It would be rather as if the scientific community, while accepting that light travels at 186,282 miles per second, nevertheless decided that there may be some benefit in conducting experiments and calculations using different speeds.

De Gaulle mentioned in his appeal for a bullion system that he drew his inspiration from the monetary regime in place before 'the world's great misfortunes', in other words the two world wars. He was suggesting some sort of return to the gold standard. Thus it is to the operation of the gold standard, the system predicated on this eternal and universal conception of gold's value, that we now turn.

Raising the standard: Myths and realities about the pre-1914 system

The gold standard sought to harness the allegedly solid and dependable value of gold bullion to the needs of an industrializing world. This supposedly objective, unchanging value stretches back in time and far into the future. It is said that, over time, gold holds its value. But that time can be very long indeed – the oft-cited statistic is that an ounce of gold buys roughly the same amount of loaves of bread today as it did during the reign of Nebuchadnezzar, king of Babylon in the sixth century BC.[8] There will, however, have been many periods in the intervening two and half millennia in which the gold-to-bread ratio was wildly out of kilter with this average, either on the upside or the downside.

Never has Keynes's dictum that in the long run we are all dead seemed more apposite. There are few nations or societies, and no individuals, who can wait hundreds of years or more for gold to re-equilibrate. The counter-argument to this view is that the smooth operation of the nineteenth-century gold standard gives the lie to such an objection and also neatly pots the notion that it is the very physicality of bullion, its quiddity as a mineral, that makes it unsuitable for any sort of monetary role.

Let us look first at what is supposedly the Victorian high noon of the gold bullion system, as sketched by the historian Niall Ferguson: 'The road to an international gold standard was indeed more tortuous than is often acknowledged. For most of the nine-teenth century two of the five great powers – Austria and Russia – had widely fluctuating exchange rates. The United States suspended convertibility as a result of the Civil War in 1862 and remained on a paper standard until 1879.'[9] Ferguson adds that in 1868, only Britain and some of its 'economic dependencies' – Portugal, Egypt, Canada, Chile and Australia – were on the gold standard, with other powers such as France and Russia adhering to a 'bimetallic' system combining gold with silver, and many other countries using a silver standard. 'Not until 1900 was the transition to gold more or less complete.' Thus, the full-blown operational gold standard lasted for just fourteen years, being suspended at the outbreak of the First World War and never properly restored.

Where did France sit in this system? As a full member, certainly: Bernstein lists the managers of the Bank of France alongside those of the Bank of England as the 'high priests' of what amounted to a monetary religion, the pre-1914 gold standard, which 'shimmers from the past like the memory of a lost paradise'.[10] Interestingly, however, France's devotion was somewhat less enthusiastic than either its embrace of the post-war gold-exchange standard or its attempts to turn the 1944–71 Bretton Woods system into a de facto bullion standard. One reason for this was Germany's use of the French indemnity of 5 billion francs, payable after its defeat in the

1870–71 Franco-Prussian War and denominated in gold, to help finance Berlin's own membership of the gold standard, which it joined that year. Another was France's continued inclusion of silver, as mentioned above, in its monetary system.

During the brief period of its supremacy, the gold standard's operations were sufficiently opaque to have generated controversy among economists ever since. As Ferguson notes, some suggest it was primarily a fixed exchange-rate system, geared to the needs of the expansion of international trade; some focus on its role as a guarantor of price stability; others see it as a mechanism 'to mediate between the international and the domestic economy by varying interest rates in response to gold flows'; and to others it was more straightforwardly a means of settling international debts, a successor to Tudor mercantilism. Furthermore, Ferguson adds, 'there is considerable evidence of outright breaches of the rules'.[11]

Nor was all necessarily well in the metropolis at the heart of the system, London. David Kynaston records that the years 1903–06 saw great concern at the low levels of reserves: 'Resources and responsibilities were clearly out of kilter,' and there was a suggestion that the clearing banks should raise their own 'special' gold reserves, to sit alongside those of the Bank of England, in order to shore up the system.[12]

If the functioning of the gold standard was neither as universal nor as trouble-free as has been claimed, neither does its existence during a period of rapid industrialization and expanding international trade give the lie to the idea that a single mineral, however precious, ought not to be pressed into service as the basis for a monetary system. Put bluntly, the gold standard 'got lucky', in that bullion output surged in the mid- and late nineteenth century, from an average of 42 tonnes a year in the 1840s to 965 tonnes in the 1850s, more than half of which came from Russia.[13]

That being said, the gold standard certainly presented an imposing face to the world in the years running up to the First World War. According to Douglas (later Lord) Jay, Labour minister in both the 1940s and 1960s, 'The whole impressive system ... rested on certain basic assumptions.' One was that 'when overall money demand fell, pay rates could in the last resort be reduced'. Another was that the system would last almost for ever, as would the dollar–sterling exchange rate. 'For since the dollar was also now fixed in terms of gold, the exchange rate between the two was immutably established at $4.86 to £1.'[14]

As became clear when the 'guns of August' heralded the start of the First World War, the system would not last almost for ever. In the deadly serious business of a global conflict, the whole notion of gold convertibility must have appeared like a mannered Victorian parlour game. The gold standard was suspended, and, as mentioned above, it was never to return in its original form.

A 'gold-exchange standard' was created at the Genoa Conference in 1922 and lasted in some form or another with diminishing membership until the eve of the Second World War. But to supporters of the gold standard, it was a poor thing indeed. John Laughland remarks that the Genoa Conference actually recommended reducing the role of gold and using foreign currency reserves instead. This meant that central banks in countries such as those in continental Europe could 'count in their monetary reserves dollars and pounds sterling, the so-called "key currencies" which remained a direct link to gold. They could use these holdings in key currencies to issue their national currency.'[15]

France, however, was to prove a stalwart of the gold-exchange standard. In 1924, in an attempt to stabilize the gyrating franc, Paris turned to the American finance house of J.P. Morgan for a sizeable loan. The terms, reminiscent of the austerity packages that were to be forced on the troubled Eurozone members ninety-odd years later, included tax increases, spending cuts and the pledging of France's gold as security. That said, the French experience after initially joining the gold-exchange standard was a positive one. As Bernstein notes, 'a flood of foreign gold and capital rushed toward Paris. That these repercussions would cause serious problems for London was more of a source of satisfaction than of concern.'[16]

France's gold stocks were rising rapidly: according to Bernstein, the Bank of France's gold holdings were double those of Britain by

1926; and two years later, the French hoard would be approaching five times the size.[17] In a pre-echo of de Gaulle's demands on Fort Knox, the US bullion depository, in the 1960s, the Bank of France threatened to turn its sterling balances in London into gold, thus depleting the UK's reserves. In the event, Benjamin Strong, president of the Federal Reserve Bank of New York, intervened to calm matters down. Even when Austria's Creditanstalt bank collapsed in May 1931, the gold-exchange standard continued to work well for France, allowing its central bank to accumulate yet more bullion by switching deposits held with counterpart institutions into gold. But the clock was ticking.

Central to the gold-exchange standard, as with the euro, was the absence of political 'interference' in the operation of the system and prickliness on the part of central bankers who felt this convention was bring breached.

As David Kynaston notes, Montagu Norman, governor of the Bank of England from 1920 to 1944, bemoaned 'the way in which monetary policy in general, and Bank Rate in particular, was becoming politicised'. Kynaston goes on:

> he reproachfully told the Chancellor, Austen Chamberlain, that 'when I call to mind your remark to my predecessor (that an independent Rise in the Bank Rate would be an unfriendly act); when I remember our continuing desire for higher rates ever since last July and indeed long before it, and your continuing unwillingness to consent, owing to political reasons ... I wonder what (in the spirit as well as in the letter) is the meaning of 'political pressure'.[18]

Ultimately, of course, Britain's relationship with the international monetary system, the relationship of which the Bank of England was, with the US authorities, the guardian and guarantor, was to suffer from political interference of the most unmistakable kind. Kynaston reports that on 23 September 1931 Norman docked at Liverpool, 'to be told formally that Britain had, in his absence, been compelled to leave the gold-exchange standard'.[19]

This effective devaluation of sterling, and the concomitant devaluation of the dollar against gold in 1933, turned the tables on France, whose membership of the gold-exchange standard began to run cold. France, along with Switzerland, the Netherlands and Belgium, clung to the gold-exchange standard, but French goods were now expensive compared with those produced by British competitors and the horrors of deflation hit hard, with a 25 per cent fall in the price level between 1931 and 1935 and the loss of a third of gross national product.[20]

By 1936, industrial and political unrest and the election of a Popular Front government ended French membership of the gold-exchange standard. In a face-saving exercise, French departure from the system was dressed up as a three-way agreement involving Britain and the United States. Similarly, in May 1983, a steep devaluation of the franc within the Exchange Rate Mechanism was presented as being, in large part, a 'revaluation' of the Deutschmark.

Into the arboretum: Bretton Woods and after

Robert Skidelsky, Keynes's biographer, writes that the failure of the gold standard had its roots in the fact that it forced adjustment on the debtor: 'Adjustment, he [Keynes] wrote, was "compulsory for the debtor and voluntary for the creditor". This allowed creditor countries to hoard their surpluses while obliging debtor countries to deflate their economies.'[21]

This indictment – uncomfortably close to the current position within the Eurozone – described a system that was to change with the coming of the new economic order to be established in the post-war world. Henceforth, debtors and creditors would share responsibility for restoring balance of payments equilibrium, through an international bank and clearing system that would oversee a system of fixed but adjustable exchange rates. That, at least, had been Keynes's hope for the conference at Bretton Woods in New Hampshire in July 1944. Some of his ideas were stillborn. Others came to fruition many years after his death. The immediate result of Bretton Woods was to establish an exchange-rate system in which currencies were anchored to the dollar and the dollar was anchored to gold, at $35 an ounce, the parity established in 1933 during the early days of Franklin Roosevelt's time in the White House.

Overseeing the system, and standing ready to provide financial assistance to countries encountering balance of payments difficulties, was the International Monetary Fund, a new type of global reserve institution within which Britain and France were equal shareholders (although it may be worth noting that five of the eleven managing directors of the IMF up to and including 2015 were French – and none was British).

No one was hubristic enough to echo Douglas Jay's observation about the gold standard and suggest that the Bretton Woods system was intended to 'last almost for ever'. There was, however, a general sense in which the IMF, like the United Nations, was quite simply a greatly superior version of what had gone before, respectively the gold-exchange standard and the League of Nations. The powerful economic recovery of the post-war years, encompassing the French, West German and Italian 'economic miracles', suggested the proof of the pudding was in the eating. Bretton Woods had indeed proved a 'real economy' system delivering higher living standards to working people and those dependent on the income from work. By the early 1960s, books claiming mass affluence was having a deleterious effect on the character of western societies appeared in increasing numbers – not a publishing phenomenon much noted, to say the least, during the immediate pre-war years.

But there was a weakness at the heart of the Bretton Woods system, one that a resurgent France, headed once again since 1958 by de Gaulle, was quick to spot. Just as with the inadequate level of gold reserves in London before the First World War, as noted by Kynaston above, so, increasingly, were America's own resources and responsibilities clearly out of kilter.

De Gaulle's February 1965 press conference suggested that Bretton Woods 'has lost its initial foundation', the backing of the dollar with the greatest part of the world's bullion. Bernstein writes: 'His facts were indisputable. By early 1965, the U.S. stock of monetary gold had fallen to its lowest level since March 1937 ... America's share of the world's total monetary gold stock had shrunk from 75 percent to less than 50 percent. By the end of the 1960s, the U.S. share would be under 30 percent.'[22]

And just as with regard to the Bank of England during the inter-war period, French thoughts turned to the advisability of entrusting their precious gold-backed assets to a foreign institution, in this case the Federal Reserve Bank of New York. It was de Gaulle's finance minister at this time, the future president Valéry Giscard d'Estaing, who attacked America's ability to use the dollar's anchor-currency status to issue debt almost without limit as an 'exorbitant privilege', a phrase often wrongly credited to de Gaulle. On 10 February 1965, Giscard gave a lecture at the University of Paris, the import of which may be seen as sounding the death-knell of the Bretton Woods system. Henceforth, he said, all major economic powers should agree to settle all payment deficits with gold, an action that would 'stop the decay of the world money system'. Bernstein records that he announced that France was taking the lead 'by starting to convert all new accumulations of dollars into gold'.[23] This gold would be shipped across the Atlantic rather than remaining in the US.

Ultimately, Bretton Woods was a game of bluff and its bluff had been called. Just like an ordinary clearing bank, there would be insufficient assets 'in the till' to pay everyone should they all attempt to withdraw everything they were owed at one and the same time. De Gaulle and Giscard's aim was to end the privileged position of the dollar, which required all Bretton Woods members to earn foreign currency or gold in order to pay their bills with the exception of the United States, which was able to settle in its own currency.

France's uncompromising decision to demand that America honour its gold pledges took place against a backdrop of increasing instability in the gold market. Central to the Bretton Woods system were two tenets: that the price of gold was fixed at $35 per troy ounce, and that American citizens were not permitted to own investment quantities of gold (nor, obviously, could they exercise the right to exchange dollars for gold, but in the logic of the system they did not need to, because dollars and gold had equivalent worth). However, by the end of the 1950s, the increasing tempo of world inflation and the arctic atmosphere of the Cold War persuaded many that bullion represented both a hedge against falling purchasing power and a safe haven in times of crisis. Fearing that private buying could push gold's price above the Bretton Woods parity, the US, Britain, Switzerland, the Netherlands, Belgium, France, West Germany and Italy formed in 1961 a gold pool based in the London market which was designed to sell gold whenever the price threatened to rise above $35.

In what can be seen as a precursor for any number of unequal financial struggles between governments and increasingly powerful markets – whether the 1985 collapse of the International Tin Council's 'buffer stock' or the travails of Europe's Exchange Rate Mechanism in the early 1990s – the 'pool' countries were fighting a losing battle. De Gaulle took France out of the arrangement in 1967 and later described it as a sham. In March 1968, the remaining pool members threw in the towel and announced that, in terms of private-sector transactions, gold would be allowed to find its own level, the corollary being that henceforth only governments and their central banks would be entitled to exchange dollars for gold, at $35 an ounce.

For the Bretton Woods system there was to be what amounted to one last throw of the dice, with not real gold but 'paper gold', the Special Drawing Rights (SDRs) created by the IMF in 1969 as 'a new international reserve asset', according to the Fund, and issued to member countries. In a sense, the SDR was a belated realization of Keynes's vision of a global mechanism, other than simple exchange-rate adjustments, that would require surplus countries to share the burdens of the debtor nations. Not only are IMF members free to trade SDRs among themselves in return for their own national currencies, but in cases of serious balance of payment disequilibrium, the Fund could (and can) instruct a surplus country to accept SDRs from a debtor country in return for the equivalent sum in the surplus country's own currency.

But this version of Keynes's abortive international accounting unit, the Bancor, came too late to save Bretton Woods. Prices in the private bullion market diverged ever more widely from the official rate, and there were fears that it would be possible for gold to leak from the intergovernmental market, at which it had cost $35 an ounce, and then be sold, in a classic round-tripping exercise, at more than $40 on the private market.

The United States broke the link with gold on 15 August 1971. At the end of 1974, the prohibition on Americans holding and dealing in investment gold came to an end. Bullion remained, and remains, an official reserve asset, but this is at the discretion of the countries concerned. In 2000, the last advanced-country reserve institution to back a portion of its circulating money issue with gold – the Swiss National Bank – broke the link with bullion.

Before moving on to the post-1971 era, the period in which international monetary systems ceased to have any explicit link to gold, it is worth reflecting on the unhappy history of this supposedly unsurpassable fiduciary measure.

One might have thought that the turbulence of the twentieth century provided the perfect conditions for bullion to show its worth as a portable, incorruptible, unchanging and universally acceptable store of value, for governments as well as individuals. But this does not seem to have happened. Instead, every attempt to yoke gold to the global economy was looser than the last, but none of these three arrangements – the gold standard, the gold-exchange standard, and Bretton Woods – proved capable of overcoming the fundamental problems of a bullion standard.

This does little to bolster confidence in President de Gaulle's 'eternal and universal' monetary asset. Rather, the trend away from monetary gold suggests that there may, after all, have been something to the objection that gold is not a particularly useful monetary asset on a large scale, that it is a metal that is pulled out of the ground, usually by commercial companies with an eye on world prices and the need to satisfy their shareholders, and that, far from representing some sort of objective bedrock on which to build monetary stability, it is just another commodity.

What's more, the much-touted argument from the supporters of
gold in our own time – that gold is a 'pure' asset because, barring
the odd dental filling, its production is unaffected by any non-
investment demand – is quite simply untrue. On the subject of gold
jewellery, the industry body, the World Gold Council, stated: 'Over
the past five years (2010–2014), it has accounted for around 50 per
cent of world gold demand, on average.' It may be argued that gold
jewellery is a form of investment asset. In terms of gold's use elsewhere, the Council notes that about 9 per cent of the world demand
for gold is for technical applications, with the electronics industry
accounting for most of this given gold's 'conductivity and resistance
to corrosion [which] make it the material of choice for manufacturers of high-specification components'. The Council adds that the
metal's 'excellent biocompatibility' has preserved it as a firm favou-
rite with the world's dentists.[24]

The interregnum: From the snake to the 'hard' ERM

As Bretton Woods broke up, the resulting turmoil convulsed the six
(from January 1973, nine) members of the European Community.
The Common Market, as was, had been launched and had flourished entirely within the Bretton Woods era. The Community was
designed as the home of a market economy, but that market was
never meant to include currencies. John Laughland, no fan of the
Exchange Rate Mechanism, describes as historically disingenuous
those opponents of the ERM, claiming that floating rates are quite
compatible with Europe's single market, given that rates were fixed
through the Bretton Woods system at the time the Treaty of Rome
was signed in 1957: 'Stable exchange rates were an integral component of the single market when it was conceived.'[25]

The ending of the post-war system spurred a search for solutions in Brussels and the capitals of the Community's member
states: 'the ensuing wave of market instability put upward pressure
on the Deutschmark ... To retrieve the situation, in March 1972,
the member states created the "snake in the tunnel".' This odd-
sounding creature, explains the European Commission website,

was an attempt to limit the fluctuations of European currencies against the dollar, the 'tunnel' being the permitted range of movement. Alas: 'Hit by oil crises, policy divergence and dollar weakness, within two years the snake had lost many of its component parts and was little more than a German-mark zone comprising Germany, Denmark and the Benelux countries.'[26]

Former European Commission official Bernard Connolly records that when the snake started operating in 1972, it included all six existing Community members as well as the four (Britain, Ireland, Denmark and Norway) that were supposed to join the Community in 1973. (Norwegian voters declined in a referendum.) 'But when economic policies and inflation rates diverged after the 1973 commodity-price shocks, Britain, France and Italy all withdrew as the system's obligations began to threaten their national policymaking autonomy.'[27]

France's withdrawal may suggest the country had abandoned its bullion-loving, hard-currency ways. In fact, the snake was too ad hoc for any nation's approach to membership to impart to the current observer very much about that country's then attitude to monetary matters. Rather more telling, perhaps, is France's decision in 1973 to issue a fifteen-year bond linked to the gold price. These so-called Giscards were designed to protect investors against any depreciation in the value of the franc, and thus ought to have acted as a discipline against any such depreciation. Unfortunately for French taxpayers, the finance minister and later (from 1974) president from whom these bonds took their name failed to foresee the huge rise in the gold price. The 1988 repayment thus ended up costing in nominal terms at least ten times what France had raised from their sale.

With the snake scotched, Community politicians – led by President Giscard and West German Chancellor Helmut Schmidt – headed off in search of something more durable. The option of freely-floating exchange rates was never seriously entertained, in part because of the belief, contested by Connolly, that the common European market simply could not function properly if swings in foreign currency acted as a further barrier to 'internal' trade, and in part because of an aversion to the whole notion of exchange-rate uncertainty, within or without the Community. This was the view encapsulated by Nigel Lawson, Britain's chancellor of the exchequer from 1983 to 1989, who believed that the exchange rate, the most important 'price' in the economy, could not be a matter of indifference to the government.

This view, and his consequent espousal of British membership of the ERM, constituted a rare example of agreement between the former cabinet minister and the great and good of Europe. By coincidence, Lord Lawson now lives in France.

The European Monetary System started life in 1977 as an initiative of the then president of the European Commission, Roy Jenkins, who saw monetary integration as a relatively pain-free method of reigniting idealism for a united Europe after the travails of the early 1970s. The baton was picked up by Giscard and Schmidt and the EMS was launched in 1978, encompassing all nine Community members. Britain, however, remained outside the 'live' component of the EMS, the ERM. In part this reflected a belief that the UK economy was in no shape to tether itself to a system dominated by the German mark. In part, it reflected disillusion with fixed exchange-rate systems in the wake of both the November 1967 devaluation of the pound and the break-up of Bretton Woods. The latter event, complained Harold Wilson, prime minister during the devaluation, allowed his successors to devalue at will, 'and not a dog barked'.[28]

That was the way Wilson's successors liked it.

Connolly notes that there was an initial period of calm after the launch of the ERM. 'The first two years of the system's operation look rather uneventful on the surface. The expected battles between French politicians and the Bundesbank failed to materialise.'[29] All that changed with the Iranian Revolution of 1978–79, the subsequent 'second oil shock' and the transformation of US economic policy in the era of Paul Volcker, the anti-inflationary chairman of the Federal Reserve. France's post-May 1981 socialist government attempted a Keynesian reflation of the economy, while at the same time Germany put up interest rates in order both to fight inflation and to defend the mark on foreign exchanges. The collision of these two policy approaches led to an October 1981 devaluation of the franc, and a second depreciation in June 1982.

The quid pro quos for these 'realignments' were, at the insistence of the Germans, controls on prices and wages. By May 1983, yet another devaluation was on the cards. This time, some of Mitterrand's colleagues decided it was time to take a stand.

Connolly records that the woes of the franc 'were stoking a titanic political battle in Paris'. Left-wing ministers wanted to stick with reflation, leave the ERM and introduce protectionist measures. 'Against them were ranged the "modernisers", Delors chief among them.'[30] Charles Grant, a biographer of Delors, takes up the story: 'Delors ... persuaded the Parti socialiste that reflation in one country, import controls and quitting the EMS were not viable policies.' The future Commission president explained to his leftist colleagues that 'private-sector companies and entrepreneurs had to be nurtured'. Grant recalls that after Delors's departure for Brussels in 1984, French governments of left and right continued the strong-franc policy.[31] Delors may have left, but his hard-money legacy lived on. Who better, then, to chair the committee established to chart the path to European Economic and Monetary Union?

Hello yellow brick road: The journey to the euro

The Delors Committee, established in 1988 and composed largely of bankers, reported in April 1989. Its report made it quite clear that the single currency – then known as the ECU, or Ecu – would be a hard currency. As described in their own words and laid down in a report presented in 1989, this would be achieved through a system committed to 'price stability'.

Ensuring the 'hardness' of the new currency, and that the ECB was to be almost completely independent, were stipulations without which Germany would almost certainly have refused to join. It would have been impossible for West Germany, as it was then, to have supported Delors's conclusions on any other basis (of which more in a moment). Here is what Jacques Delors and his colleagues had to say under the heading 'Mandates and Functions' of what was then described as 'a new monetary institution . . . what might be called a *European System of Central Banks*' to manage the single currency, now, of course, known as the ECB: 'The System would be committed to the objective of price stability.'[32] It adds: '*Subject to the foregoing*, the System should support the general economic policy set at the Community level by the competent bodies [our emphasis].'[33] So there was to be a hard currency as top priority and support for economic policy as a secondary aim. But the economic policy in question would be a Europe-wide policy, one which, as we shall see later, would bolster the uncompromising commitment to shielding what would become the euro against those forces that could weaken it.

It is worth noting at this point that the report had nothing to say about the 'social dimension' that would later be claimed to be an indispensable aspect of economic and monetary union. Rather, the report stressed the insulation of the central bank from political interference: 'the ESCB [European System of Central Banks] Council should be independent of instructions from national governments and Community authorities; to that effect the members of the ESCB Council, both Governors and the Board members, should have appropriate security of tenure.'[34]

The Bundesbank's influence in establishing the constitutional position of the ECB can be seen in the institution's negative reaction to the spread of 'inflation targeting' in the 1990s and beyond, a straightforward (if ultimately flawed) system whereby the monetary policy would no longer seek price stability through the pursuit of 'intermediate' targets, such as the money supply or the exchange rate, and would instead target the inflation rate itself. German central bankers had rather less objection to the notion of inflation targeting, as in the widespread idea, based on the admired New Zealand model, that the inflation target would be set by the government rather than by the central bank itself, with the latter left merely to figure out the best way to reach this goal – in the jargon, 'operational independence' rather than 'target independence'.

Connolly explains the difference as being that the central bank, 'far from being a great estate of the realm', was comparable to a contractor 'supplying, say, office furniture ... The government would include specification in the contract, a price would be agreed, and there would be provisions for review of performance.' In this unglamorous (for central bankers) state of affairs, the company could carry out its duties any way it liked 'but could not exercise any independent political power'.[35]

Indeed, there was perhaps an early hint in Gordon Brown's chancellorship that neither he nor his economic adviser Ed Balls was in any rush to join the single currency, contrary to the then widespread view that Brown was, if anything, more gung-ho for the euro than Tony Blair. It was explained to the authors at the time that the much-touted 'independence' of the Bank of England, in which politicians set the inflation target and the Bank had a five-to-four majority on a committee that set interest rates, may seem radical and daring in the UK but would not pass muster in Brussels as representing central-bank independence of the sort required to join the single currency. (Sweden gave itself a de facto opt-out by making Eurozone-style independence for the Riksbank subject to a referendum: voters said No in 2003.) The manoeuvrings in the UK on this subject are examined fully in Chapter 6.

This insistence on central bank independence underlined a common theme linking the gold standard and the euro: the need for and desirability of removing monetary policy from the hands of politicians. Niall Ferguson notes that the Brussels Conference of 1921, ostensibly established to discuss possible aid for famine-stricken Russia, insisted that 'all "banks of issue should be freed from political pressure" – and proclaim[ed] their faith in the "rules" of the restored gold standard'.[36]

Writing in the *Spectator* on 20 July 1990, the distinguished British economist Samuel Brittan put the case enthusiastically and concisely, and his remarks are worth quoting in full:

The most important reason for favouring a European Monetary Union run by a European central bank (known to its friends as Eurofed) is precisely the reason why it is loathed by some politicians (such as Mrs Thatcher): namely its independence of

national governments. The fact that it is European or supranational is secondary. The main thing is that it puts money at one
remove from the control of elected politicians who will always
be tempted to pursue inflationary policies, out of wishful
thinking as well as for crude electoral reasons.

Indeed, it could be argued that the ECB has more successfully
defended its autonomy than did central banks during the last days
of the gold-exchange standard, given that, as we saw, it was politicians who took sterling off gold, in defiance of the wishes of the
Bank of England.

It is also true that the ECB has always had to face the possibility
that the Eurogroup – the council of Eurozone finance ministers –
could join forces with the European Commission to seize control of
monetary policy provided it were able to justify this on exchange-
rate grounds. This was the 'nuclear' Article 111 of the Maastricht
Treaty, now Article 219 of the consolidated Treaty on the Functioning
of the European Union, which states that the Eurogroup, 'either
on a recommendation from the European Central Bank or on a
recommendation from the Commission and after consulting the
European Central Bank, in an endeavour to reach a consensus
consistent with the objective of price stability', may commit the euro
to an exchange-rate system 'in relation to the currencies of third
States'. What is more, should there be no formal exchange-rate
system between the Eurozone and third-party countries – presumably envisaged as a sort of latter-day Bretton Woods – the Eurogroup,
again after consultation, 'may formulate general orientations for
exchange-rate policy in relation to these currencies'.[37]

There was some suggestion of a Eurogroup coup in the autumn
of 2000, when the euro was sliding against the dollar and had to be
rescued by a co-ordinated foreign-exchange market intervention by
the 'Group of Seven' leading nations, then meeting in the Czech
capital Prague. But there was never a consensus for such a move, not
least because it was unclear how the assembled finance ministers
would prove more orthodox – and thus more supportive of the
exchange rate – than ECB president Wim Duisenberg and his

colleagues. What is more likely is that the Eurogoup politicians would try to use an exchange-rate justification to force the ECB to loosen monetary policy, thus making life easier for their constituents. But this would invite a challenge under Article 219, specifically this sentence: 'These general orientations shall be without prejudice to the primary objective of the ESCB to maintain price stability.'

Ultimately, the euro was supposed to be insulated from political control. Ann Pettifor notes: 'The plain truth is that the euro is a product of utopian neo-liberal economists and their ambitions for a monetary system governed only by market forces. According to the ideology, market forces must be beyond the reach of any European state.'[38]

Significantly, the Delors Report cited 'the lack of sufficient convergence of fiscal policies as reflected in large and persistent budget deficits in certain countries' as providing part of the impetus behind the move to monetary union, the point being that the existing halfway house of the European Exchange Rate Mechanism was being undermined by the spendthrift countries, and only going 'all the way' to a single currency would bring them to heel.

It can be argued that while the gold standard imposed this discipline on member countries because of the intrinsic nature of a bullion-based monetary system, the causality was the other way round with the euro, with the discipline being the precondition for the participation of the one country without which the bloc could not come into existence: Germany. Here is what an IMF paper of June 2004 had to say on the subject: 'Given many prospective EMU members' apparent inability to maintain fiscal discipline, Germany, in particular, insisted on a common fiscal framework to rein in the spending of profligate countries before the euro was allowed to replace national currencies.' It adds that these demands gave rise to two fundamental provisions in the Maastricht Treaty: that fiscal deficits should be kept below 3 per cent of GDP, and that debt ratios should not exceed 60 per cent.[39]

There is a certain irony, of course, in the fact that the first two countries to breach these 'key provisions' were not from the lotus-eating European south, but were France and Germany, in 2003, who did so while persuading their fellow Eurozone members that they ought not to face any penalties.

More broadly, however, it makes little difference whether the 'salutary check in the extravagance of governments' is intrinsic to a monetary system or a deliberately constructed adjunct to it. Nor does the fact that large, powerful members of the system can break the rules with impunity greatly diminish the importance of the disciplinary mechanism, which – as Portugal, Ireland, Spain and Greece have found – remains very much in force for smaller, less powerful members of the system.

Pettifor outlines that 'Eurozone member countries must . . . agree to limit (under almost all economic circumstances) government annual deficits'.[40] It could be noted that the French-inspired Delors disapproval of annual deficits sits ill with France's own record, a country that has not run a surplus on its government finances since 1974. But this does not at all affect the fact that French officialdom is wedded to hard money, that 1981–83 represented the briefest departure from this stance, and that Mitterrand's leftists were put to the sword by Delors in May 1983. Nor did Delors emerge from nowhere; he represented a tradition of French finance ministers, as did a recent predecessor, Raymond Barre, who combined the job with that of prime minister and whose abrasive anti-inflation policy Barre summarized as '*rigueur*'.

Long after both Barre and Delors had quit the finance ministry, French officialdom was still singing the old golden tunes. By the late 1990s, when countries such as Britain were getting ready to dispose of much of their gold holdings, the 1998 annual report of the Bank of France declared: 'Above all . . . holding gold is, from the political point of view, a sign of monetary sovereignty [and] an insurance policy against a major breakdown in the international monetary system.'[41] Unsurprisingly, then, the ECB, being established at this time along the Delors principles, elected to keep 15 per cent of its reserves in gold.

Again, the Janus face of France, the search for 'real', unchanging values – for money, for measurements, for social principles – from a country many of whose philosophers and other intellectuals have made big waves (and sometimes handsome livings) from asserting that more or less everything is a 'social construct', from elementary morality to the 'illusion' that literary novels may actually need authors to bring them into existence. One element that largely escapes this relativist scrutiny is the monetary system. Yet here, surely, the pitiless gaze of the Gallic radical would be beneficial?

After all, hard money, whether arising from the gold standard or the euro, favours the holders of wealth over other sections of society. If one of the variables in the economic mechanism – the value of money – is not allowed to move, everything else, such as employment, living standards and export sales, must move more violently. Hard money ensures that the burden of 'adjustment' to each economic shock falls on those in work and those otherwise dependent on the income from work, rather than sharing the pain across society with some rise in inflation and a depreciation of the currency, thus allowing the internal and external value of the currency to absorb some of the sting. Finally, hard money favours creditors over debtors.

Ultimately, where one stands on the question of hard money will reflect one's view of where holders of wealth ought to sit in relation to the other actors in the economy and the wider society. Those who believe that wealth ought to have an objective standard of value, whether expressed in gold or hard currency, may be chasing a will-o'-the-wisp, given that these stores of value themselves have a value, which moves around like any other price. But they can do great damage in the meantime to the real economy, as is being seen in the Eurozone now.

The gold standard failed because it was a fair-weather construct that fell apart once balmy economic and political conditions disappeared. The euro will go the same way.

A last word

To end where we began, at the International Bureau of Weights and Measures outside Paris. The kilogram is in trouble. Not the kilogram in everyday use in the majority of countries round the world, but the kilogram locked up in the vault. Its mass appears to be changing, and scientists are currently trying to find an alternative way of measuring the same thing. As an unchanging, unalterable standard, it would seem that platinum and iridium are scarcely more reliable than gold.

Our next chapter draws comparisons with the world of schooling, another arena that sets great store by standards. But, as we shall see, one country's idea of high-quality education can be very different from that of another.

CHAPTER 4

NO END OF A LESSON

Schools of thought collide in the Eurozone

And mind now, I say again, look out for squalls if you will go your own way, and that way ain't the Doctor's, for it'll lead to grief. You all know that I'm not the fellow to back a master through thick and thin . . . [but] he's a strong, true man, and a wise one too.

Thomas Hughes, *Tom Brown's School Days*

There had been plenty of anxious hours spent pacing round the maternity unit's waiting room. Doom-mongers said the child should never have been conceived. Now that the baby was due, they said it would have a short and unhappy life. But the fears were misplaced. When the euro finally came into the world on 1 January 2002, the changeover from national currencies could hardly have been smoother. It was a textbook birth. True, the single currency had been present in virtual form for three years, but this was the day when marks, francs, pesetas, guilders, drachmas, escudos, schillings, punts and markkas started to be phased out in a faultless logistical operation that involved the printing and distribution of 8 billion euro notes and 38 billion euro coins to eleven countries.

Three days into the new year, 96 per cent of hole-in-the-wall machines were dispensing euros, and by the end of February the transition was complete. Predictably enough, there were a few scams as retailers jacked up prices in order to take advantage of confusion about the rates at which francs, marks and pesetas had been exchanged for the euro. The new currency was the equivalent of a test-tube baby: nothing quite like it had ever been tried before and there were plenty of experts happy to state that the science was flawed. But the doubters were wrong. The baby appeared on time and seemed entirely healthy. Europeans were proud of the new arrival, seeing it as the fruit of a long and happy marriage. There was no real evidence that what Jean-Claude Juncker called the 'unwarranted and unjustified' price rises did serious long-term damage to the currency, as he later asserted.[1]

Instead, a better guide to the mood in the countries that were founder members of the single currency was the scene in Rome, a city that had been at the heart of an empire that had spawned Europe's first attempt at a single currency. Tradition has it that a coin thrown in Rome's Trevi Fountain guarantees that a visitor will return. But the Italians who tossed their lire into the water when the new year dawned in 2002 had something else in mind. They were getting rid of Italy's old currency and never wanted it back. In the Eternal City they were enthusiastic for what was billed as the eternal currency.

Nor was the feeling of pride confined to Italy, a country that had debauched its currency on many occasions from Ancient Roman times onwards. There was a sense that the single currency symbolized both the past and the future: the steps taken over more than half a century to bring the continent closer together, and the idea that it would allow Europe to challenge America's economy and geopolitical hegemony. This glorious optimism did not last long, but the later problems of the euro had little to do with Venetian gondoliers overcharging for a trip down the Grand Canal or Bavarian beer cellars marking up the price of a Pilsner lager. Rather, the difficulties were caused by genes and by environment: the wrong parents, the wrong sort of upbringing and – in particular – the wrong sort of schooling. Concealed during its early years, the fundamental problems of the euro became all too evident during the crisis that broke during its second decade. From 1999 to 2007, the story was of weaknesses disguised, conflict postponed and cracks papered over.

This chapter will look at the contradictory expectations of the euro from different countries in the Eurozone, using the conceit of a clash between schooling of the character-building variety and the progressive notion of child-centred education.

Gordonstoun and Summerhill

Precious few people spoke out against Adolf Hitler after he became chancellor of Germany in January 1933, but Kurt Hahn was one of them. While many stayed silent at the suppression of democracy and the flouting of the rule of law, Hahn denounced the Nazi leader personally after the SA killed one of his pupils in front of the child's mother. In return for his courage, Hahn was imprisoned, and was then sent into exile after British Prime Minister Ramsay MacDonald intervened on his behalf.

The reason MacDonald made the plea to Hitler was that Hahn was an educationalist of international repute. On arrival in Britain he wasted no time in setting up a school near the Moray Firth. Gordonstoun received its first pupils in 1934 and soon won a reputation for its rigorous approach. The bleak location appealed to Hahn, who wanted a school that would make men out of boys. He didn't care that the wind howled in off the North Sea when the weather was bad, which it often was. His establishment would also be bracing; it was founded on the belief that unless boys were kept on the straight and narrow they would be corrupted by an imperfect world.

Hahn was strongly influenced by Plato's *Republic*, even though Gordonstoun's regime owed more to Sparta than to Athens. The school was famous for its outdoor activities, the marches across the Highlands, the cold showers in the morning, and the cross-country runs. Discipline was notoriously harsh. The duke of Edinburgh was a Gordonstoun alumnus and decided it was just the school to toughen up his son, Prince Charles. The actor Sean Connery thought that a school that had as its motto 'Plus est en vous' ('There is more in you') was right for his son Jason.

Germany wanted the single currency to be run along the lines of Gordonstoun so that it could teach the rest of Europe the right sort of economic values. As with Hahn, there was a fear of corrupt influences: inflation, budget deficits and debt-financed growth. Such decadent temptations would be countered by Germanic values: sound money, self-improvement and budgetary rigour. The equivalent of the tramps through the heather for the boys of Gordonstoun under the eyes of watchful teachers would be structural reform of European economies grown soft on a diet of devaluation and unsound money. The cold showers would be provided by a European Central Bank, modelled on Germany's beloved Bundesbank, which would not be swayed by the desperate pleas of politicians for the warm tap to be turned on. The discipline would be administered by a Stability and Growth Pact that would punish those who dared to think they could escape the tough regime by running up budget deficits.

That, at least, was the theory. There was, however, another experimental school set up between the two world wars and it too acted as a model for monetary union, although nobody would ever admit as much.

Summerhill School pre-dated Gordonstoun by thirteen years and in many ways was its mirror image. Founded in Germany by an English educationalist A.S. Neill, the school moved to Lyme Regis in Dorset in 1923 before ending up in its present location in Suffolk in 1927. The wind can also blow cold off the North Sea in East Anglia but Neill's aim was to protect his pupils from its buffeting. His ethos was that children learned better if they were free to choose when – and if – they attended lessons. Pupils would decide what to do with their own time, and have the same say as the staff in the running of the school. Children developed at their own pace; classes were often made up of pupils of different ages, depending on how fast their progress was in specific subjects. Neill was not particularly interested in teaching methods and was reputed to have been an awful teacher. His prime aim was to ensure that the children at Summerhill were happy. His credo was 'Freedom not licence', meaning that children could do what they liked so long as it did not affect the liberty of somebody else. Summerhill, although seen as a beacon of liberalism in the 1960s and early 1970s, was not the sort of school likely to endear itself to educational traditional-ists, and it was inspected nine times in the 1990s. Tony Blair's first education secretary David Blunkett found the idea of optional lessons particularly upsetting, and, following a major inspection by OFSTED (the Office for Standards in Education, Children's Services and Skills) in 1999, Blunkett issued the school with a notice of complaint, objecting to non-compulsory lessons. Schools that fail to respond to a notice of complaint are usually shut within six months, but Summerhill fought Blunkett in the courts – and won.

The story of the first decade of the euro is the clash between these two irreconcilable approaches. While some of the pupils were doing their homework, others decided not to turn up for class. Only gradually did it become apparent that the Gordonstoun approach did not suit all European countries. A decade went by before the Germans realized to their horror that there was more than a little of Summerhill about the place, particularly in the way that countries developed at their own pace and were free to skip the lessons they did not fancy all that much. By the time the penny finally dropped, much of Europe had been laid low by the financial and economic crisis that began in 2007. At that point, belatedly, and disastrously, Berlin insisted that the cure for a bad dose of influenza running through the school was cold showers and cross-country runs for everyone, even those pupils confined to the school sanatorium.

Entrance exam

There are two types of British public schools. The highly academic ones ask that applicants for entry sit and pass a series of tests in English, maths and verbal reasoning. The ones for plodders merely require that the parents can open a chequebook at the start of every term. Germany was unashamedly elitist in its vision for the euro. Fearful that the euro would be the sort of establishment that might attract the wrong sort of clientele, it insisted on a process that would weed out the duffers.

Germany's concerns were understandable. The rebuilding of Europe's strongest economy from the ruins of the Second World War had been symbolized by the independence of the Bundesbank and the strength of the mark. Where the Americans revered their flag, the Germans revered their currency. The attachment to the mark ran deep, and in the 1970s and 1980s a succession of German politicians and presidents of the Bundesbank warned against rushing into monetary union. The feeling in Bonn, the capital of West Germany, and in Frankfurt, the home of the Bundesbank, was that there should only be a single currency once Europe had progressed much further down the road towards a political union that would allow for the harmonization of tax, spending and wage policies. With hindsight, it would have been better had the warnings been heeded, but other European countries thought Germany already wielded enough power and were unwilling to cede any more sovereignty. Germany was the anchor for that European Exchange Rate Mechanism, a system whereby countries had to raise (or lower) interest rates if there was a danger that their currencies would deviate from a small permitted range against the mark. For the French, in particular, this proved to be a traumatic process, with high unemployment being the price paid for the frequently doomed attempts to maintain the parity of the franc. The French saw monetary union as a way of regaining some control over Germany. Paris, eager to win back some of the economic sovereignty it had ceded to its more powerful neighbour, wanted monetary union to come first.

Negotiations in the run up to the Maastricht Treaty that set the timetable for monetary union were complicated by the tearing down of the Iron Curtain in late 1989 and the reunification of Germany a year later.

The French president at the time, François Mitterrand, was in no position to halt reunification, but he did have the ability to delay the process. The bargain he struck with Chancellor Helmut Kohl involved France giving its blessing to reunification in return for Germany agreeing to go ahead with monetary union without political union. Kohl was aware, however, that he would never get such a deal past the Bundesbank (or the German people, for that matter) without conditions attached, and he knew that Mitterrand had a more pressing need for monetary union than he did. So, he made sure that the entrance exam for membership of the single currency would be difficult. To make doubly certain, he insisted that the questions would be set by the Bundesbank.

And so the Maastricht convergence criteria were born. Countries that wanted to participate in monetary union would need to sit and pass five papers, all of which reflected the economic wisdom that had been distilled by German officialdom during four decades of post-war economic success and which reflected the orthodoxy of the 1980s.

Test number one involved Germany's preoccupation: the importance of keeping inflation under control. For a country that had suffered two traumatic bouts of hyperinflation – one in the 1920s and one in the years immediately after the Second World War – this was perhaps understandable. Also relevant was Germany's record during the 1970s, when it was far less damaged by the two oil inflationary shocks than many of the other leading industrial nations, including the United States, Britain and France. A successful country would need to have an inflation rate no more than 1.5 percentage points higher than an average taken from the three EU countries with the lowest rates. The Germans fully expected many of the weaker European countries, the inflation-prone Italians for example, to flunk this paper.

The next two linked tests involved fiscal policy, the mixture of tax and spending that determines the balance of a country's public finances. A country where the government spends more than it receives in tax runs an annual budget deficit. These deficits accumulate over the years into national debt, the total amount of money a nation owes its creditors. Both the deficits and the national debt are usually expressed as a percentage of a country's annual output or gross domestic product. The Maastricht Treaty said a country would only be allowed to join the monetary union if its budget deficit was no more than 3 per cent of GDP and if its national debt was below 60 per cent of GDP (or falling steadily towards 60 per cent if above that level).

The Germans had two reasons for insisting on these tests. Firstly, sound public finances were seen as important in themselves. The German word for debt is *Schuld*, which is also the word for guilt, and there was a suspicion of attempts by governments to spend their way out of trouble by financing public spending through budget deficits. Keynes had never been big in Germany and the Bundesbank was wary of those governments that did adhere to his theories. So, when Helmut Schmidt agreed to take part in a co-ordinated attempt to reflate the global economy in 1978, Germany's involvement was half-hearted and short-lived. Secondly, any country that sought to meet the inflation test by deflating their economies would fail the fiscal papers. The reason was that, while slowing an economy bears down on the cost of living, it also leads to bigger budget deficits by reducing tax receipts and increasing welfare payments.

There were two final tests. These were designed to ensure that a country that had qualified for monetary union would be able to keep up once it had given up the right to set its own interest rates and devalue its own currency. Achieving low inflation and healthy-looking public finances temporarily was one thing, but the Germans wanted to ensure that they would last. A country seeking membership was required to be a member of the Exchange Rate Mechanism for a minimum of two years and to have long-term interest rates in the year before entry no more than two percentage points higher than the average of those in the three countries with the lowest inflation rates. This fifth exam was considered important because long-term interest rates are not set by finance ministries or by central banks, but by financial markets. If the markets have confidence in a particular government's economic policies they will allow that country to borrow more cheaply.

Taken together, Germany was confident that the Maastricht Treaty would separate the sheep from the goats and so ensure that the single currency had a small membership. Other countries would be welcome to join but only at a later stage, once they had shown the necessary rigour.

But by making the euro exclusive, the Germans made membership more alluring. Spain, Portugal and Greece were not at all keen on the idea that they should be placed in a remedial class while the favoured few forged ahead. They set out to pass the five tests and were not daunted by the fact that no country, not even Germany, found it easy to pass the Maastricht entrance exam.

The mid-1990s were a difficult time for the German economy. The post-reunification boom was over, in part because the Bundesbank had raised interest rates to keep inflation in check and in part because the temporary suspension of the ERM in 1993 led to a revaluation of the mark, which made German exports dearer. France was deflating its economy in order to qualify for the single currency and Italy was also struggling. Accordingly, continental Europe's three biggest economies all had recourse to some creative accounting in order to pass the fiscal tests. France only passed the budget deficit test by raiding the pension fund of France Telecom; Italy's budget deficit mysteriously came down from 6.7 per cent to 2.7 per cent of GDP in the year the papers were marked.

Even then, Italy should have been failed by virtue of its national debt, which at 120 per cent of GDP was double the Maastricht limit. Belgium's debt level was even higher at 130 per cent of GDP. But both countries had been founder members of the Common Market in 1957, and Belgium was going to get in due to its existing monetary union with Luxembourg, which comfortably qualified. The Bundesbank had deep misgivings, but if Belgium was going to be a founder member, was it possible to exclude Italy? The reality, as David Marsh notes, was that it was 'arithmetically valid, but politically impossible'.[2]

The German attempt to limit the initial size of monetary union was a failure. It underestimated the desire to be part of The Project and the enterprise that countries would show in order to pass the tests. There was, however, an even bigger problem with the convergence criteria laid down at Maastricht: they did not lead to convergence. The tests were tough – and would have been tougher had they not been fiddled – but they were the wrong tests, for the wrong countries, at the wrong time. As one critic put it:

Convergence among the disparate economies of the countries that joined the euro was necessary for monetary union to work, and the euro was supposed to force structural reforms and bring about this convergence. The painful structural reforms many countries had avoided taking for a very long time would now be expected to magically happen and their disparate economies would look more and more like clones of each other.[3]

However, this 'incredible assumption' was supposed to hold together EMU, and there was no Plan B in case such convergence was not achieved. 'The Maastricht Treaty specifically prohibited bailouts: its founders thought that no bailouts would thus be needed and that fiscal discipline would be the natural outcome of having assigned theoretical limits to budgetary deficits and debt levels.'[4]

Germany imagined that the Maastricht Treaty would turn a class made up of eleven countries (rising to twelve in 2001 with the addition of Greece, and to nineteen today), of mixed abilities, into model students – but it was wrong. As with a school entrance exam, the judgement should have been whether the pupil could keep up with the rest of the class. This would have involved seeing whether all the countries were likely to see similar increases in their labour costs so that they remained competitive against each other. A country might have a low inflation rate, it might be running a budget deficit of below 3 per cent of GDP and have a debt-to-GDP ratio of less than 60 per cent, but it would quickly lose competiveness if its labour costs were rising at 3 per cent a year while a rival country's were rising at 1 per cent a year. As Heiner Flassbeck and Costas Lapavitsas note, the convergence criteria have proved 'irrelevant' to the events that have subsequently threatened the existence of the single currency.[5]

Indeed, it was a bit like a school deciding that to pass the entrance exam, the test would be whether the hopefuls could lose enough weight to fit into an ultra-tight school uniform. Many nations did indeed go on crash diets to ensure that they could button up their trousers and squeeze into their blazers. Others could not manage, even when it was clear they were cheating the examiners. At that point, the criteria were relaxed because it was seen as unacceptable that families who had supported the school from its foundation in 1957 should be excluded from the next phase of its development.

Curriculum

George Soros is a passionate European. The speculator who made his name by betting against the Bank of England and who drove Britain out of the Exchange Rate Mechanism in 1992 was part of the post-war generation that saw closer European integration as a way of preventing a repeat of the extremism, persecution and war that had blighted his early life. Soros was a strong and vocal supporter of monetary union, so it was with a heavy heart that in 2014 he delivered his critique of how the single currency had evolved.

In a series of interviews (collected together in a book[6]) with Gregor Peter Schmitz, Europe correspondent for *Der Spiegel*, Soros was asked whether he agreed with the statement that Germany 'used to be the eager pupil in Europe, and now it acts like a strict schoolmaster.' Soros: 'It is an apt description because the Germans want the rest of Europe to learn to be like Germany. But that is impossible. Germany has the best-performing economy in Europe today. But everybody cannot be first at the same time.'

This, though, was how Germany envisaged the single currency. Monetary union would be used to force through the structural changes that it considered had been ducked by too many countries for too long. Europe had prospered during the Bretton Woods period of fixed but adjustable exchange rates that existed from the end of the Second World War to the early 1970s, in large part because strict capital controls allowed countries to pursue full employment without the fear of being blown off course by currency speculation.

Germany, which operated with an undervalued mark during much of this period, was a beneficiary of the Bretton Woods regime, but preferred to see its success as purely the result of hard graft. As a result, there was never any intention that countries should be afforded the sort of protection from speculation that Germany itself enjoyed in the 1950s and 1960s. The Eurozone had no controls on the free movement of capital either between its members or between it and the outside world. Deprived of the easy option of devaluation and without recourse to ever-higher budget deficits, the only course of action would be to knuckle down to reforms that would make economies more efficient. At regular intervals since the Second World War, politicians in Britain have called for schools to return to the so-called three Rs of reading, writing and arithmetic. Germany, with the strong backing of the European Commission in Brussels, wanted monetary union to follow an identical approach: teaching by traditional German methods.

To make sure that all the members of monetary union got the message, the ECB's mandate in 1999 was to keep inflation below 2 per cent a year, an even more explicit definition of price stability than the one used by the Bundesbank. German lessons also meant that the ECB had to target the money supply, in the way that the Bundesbank always had, and that it approached the setting of interest rates in the same way, and using the same techniques. Germany's only real concession to its new pupils was to join the single currency at an uncomfortably high exchange rate that disadvantaged its exporters, but after that it was meant to be a case of hard graft for everybody.

There was an economic rationale to this approach, namely that the inflexible nature of European labour markets meant that any attempt to boost growth through expansionary macroeconomic policies – lower interest rates or looser fiscal policy – would feed through into higher inflation rather than stronger output. This sort of approach might work in the US, but only because it was easier to sack Americans and cut their pay. In Europe, with its stronger trade unions and its more generous welfare safety net, it was asking for trouble.

The problem with this theory was simple: it was just a theory, and did not work in practice.

Paul De Grauwe and Cláudia Costa Storti explored the idea that stimulus from the ECB was less effective than stimulus from the US Federal Reserve Board in 2005.[7] Their research was exhaustive, embracing eighty-three separate studies that explored the impact of policies designed to boost demand on output and inflation, in both the short and long term, in both Europe and the United States. De Grauwe and Costa Storti were looking for evidence to back up the idea that the ECB was somehow constrained by Europe's economic inflexibility and rigidities, and in particular that stimulative policies meant higher inflation and less growth in the Eurozone than it did in the US. Their conclusions were unambiguous: there was nothing to show that when the Fed changed monetary policy it achieved better results than the ECB. It was not true that any attempts to stimulate the Eurozone economy would feed through into higher inflation than in in the US, with less of an impact on growth. The ECB might have other reasons, such as the need to build up its anti-inflation credibility, for not wanting to adopt stimulative policies, but there was simply no evidence that it was 'handicapped by the existence of structural rigidities in using monetary policy for the purpose of stabilizing output compared to the US.' And the popular argument that, due to the existence of rigidities, the ECB is less powerful than the Fed in stabilizing output is, they say, unfounded. 'Therefore, the lower degree of activism of the ECB compared to the Fed cannot be justified on the grounds that the ECB cannot affect output because of the existence of rigidities.'

In the same year that De Grauwe and Costa Storti published their findings, the ECB held a conference in Frankfurt to which it invited the UK academic Stephen Nickell, then a member of the Bank of England's Monetary Policy Committee. It was Nickell's job to comment on a paper by Romain Duval and Jørgen Elmeskov which had explored the effect of monetary union on structural reform in the Eurozone. If the ECB had been expecting to find that six years of monetary union had encouraged structural reform, it was disappointed. Reforms, said Nickell, were more likely to be undertaken in small countries than in large ones. Bigger economies only tended to introduce structural reforms when they ran their own affairs, a freedom they had given up when joining monetary union.[8] Nickell's point was that structural reforms were an easier sell when they took place in a growing economy. This could happen if a country was setting its own interest rates, which could be cut to compensate for any loss of income or demand caused by the reforms. For a large country operating in a currency union, the impact of reform will be slow and there will be no offsetting boost from lower interest rates. This led, Nickell added, to the 'rather depressing conclusion that one of the effects of EMU is to weaken the incentives for structural reform in the larger member countries'.[9]

As it happened, this was not entirely true. There was one large member country in the Eurozone that had embarked on serious structural reform, but it was not France, Italy or Spain. It was Germany.

Term starts

The euro's arrival in 1999 coincided with a period of rapid economic growth, in part stimulated by the collapse of oil prices to below $10 a barrel and in part explained by the technology boom that was concentrated in the US. After the hardship endured to qualify for the single currency, the pick-up in growth and the decline in unemployment was a relief. The improvement for countries such as France and Italy was aided by Germany's willingness to join the single currency at an overvalued exchange rate. As it happened, Germany could afford to be generous, because almost as soon as it was launched in virtual form in 1999 the euro started to fall in value.

This wasn't quite what the Germans had predicted or wanted, wedded as they were to a belief in a strong currency. But the 30 per cent drop in the value of the euro against the dollar between January 1999 and September 2000 meant German goods were highly competitive in markets outside the Eurozone. China, which was rapidly industrializing, was a ready market for the machines needed to fit out its factories, many of them made in the *Mittelstand* companies of Germany.

It was, however, a short-lived respite. True to its mandate and to its Bundesbank lineage, the ECB responded to a weaker currency in predictable fashion, by raising interest rates. A weaker exchange rate works in two ways: it makes exports cheaper but imports dearer. The ECB believed that the 30 per cent fall in the euro posed a threat to inflation and was determined to establish its credibility as a central bank that was serious about maintaining price stability. It raised interest rates steadily for the first two years of the single currency, and in doing so led to a sharp slowdown in Eurozone activity at precisely the same time as the IT bubble of the late 1990s burst.

At the helm of the ECB in its difficult first few years was Wim Duisenberg, who had until 1997 been running the Dutch central bank. There had been little real controversy over the name chosen for the single currency, since all governments understood that something neutral was required. Appointing someone to run the ECB was another matter; the French government held up the appointment until it was agreed that Duisenberg would not serve his full eight-year term but would stand down in favour of Paris's nominee, France's own central bank governor, Jean-Claude Trichet.

The French objection to Duisenberg was that he was a German in all but name. In the years leading up to the creation of monetary union, the interest-rate policies of the Bundesbank and the Nederlandsche Bank were identical. When Germany raised the cost of borrowing, the Netherlands immediately followed suit. So much in step were the two central banks that Duisenberg won the nickname 'Mr Fifteen Minutes' because that was how long it took for the Bundesbank decision to be followed by the Dutch. It was not politically feasible for Helmut Kohl to insist that a German should run the ECB, but he got the next best thing. The authors of this book discovered at first hand how steeped Duisenberg was in Bundesbank thinking at a meeting of the International Monetary Fund in 2001. At a press conference held while the Eurozone economy was going through a sticky patch, Duisenberg would not accept that monetary policy and fiscal policy were too tight. The conversation between Duisenberg and one of us went as follows:

Q: So, Mr President, are you saying that monetary policy is set
   fair for growth?

A: That is correct.

Q: And fiscal policy is also set fair for growth?

A: That is also correct.

Q: So why is there no growth?

Duisenberg was for a moment left speechless by this final question.
Then, with the air of a headmaster lecturing a rather obtuse pupil,
he launched into a talk about the need for Europe to raise its growth
rates through structural reform. There could be no better man, as
far as the Germans were concerned, to safeguard the independence
of the ECB.

As it happened, the Duisenberg-led ECB went too far. It tightened policy too aggressively at a time when the global economy
was weakening anyway. The slowdown was particularly hard on
Germany, because Europe's biggest economy was faced with higher
interest rates, a recovery in the value of the euro and weaker global
demand for its goods all at the same time. Germany responded by
taking steps to make itself leaner and fitter. Workers accepted pay
rises that were below the rate of productivity growth, thereby
boosting corporate profits. The German government embarked on
reforms of the labour market and the welfare state designed to
make labour markets more flexible and the welfare system less
expensive. If the rest of Europe was like schoolboy Billy Bunter in
the stories by Frank Richards, always waiting for his postal order to
turn up, Germany was like the school swot, burning the midnight
oil in order to retain its position at the top of the class.

The sacrifices made by German workers were considerable. In
the first decade of the euro's existence, wages and salaries rose by
20 per cent, representing a real cut in living standards once inflation was taken into account. By way of comparison, the equivalent
figure for Greece was 140 per cent: even after a slump that reduced
the size of the economy by 30 per cent in the five years between
2009 and 2014, wages and salaries have still risen by more than they
have in Germany over the period from 1999 to 2014.

Reforms of the labour market were extensive, and were overseen by Peter Hartz, a Volkswagen executive. There were four parts to the programme, which included additional wage subsidies, the creation of new job opportunities and, most controversially, deep cuts in unemployment benefits for the long-term unemployed. The shock treatment was seen as necessary to rid Germany not only of the highest unemployment since the early 1930s but also of its unwanted reputation as the 'sick man of Europe'. The jobless rate had been 4 per cent in the 1970s, but had averaged 9 per cent in the decade from 1995 to 2005. Unemployment moved up and down according to the state of the economy, but the trend had clearly been rising for three decades.

The Hartz reforms affected the German labour market in two ways. Firstly, the combination of sticks and carrots led to a fall in unemployment. Between 2005 and 2008, the jobless rate fell from 11.5 per cent to 7.5 per cent, and there was no sharp increase – as there was in the US and the UK during the Great Recession of 2008–09. German workers found that their hours were cut, but the use of wage subsidies by the government limited the number of redundancies. Unemployment continued to fall as the Germany economy stabilized, reaching 5 per cent currently, less than half the Eurozone average. One estimate suggests that the Hartz reforms were responsible for knocking three percentage points off Germany's structural unemployment rate.[10]

The other effect was on wages. Increasing the supply of labour at a time when unions were already adopting a policy of restraint had predictable consequences: real wages fell by around five percentage points in the three years after 2005 and have still not recovered to the levels they were at when the euro was launched. It was also easy to understand why the Hartz reforms were not wildly popular among the German working class and why there was a lack of sympathy for workers in Greece, Spain and Portugal when their wages came under pressure during the Eurozone's sovereign debt crisis.

Tom Krebs and Martin Scheffel note that there would be two difficulties in exporting the Hartz reforms. The first was similar to the point made by Nickell: it is hard to convince people of the desirability of reforms when unemployment is high. There is an unwillingness to take risks and the gains and losses of change are unevenly distributed at a time when confidence is low. The second point is that cutting social insurance for the long-term unemployed might be less effective in other countries. As Krebs and Scheffel put it: 'The benefits paid to the long-term unemployed are already low in France and very low in Spain, and reducing these unemployment benefits to even lower levels is not likely to have large incentive effects. In contrast, the German unemployment-insurance system was very generous to the long-term unemployed before the Hartz IV reform, and in this case efficiency gains from implementing the reform were quite large.'[10]

Streaming

The German approach was not copied across the Eurozone. In some countries, such as Italy, the loss of freedom to devalue the currency started to have an impact immediately. Italy had always tended to run a higher inflation rate than Germany, and now it steadily lost competitiveness. In other parts of the Eurozone, though, joining a single currency with a one-size-fits-all interest rate led to the availability of much cheaper credit. If the interest rates set by the ECB were for the struggling Germans a little too high for comfort, they were too low than was strictly desirable for the Irish, the Portuguese, the Spanish and the Greeks. Had these countries retained their own independent central banks, all would have had higher official interest rates in the early years of the euro.

The quite different effects of a single interest rate on the variety of countries using the euro quickly became obvious. In 2002, work by the EU Commission and the UN Economic Commission for Europe estimated the difference between the optimal rate of interest for each member state and the rate of interest set by the European Central Bank in 2000 and 2001. It found that in both years, interest rates had been set half a percentage point too high for Germany and France, and one percentage point too low for Portugal. They were too low for the Netherlands by half a percentage point in 2000 and by one and a half points in 2001. In Ireland, the disparity between the actual and the optimal level of interest rate was even more marked and makes the subsequent property bubble easily understandable: official borrowing costs were three points too low in 2000 and four points too low in 2001.

There was more to it than that, however. Long-term interest rates, the ones set not by central banks but by the financial markets, continued to converge after the single currency's launch. The reason was that financial markets bought the hype. Investors believed that because there was no longer any question of Spain, Ireland or Greece devaluing their currencies, there was really not much difference between a German bond and those sold by Madrid, Dublin or Athens. The ECB insisted that a common monetary policy coupled with structural reforms would lead to convergence and the financial markets assumed that because the central bank had spoken that it must be so. It wasn't.

A study conducted by the House of Commons Library in 2002, when the UK was contemplating joining the single currency, found that inflation rates had bunched before the euro was launched, varying by less than 1.5 percentage points, but had diverged subsequently.[11]

Monetary union led to divergence, not convergence. Lower interest rates papered over the cracks in some of the weaker countries of the Eurozone, allowing them to go on borrowing binges. The idea was that the abolition of all exchange controls would lead to a more efficient allocation of capital within the Eurozone. Instead, there was misallocation of capital on an epic scale, with money pouring into real estate and construction.

Spain provided an example of how the euro fostered a bubble mentality. Property prices rose fivefold in a decade, and as the price of real estate went up people had to borrow more to buy a home. Private debt as a proportion of national income stood at 80 per cent in 1980; by 2007 it had almost tripled to 230 per cent – higher even than in the land of perennial housing bubbles, the UK. At its peak, 13 per cent of Spain's employees worked in a construction sector that accounted for 18 per cent of GDP.

Rapid, property-driven growth made a country like Spain attractive to overseas investors, particularly those living in Germany and France, whose domestic economies were struggling. As a result, the Spanish housing boom was given extra momentum. There was never the remotest possibility that Spain would embark on the structural reforms expected by the ECB and the European Commission while the party was still in full swing.

There was, therefore, quite a contrast between the core of the Eurozone and the periphery in these early years of the euro's life. In the first decade of the single currency, growth rates in its 'Big Three' changed very little. Germany grew by 1.5 per cent on average, up 0.1 points on the last five years of the mark between 1993 and 1998. France grew slightly quicker than it did during the period when it was deflating its economy to qualify for the euro, by 2.1 per cent on average against 1.7 per cent. Italy's growth rate remained unchanged at 1.3 per cent.

The reason the euro as a whole expanded at a faster rate than it had in the 1990s (2.1 per cent against 1.9 per cent) was due to the pick-up in activity in some of the peripheral economies, with Spain's average expansion of 3.6 per cent failing to keep pace with Greece (4 per cent) and Ireland (6 per cent). But these growth rates belied an underlying weakness, which was that the housing booms were leading to higher inflation in countries such as Spain, meaning that they were increasing their costs at a time when Germany's were coming down. Europe's strongest economy became even more of an export dynamo in the years leading up to the Great Recession, increasing its competiveness by 10 per cent against all other countries during a period when Italy's competitiveness fell by 34 per cent.

China became more of a factor as time wore on, especially after it was admitted to the World Trade Organization in 2001, because the high-quality capital goods it needed to fit out the factories of the Pearl River Delta and elsewhere were Germany's specialism.

For many decades, exports had accounted for around 30 per cent of Germany's national output, but after the introduction of the euro the share rose steadily, peaking at 50 per cent of GDP after the global financial crisis. German exports to the rest of the Eurozone rose by 10 per cent a year in the first decade of the euro's life, a far stronger performance than managed by its euro partners. The upshot was that Germany had a rising trade surplus while deficits grew bigger in Spain, France, Italy and Greece.

This was not quite what had been envisaged. It had been assumed that capital flows would be used to build up the productive capacity of the weaker Eurozone countries, not to build second homes for BMW workers from Munich. Current account deficits soared in those countries that had the biggest housing bubbles, from 3 per cent to 9.6 per cent of GDP in Spain, and from 0 to 6 per cent in Ireland, a country that was the European home of many US multinationals attracted by the country's low rate of corporation tax. One way of looking at it is, as Adair Turner puts it, that foreign investors were content 'to invest in peripheral country debt securities or to lend money to their banks, households and companies'.[12]

We would put it another way: Billy Bunter got his postal order. And spent it in the tuck shop.

Cheating

The Germans were not in much of a position to do anything about this. They had set up the ECB to be a clone of the Bundesbank. They staffed it with officials who accepted the Bundesbank view of the world. And they had in place a Stability and Growth Pact (SGP) designed to prevent member countries from running up excessive budget deficits. Only at the insistence of Jacques Chirac during the preparations for monetary union were the Germans prevented from instigating automatic fines for those that breached the SGP.

From a German perspective, the Stability and Growth Pact was needed to avoid cheating. Monetary union was supposed to prevent countries from going it alone, but that discipline could be avoided if countries were able to let rip with their budget deficits. There was to be no use of lax fiscal policy to avoid the strictures imposed by the ECB, and penalties for anybody who tried.

The debate over the Stability and Growth Pact underlined the German wariness of anything that smacked of Keynesianism. But Keynes said a degree of budgetary leeway was even more important if a country was giving up monetary autonomy, and that this would become apparent during a period of weak growth.

This was indeed what happened in 2003, when the first breaches of the SGP occurred. Contrary to expectation, the culprits were not the Portuguese, the Spanish or the Greeks – they were all humming along as a result of the stimulus provided by low interest rates. Artificially high growth meant the governments in Lisbon, Madrid and Athens had little trouble in keeping their deficits below 3 per cent of GDP (although it transpired that in the latter case, compliance was aided by a curious interpretation of the rules of arithmetic). Instead, as Keynes would have predicted, the problems arose for those countries that had low growth and high unemployment, because that led to downward pressure on tax receipts and upward pressure on welfare payments. In both 2002 and 2003, Germany and France ran deficits in excess of the SGP's 3 per cent limit.

The European Commission responded by announcing that it intended to fine the euro's two largest states. Romano Prodi, the president of the Commission, was put in the position of a teacher who is disappointed to find that his most promising – and previously blameless – students have been caught behaving badly and feels that he has no choice but to treat them in the same way as he would serial offenders. The rules stated the Germans and the French should hand over an interest-free deposit to the Commission, which would be surrendered if they failed to reduce their deficits below the permitted limit. Germany and France decided that the rules should not apply to them and refused to pay. The finance ministers of the Eurozone rallied behind Berlin and Paris, and voted the Commission down. As Prodi said later: 'Clearly I had not enough power.'[13]

The impact of the breach of the Stability and Growth Pact was profound. In economic terms, the Franco-German breach of the SGP was sensible, because higher budget deficits helped support the economy when growth was weak. But politically the behaviour of the Eurozone's two biggest countries suggested that neither took budgetary discipline all that seriously. It gave other countries to think that they too could break the rules with impunity. And it sent out a message that national governments were determined to keep control of their own budgets. For the Germans, who in the 1990s had campaigned for budgetary decisions to be pooled at a supranational level, the flouting of the Pact was a short-term victory but a long-term defeat.

Inspection

Schools are inspected regularly and so are countries. Each year, a team from the International Monetary Fund in Washington conducts what is known as an Article IV consultation with each of its members. Although the Eurozone is not strictly speaking a country, the IMF provides a report card for the single-currency area as a whole as well as one for each individual member state.

Had a parent received the report the IMF wrote on the Eurozone in July 2007, he or she would have flushed with pride. 'The outlook is the best in years,' the Article IV report noted. 'The economy is poised for a sustained upswing, partly because of cyclical considerations, but also due to policies, which up to now have had a forward-looking cast.'[14] There were big ticks for the Eurozone's commitment to structural reform, for its strong public finances and for its record on bringing down unemployment. Within a month, a financial crisis would break which would lead to four countries being put under IMF structural adjustment programmes and threaten monetary union's very existence, but the IMF seemed entirely oblivious to the dangers. In educational terms, it was as if a school, within a year of being branded a failing establishment, had been given a glowing report from inspectors too blind to see what was actually going on.

A later IMF survey, conducted after the global recession and the Eurozone debt crisis, came to a different conclusion. This 2013 analysis helped to answer a simple question: would the countries on the Eurozone's periphery that went from boom to bust have been better off not joining the euro in the first place? Neither the housing bubbles nor the economic divergence between the euro's core and its periphery during its early years by themselves provide conclusive proof that countries such as Spain and Portugal would have been better off running their own independent monetary policies. For that to be shown, there would need to be a counterfactual, a country or a group of comparable countries that did better by staying outside monetary union.

The IMF report provides precisely that, since it compared four former Soviet bloc countries with a selected group of countries from the Eurozone's periphery. The Czech Republic, Hungary, Poland and Slovakia make up what the IMF calls the Central European 4 (CE4), while the Selected Periphery (SP) includes Greece, Italy, Spain and Portugal. In what was akin to a high-flying academy doing outreach in struggling schools on the wrong side of town, ten new countries – including the CE4 – had joined the EU in 2004. All had much lower incomes per head even than the poorest countries on the Eurozone's periphery. The IMF's findings were unequivocal. Despite the claims in advance that the single currency would bring member states closer together, there had been more lasting convergence between Germany and the CE4 through the creation of a German Central European Supply Chain (GCESC) than between Germany and the SP. The reason for that, the Fund said, was that Poland, Hungary, the Czech Republic and Slovakia attracted foreign direct investment that built factories and created lasting economic benefit, while Italy, Spain, Greece and Portugal attracted speculative cash that pumped up housing bubbles.[15]

All this was happening at a time when the exchange rates of the CE4 were fluctuating wildly and the exchange rates of those countries in the Eurozone remained unchanged. In other words, being inside the Eurozone did not bring the convergence-boosting investment that was promised, while being outside the euro proved no barrier to the development of new greenfield sites that led to a marked narrowing of the gap in living standards between Germany and its former communist neighbours.

Indeed, the evidence is that the CE4 countries were better able to cope with the downturn that began in 2008 because three of them retained control of their own monetary policy and the fourth – Slovakia – only joined the Eurozone in 2009. In 1995, the Czech Republic, consistently the richest of the CE4, had per capita incomes that were just 19 per cent of Germany's. By 2014 they had risen to 42 per cent of Germany's. Over the same period, Greece had seen its GDP per head rise from 41 per cent to 46 per cent of Germany's, while Portugal's had risen from 37 per cent to 46 per cent of that of Germany.

'These successes were exactly what the architects of the euro area hoped would happen to poorer members after joining the single currency', Matthew Klein noted in the *Financial Times*. 'The founders dreamed of building a unified European economy with transnational supply chains centred around the core of Germany, Austria, and the Benelux countries. Technology transfers, foreign management, and new investment in plants and equipment would foster convergence across the bloc.'[16]

Strangely, it seemed to have escaped the attention of the euro's architects that countries can have close links even if they are not in a monetary union. There is, for example, more convergence between Norway and Sweden, two countries that have their own currencies, than there is between Finland and Greece, which both use the euro. There is no single currency for Australia and New Zealand, and both Canada and the US have their own central banks and their own dollars.

Klein sums things up succinctly: 'Contrary to what the euro's founders believed, it now appears the absence of monetary union is what's needed to channel capital flows most productively across borders. That's the real tragedy of the single currency: it was pointless from the start.'

Test

It is one thing performing in practice, quite another to deliver when the pressure is on. Nice essays served up in class count for nothing in an examination. Under the spotlight, all sorts of weaknesses are exposed. Such was the case for the Eurozone in August 2007, when what had been considered a local and containable problem in the US housing market soon turned into the most acute financial crisis since the 1930s. The single currency failed the test.

Europe was relatively ill-prepared for the searching examination it was about to receive. None of the three biggest economies – Germany, France and Italy – had performed that strongly in the first eight years of the euro's life, and this had opened up a divide between monetary union's sluggish core and its fast-growing periphery. As Marsh notes, neither France nor Italy were able to take advantage of Germany's willingness to join the single currency at an overvalued rate.[17]

But the economic divergence was a symptom of an underlying problem rather than its cause. Given its eclectic membership, it was always going to be a challenge to turn monetary union into a cohesive bloc. That would have been the case even had a single interest rate been accompanied by centralized control over budgets, which is what the Germans originally wanted.

In Soros's view, the cause of the crisis dates back to the introduction of the euro itself, a move that was seen as making the surpluses and deficits of individual Eurozone countries irrelevant. Germany ran ever-higher trade surpluses at the expense of other Eurozone countries as the 2000s wore on. The Germans were doing extra lessons while the rest of the class enjoyed the kudos that came with being allowed into such a prestigious school. Spain, Portugal and Greece abided by the school's uniform code, but too little attention was paid to whether they could keep up with the lessons.

The loss of competitiveness accumulated over time, so that by the end of the euro's first decade the cost and price difference between Germany and southern Europe was 25 per cent. Monetary union had abolished exchange rates between Eurozone members, but it had not abolished real exchange rates – the exchange rate adjusted for variations in unit-labour costs. By this measure, Germany had seen a substantial depreciation.

As Flassbeck and Lapavitsas note, Greece had been living above its means, but not by as much as Germany had been living below its means.[18] Unit-labour costs rose by an average of 0.4 per cent a year in the first decade of the euro, compared to an inflation target of just below two per cent. Germany's current account surplus continued to grow, but the rules of mathematics mean that not all countries can run surpluses at the same time. One country's surplus is another country's deficit.

Flassbeck elaborated on the notion that Germany was at the root of the Eurozone's problems through its pursuit of a beggar-thy-neighbour approach when he spoke at the economics festival Kilkenomics in Ireland in 2015, also attended by one of this book's authors. Cutting the price of potatoes, he said, led to an increase in demand for potatoes. But cutting wages affects the ability of workers to purchase other goods and services. 'People are different from potatoes.'

What happened was that Germany ran bigger and bigger trade surpluses at the expense of the other members of monetary union. It then re-recycled these surpluses back across the Eurozone, often in the form of investment in real estate. The flaw in this model is that it only works so long as the capital keeps flowing from the surplus country to the deficit country. Once the money stopped flowing, the financial markets started to fret about the size of the trade deficits that were being run in some of the peripheral Eurozone economies and investors demanded a higher interest rate when they lent money to their governments. Warren Buffett once famously said that it is only when the tide goes out that it is possible to see who has been swimming naked, and this was certainly true of the Eurozone. It became clear that there was, after all, a difference between the security provided by a German bond and an Italian bond, and interest rates reflected that difference. The Eurozone's faith in unhindered capital flows proved misplaced: it resulted in too much capital going where it was not needed, and allowed some governments in the Eurozone – Greece being a prime example – to disguise the true state of their public finances.

The crisis did, however, determine what sort of establishment the Eurozone was going to be. It was Germany that provided the funds to keep the school going when the crisis broke and so the school would be run along German lines. That meant obeying the rules: no more cheating in class; no more smoking behind the bike sheds; no more idling around waiting for postal orders to turn up. From now on, there would be cold showers, more frugal mealtimes, punishments for failing to attend lessons. At this point, some of the weaker members of the Eurozone could sympathize with Prince Charles when he described Gordonstoun as 'Colditz with kilts'.

Happy-go-lucky Ireland would be one of the first countries to be called to the headmaster's study.

CHAPTER 5

IRE AND ICE

Two crises in a cruel sea

Ireland's boom is in full swing.
Rows of numbers, set in a cloudless blue
computer background, prove the point.

Dennis O'Driscoll, 'The Celtic Tiger'

Future historians may marvel at the fact that, in the late twentieth and early twenty-first century, two island nations previously best-known for primary industrial output – agricultural produce in one case, fish in the other – appeared to have stumbled on a winning formula that guaranteed dizzying levels of economic growth. In both cases, that of Ireland and Iceland, the key ingredients included lower taxes on business, a strong inflow of foreign capital and an asset-price boom (in real estate and equities respectively) that allowed those riding the wave of economic expansion to claim that huge levels of borrowing were properly collateralized. Those future historians may wonder also at the similarities between the economic crashes that befell both countries, whose capital cities are 900-odd miles apart across the grey waters of the North Atlantic. Doubtless they will come across that rather tired wise-crack from the years of the global Great Recession, that the only difference between Iceland and Ireland was six months and one letter.

And, should they be doing their jobs properly, our future histo-rians will conclude that this was not really true, that for all the simi-larities between the two countries there was one huge difference, which is that Ireland was a member of the Eurozone and Iceland was not even a member of the European Union. This gave Iceland a free hand denied to Ireland in terms of letting its banks go bust, inflating its currency, effecting a steep devaluation of the exchange rate and imposing capital controls. Ireland, by contrast, felt obliged to guarantee its banks' assets and apply deflationary austerity measures as a condition of support from its creditors.

In this chapter we track the outcomes of these two very different responses to the financial crisis and try to draw some lessons from them.

No comparisons are ever exact, there being, inevitably, what asset managers call 'basis risk', the extent to which one thing does not match up with the other. Iceland's population, for example, is just 332,000, against Ireland's 4.9 million. But the cases of Ireland and Iceland, while not making for a perfect read-across, provide a compelling test case of the claim that membership of the single currency supplies a safe harbour for smaller economies, sheltering them in an uncertain world of colossal, sometimes violent, capital flows and giving them access to the vast resources of the European Central Bank, headquartered in that fortress of continental capital stolidity, Frankfurt. Given that supporters of the euro had been known to include the UK in their definitions of 'smaller' economies, it was surely important to them that Iceland, whose entire popula-tion would fit into the city of Birmingham nearly three times over, was seen to fail to manage its own recovery and to do so in compar-ison with a successful performance from euro-member Ireland.

Nor does the population difference between the two countries invalidate economic comparisons. Policy choices in the United States and the United Kingdom have been profitably compared and contrasted since at least the Second World War, despite the fact that at the time of writing America's population stands at 321.4 million against 64.1 million for the UK.

From a leftist perspective, too, it mattered that Ireland be shown to bounce back successfully from its difficulties. In the eyes of the European left, Ireland's membership of the single currency was one of a suite of bold and praiseworthy policy moves, which included the legalization of same-sex relationships (1993), a ban on smoking in the workplace, including pubs and restaurants (2004) and legislation providing for divorce (1996). By contrast, Iceland was a nearby country of which they knew little, beyond the fact that its recent governments had been headed by those of an apparently deep-dyed free-market disposition. Its self-imposed exclusion from the EU was itself a sign of suspicious eccentricity, and its best-known international dimension was (pre-2006, when US forces were withdrawn) as an important US military base – hardly likely to endear the country to the left.

Furthermore, the 'Iceland first' response to the crisis betokened the sort of narrow nationalism that leftists have traditionally deplored. In deciding which horse to back in the North Atlantic recovery stakes, there was really no contest.

Notes from two small islands

For a radio panel show more used to holding its weekly sessions in village halls and school assembly buildings, BBC Radio 4's 'Any Questions?' had certainly come up in the world. The National Gallery of Ireland is one of Europe's great museums, with a collection spanning most schools of art from the fourteenth century to the twentieth. Situated in Merrion Square in Dublin, it is close to Upper Merrion Street, coincidentally home to the Irish Republic's Department of Finance.

It was 23 March 2007 and, as the programme's chair Jonathan Dimbleby explained, they were in Dublin as guests of the European Commission Representation in Ireland, given that the programme was being put together 'as the EU celebrates the fiftieth anniversary of the Treaty of Rome, which pledged the member states to lay, I quote, "the foundation of an ever closer union among the peoples of Europe".' Peter Mandelson, then Britain's EU commissioner, had been due to appear on the panel but, explained Dimbleby, 'he dropped out at the end of last week apparently because of a meeting in Indonesia'. In his place 'we are graced by the presence of another enthusiast for Europe', the UK's former Europe minister, Labour MP Denis MacShane. He was joined by Professor Brigid Laffan, 'dean of the European Institute at the University College Dublin and the Jean Monnet Professor of European Politics', and by the chief executive of budget airline Ryanair, Michael O'Leary. The final panel member was an oddity in that he was neither Irish, nor pro-European Union: the former Tory cabinet minister John Redwood, then chairing opposition leader David Cameron's long-forgotten 'Economic Competitiveness Policy Group'.

In retrospect, it can be seen that the panel was meeting at a time of uncertain crosscurrents in British, Irish and European affairs. The 'European Constitution', painstakingly stitched together by the former French president Valéry Giscard d'Estaing, had been rejected by voters both in Giscard's native France and in the Netherlands, a country so traditionally pro-EU as to have provided the origin of the phrase 'federasty' (a label that, to be fair, the Dutch are thought originally to have stuck on themselves). In its place, an (allegedly) more modest instrument was being drawn up, one that could avoid the scrutiny of electorates. It was to emerge as the Lisbon Treaty.

The strong tide that had seemed destined to carry Britain into the single currency had abated. True, euro member Ireland was firing on all economic cylinders – the previous year, Prime Minister Bertie Ahern had declared, 'The boom is getting boomier.' But Britain was growing strongly as well, although the requirements of domestic politics meant that the boom had to be described as a non-boom; there was to be, declared Chancellor Gordon Brown (on the brink of assuming the premiership), no return to boom and bust.

Back in the UK, the issue of joining the single currency – 'abolishing the pound', in the stark phrase preferred by Redwood and fellow Eurosceptics – had, as we shall see in detail in Chapter 6, faded, the bitter battles of the late 1990s and early 2000s starting to recede from the rear-view mirror. Signing up for the euro club had been a project associated with Tony Blair, the outgoing prime minister. Blocking his ambition had been largely the work of his expected successor, Brown. But if the British, by and large, were content to see sterling and the euro go their separate ways, this was far from being a universal view in Ireland.

Part way through the programme, one member of the audience, Michael O'Mara, asked: 'Will the British government ever grow up and adopt the euro currency?' The answers, as taken from the BBC transcript, were as follows. O'Leary declared: 'Absolutely . . . I think in time, yes, it's inevitable.' Laffan was more cautious: 'I'm not so sure it is inevitable. I would have hoped it would be . . . because I'd like to be able to go to London and not have to change currency' – which drew claps from the audience. MacShane admitted that to have joined the single currency in recent years 'certainly hasn't been right for us' but 'to rule it out forever would be a huge strategic error'. Redwood, unsurprisingly, did not think it right for Britain to join the euro, and equally unsurprisingly encountered what the BBC transcript described as '(AUDIENCE NOISE)'. One may have thought that, were the euro to have proved such an unambiguous blessing to the Irish economy, the country's inhabitants – or at least that section of the population that turns up for current affairs discussion programmes – would have been indifferent to the likelihood or otherwise of the UK deciding to join. One possible reason why this was not the case was given a little later in the programme by Brigid Laffan: 'It would also be important from an Irish perspective if the United Kingdom was a member of the euro because we trade a lot with the UK and it would remove the uncertainty of the exchange rate.'

Indeed, Britain is one of Ireland's largest trading partners – the largest, on some figures – and life would certainly be easier for importers and exporters were the two countries to share one currency. But this cannot have provided the whole explanation, given that Anglo-Irish trade had taken place across an exchange rate since Ireland left the sterling area in 1978 and established its own currency, the Irish pound, also known as the punt or the IRL.

Perhaps there was a more deeply-seated psychological irritation at seeing the British flouting European etiquette in this way, shamelessly parading their difference and acting as if they knew better than everybody else.

Regardless, it is notable that no-one on the panel or indeed in the audience had the bad taste to ask what was so 'grown-up' about handing over control of monetary and exchange-rate policy to a large, unaccountable institution based in a foreign country. Perhaps the Irish held a different notion of adulthood from that of their nearest neighbours – not to mention from that of their traditional close friends, the people of the United States, who, then and now, showed no urge to do anything so 'grown-up' as to abolish the Federal Reserve and outsource US monetary policy to non-Americans.

As the 'Any Questions?' panel debated these and other matters, the Icelandic authorities were busy stoking their own boom with a series of measures to make life more fiscally agreeable for the country's population. In the very same month, March 2007, the government cut the reduced rate of VAT charged on food and some other items from 14 per cent to 7 per cent. The Organisation for Economic Co-operation and Development (OECD) reported: 'At the same time, excise duties on several food items were abolished and import duties on meat were reduced.' These were the latest in a series of tax reductions, according to the OECD report: in 2005, the wealth tax was abolished and in 2007 the corporate income tax was reduced from 30 per cent in 2001 to 18 per cent. Corporate income tax was cut again in 2008 'as the authorities, despite warnings that the economic situation was quickly deteriorating, wanted to strengthen Iceland's attractiveness as an international business location ... Some of these tax cuts might have seemed justified at the time by the belief that the boom in revenues was permanent.'[1]

If euro membership was being touted for Britain before the crash, it was being urged on Iceland after it, not least by the OECD. In the same report, the OECD declared that Eurozone membership 'appears to be the best solution for Iceland among its long-term options for monetary policy'. Joining the single currency, it admitted, 'will require difficult decisions, such as the negotiations over Iceland's fisheries'. But it would be worth it because 'the economy should noticeably benefit from the enhanced macro-economic stability and the reduction in real interest rates'.

If this seems almost beyond parody from the perspective of the present, after all the travails of Greece and other Eurozone countries, we need to bear in mind that back then, euro membership or unilateral 'euroization' of the Icelandic economy were being touted in official circles in Reykjavik. But however fair-mindedly one looks at the OECD recommendations, it is hard not to detect a grim determination to cling to the alleged benefits of the single currency – the Ireland model – and ignore at all costs the hint of a suggestion that the euro may have helped to cause the crisis rather than to have supplied the solution.

The OECD noted the difficulties of running a monetary policy 'in a very small open economy', adding that joining the Eurozone would 'eliminate the exchange-rate risk and open access to the large euro capital market'.

Time, apparently, for Iceland to 'grow up' in the approved Irish manner. That it declined to do so, and preferred a successful adolescence, is the theme of this chapter. What may be described as 'official Europe' and its allies in the OECD, the IMF and elsewhere were given the comparison they were seeking between the fate of a small, trouble-hit Eurozone member and a small, trouble-hit non-member. However, the results were not what had, presumably, been hoped for.

Breaking free: From strait-laced societies to turbo-charged economies

If the working out of their respective economic crises – not least because of their sharply divergent monetary arrangements – sets the two countries apart, their emergence, however fleetingly, as fast-paced nimble-footed economies with much to teach their larger brethren demonstrates much more commonality. In part, this can be traced to some key similarities in the social and political backgrounds of the two economic booms.

Iceland and Ireland shared a recent history of strait-laced semi-puritanism, not least with regard to the consumption of alcohol: strong beer was prohibited in Iceland until March 1989 and Ireland's 'Holy Hour' closing of pubs from 2 p.m. to 4 p.m. on Sundays lasted until 1999. By the early 2000s, both countries had reinvented themselves as hotspots of hedonism, with Dublin a major centre for stag weekends and Reykjavik routinely praised for its 'vibrant club scene'.

Both countries were traditionally keen to keep television in its place: Iceland banned all transmissions on Thursdays until 1987, apparently to ensure a day for family and social life, while Ireland's public broadcaster RTÉ continues to transmit the minute-long Catholic call to prayer, the Angelus, daily at 6 p.m., giving rise to a unique Irish institution, the 'Six One' evening news.

Iceland and Ireland have generally shared a coalition-based consensual political culture, with a number of parties holding apparently conflicting sets of beliefs nevertheless able to agree on most matters likely to arise in terms of public administration, with their remaining differences aired in sometimes eccentric ways. More than thirty years ago, Richard West noted of Iceland, 'the government is a coalition of Communists and Conservatives, the two groups that also run the trade unions. Both parties apparently get their votes from the well-to-do and the middle classes. The working classes vote for the Socialists, who appear to be rather right-wing and refuse to join in the government.'[2] Today, one of the country's largest political groupings – not in government – is the Pirate Party, dedicated to 'internet freedom'.

Ireland at the time of preparations for euro membership in the mid-1990s boasted no fewer than six main parties – Fianna Fáil, Fine Gael, Labour, the Progressive Democrats, the Green Party and the Democratic Left – all of which believed much the same sorts of things, belying Ireland's self-image as a disputatious country with a strongly rebellious streak. All certainly shared the political establishment's enthusiasm for the European Union. To escape the somnolent pro-Brussels consensus meant supporting the handful of Eurosceptics including the failed presidential candidate and successfully elected MEP for Connacht–Ulster from 1999 to 2004, Rosemary Scallon, better known as the singer – and, perhaps ironically, winner of the 1970 Eurovision Song Contest – Dana.

Both countries have been touchy on the subject of their relatively recently acquired independence, from Denmark in 1918 in the case of Iceland and from Britain in 1922 in the case of Ireland. Both countries, although independent, initially maintained the crowned head of the former governing power as head of state, opting for republican status only later – 1944 in Iceland and 1949 in Ireland.

Both were of considerable strategic interest to the UK during the Second World War. For Iceland this triggered a flagrant violation of the country's sovereignty and neutrality when UK forces arrived in May 1940 in defiance of a rejection by Iceland of offers of help. Ireland itself may have suffered a similar territorial violation, with regard to the three former 'Treaty Ports' of Berehaven, Cobh (also known as Spike Island) and Lough Swilly, which had been retained as British naval and air bases after Irish independence but had, with unfortunate timing, been returned to the Irish government by the Neville Chamberlain administration in 1938.

On 5 November 1940, Winston Churchill described Britain's inability to use the Irish ports as 'a most heavy and grievous burden and one which should never have been placed on our shoulders, broad though they may be'. Sir Max Hastings writes that Churchill 'was tempted by the notion of reinforcing his country's claims upon these naval bases and air bases'.[3] The temptation was resisted.

All of which takes us to another feature shared by the two countries: their sometimes difficult respective relationships with their much larger North Atlantic neighbour, the United Kingdom. The so-called 'cod wars' of the 1970s between Britain and Iceland over the latter's extension of its fishing grounds are now a distant memory, recalled if at all as a somewhat farcical conflict, comparable perhaps with the 'invasion' of Anguilla in the West Indies in 1969 by a squad of Metropolitan Police officers. Easily forgotten by the public at large is the exchange of live ammunition and the life-threatening ramming of fishing trawlers, as is the threat by Iceland to shut down vital US military facilities, a threat that persuaded Washington to put enormous (and successful) pressure on London to give way. In fishing circles, however, it has not been forgotten. The shore fishing information site British Sea Fishing recalls: 'The loss of access to these fisheries devastated many British fishing communities such as Hull and Grimsby and many Scottish ports, with as many as 1,500 fishermen and several thousand shore-based workers from these areas losing their jobs.'[4]

Despite this, and despite the loss of two lives, one British and one Icelandic,[5] there was no real comparison in terms of scale with the main bone of contention between Britain and the Irish Republic in the 1970s and early 1980s. Britain's handling of the conflict in Northern Ireland was ultimately to claim more than 3,600 lives between 1968 and 1998. Yet, despite the tendency of British soldiers to 'get lost' and stray into Irish territory in hot pursuit of alleged terrorists, there was no sustained head-on clash between representatives of the two countries, no equivalent of the Cod War confrontations. The so-called Troubles were not a direct dispute between Britain and Ireland but a security crisis largely within (contested) British territory that could not help but overshadow relations between the two countries.

This may have been compounded by the realization that Britain had the economic and military resources to keep a lid on the cauldron of Northern Ireland, and the Irish Republic, for all its (then) constitutional claim to the territory of the North, did not. Furthermore, the Irish Republic generated significantly lower output per head. Joe Haines, senior aide to the British prime minister, noted: 'If the standard of living of the people in the North was to fall to that of the South, it would be a catastrophic fall. Dublin may be more romantic, but it is scruffy and seedy compared with Belfast, even bombed as severely as it has been.'[6]

But it is at this point that a key difference emerges between our two 'small islands'. Iceland was always prosperous, and had little difficulty finding work for all its people. Richard West's article noted that Iceland was one of the richest countries in the world, after Sweden, adding: 'The country thrives; there is no unemployment, in fact there is minus unemployment since lots of people seem to have two or three jobs.' He found Icelanders to be 'very nationalistic' with no wanderlust in terms of wishing to emigrate – an irony, given the 'Viking raider' myth that was to be cherished during the boom years. This stay-at-home mentality was confirmed by the country's highest public official: "'We've had our people," President Vigdís [Finnbogadóttir] told us, "who tried their luck in Australia and Canada, but they came back."'[7]

The contrast with Ireland in terms of the population's ability to find work could scarcely be starker. Ireland was marked by mass emigration, notably in the nineteenth century, the 1950s and the 1980s. The 'Irish diaspora' – from Chicago and New York to Sydney and Melbourne – was and is such an established feature of international culture that, by the 1990s, enterprising types in those cities without a sizeable Irish presence, such as some in China, could order 'kit pubs' allowing 'genuine' Irish bars to be assembled from scratch.

Presaging the spirit of the 'Celtic Tiger', in the early 1980s Ireland's Industrial Development Authority tried to turn a growing problem – the lack of jobs for the rising generation passing through the education system – into an attraction, one presented with a bravura national self-confidence that was to become common a decade or more hence. As noted by the *New York Times*, international travellers arriving at Dublin Airport were greeted by a poster depicting 'four clean-cut students strolling across the cobblestone courtyard of Trinity College' with the caption 'We're the young Europeans'. The paper explained that the advertisement was part of a new campaign to attract foreign investment, and 'reflects Ireland's attempt to cope with an awkward, urgent problem. For Ireland's greatest selling point – a growing population of well-educated young people – is also rapidly becoming its most critical national concern.'[8] Some suggested that this difficulty in finding work for all its people marked Ireland as a 'failed state', vindicating Churchill's prediction that the independence of the twenty-six southerly counties had not only meant a 'woeful curtailment' of the 'harmony and strength' of the British Empire but had 'condemned Ireland to a melancholy fate'.[9]

There is, of course, much more to the recent economic histories of Iceland and Ireland than their relationship with Britain. But for geographical and historical reasons, their burgeoning economic status would express itself in part at least through a British prism. And while the ultimate expression of the two economic booms looked very similar – with the aforementioned cuts to business tax, inflow of foreign capital and soaring asset values – the starting points were very different. Put simply, the Irish were framing an economic policy in (apparent) contrast to that of the UK, whereas the Icelanders were far more interested in buying so-called 'trophy assets' in Britain and elsewhere. As has been pointed out in Michael Booth's 2014 study of the Nordic countries, *The Almost Nearly Perfect People*, Iceland was distinguished from its fellow Nordics by an almost Wild West mentality.[10] Ireland, by contrast, set out on its road to boom and bust in a mood of high seriousness. It is to the latter nation that we turn first.

Ireland: Stooping to conquer?

Ireland's monetary union with the UK was sufficiently tightly bound that the two countries' coins were the same size, of a very similar design and were virtually interchangeable. Even after the IRL broke free from sterling, British banknotes remained acceptable in the Republic in a one-to-one exchange on the basis that the sterling–punt rate rarely moved too far either way: what was lost on the swings tended to be gained on the roundabouts. Change would be given, obviously, in Irish coinage.

But this easy-going attitude was not replicated in high policy-making circles. Here, the 1978 breakaway from sterling was treated as being of the utmost importance. Economist Richard Douthwaite described how 'the Department of Finance file of correspondence with the British Treasury about the common currency, sterling, was sent down to the vaults and never called for again. The Irish pound was free.' Independence for the Irish pound meant 'the last link with the United Kingdom had been broken', something of an over-statement given that the two countries were to remain entwined in a range of institutions ranging from cross-border bodies in Northern Ireland to the provision of lighthouses. That said, Douthwaite identified correctly the significance ascribed in official circles to departure from the sterling area – 'Ireland has finally fought its way out of Britain's shadow' – and also the lift to national self-confidence that came from the country's European identity: 'Irish people at all levels have dealt with their European counterparts and proved to themselves that they can operate at least as well [as the British].'[11]

In fact, 'the Irish pound was free' only in the sense that it was no longer tied to sterling. It was now tied instead to a number of currencies within the European Exchange Rate Mechanism, a monetary bloc anchored to the German mark. In a foreshadowing of Ireland's enthusiasm for the euro, membership of the ERM was deemed a vast improvement on any link to the British currency.

The UK had a 'derogation' from ERM membership, which differed from its opt-out from the euro in that it was supposed to join at some point, which indeed it did. Ireland wanted to join straight away, having concluded after five years of EC membership – it joined in 1973, along with Britain and Denmark – that, as Douthwaite notes, the European club enhanced the country's status, whereas the British tended to the opposite view. 'The former British politician and President of the European Commission, Roy Jenkins, once described the way that Ireland conducted its first European Presidency as "a model of triumphing over the limitations of small-power resources to exercise skilled and authoritative diplomacy . . . [which] succeeded in making London look peripheral to Europe, while Dublin was metropolitan".'[12]

The Irish capital had come a long way in a short space of time since Joe Haines noted its 'seediness'. Central to this advance was its full immersion in the institutions of the European Union, including the ERM and later the euro. Each stage of political estrangement from the UK and monetary integration into Europe took it further away from its state of supposed adolescence, still attached to its former imperial parent, Britain. First to be shed was 'dominion status': sovereignty under the Crown, which still holds sway in sixteen independent countries including Canada. Then came the leaving of the sterling area. Now, with euro membership, the break would be decisive and visible, the monetary equivalent of the switch to kilometres on the road signs once the border from Northern Ireland was traversed.

Here we are at the heart of the notion of euro membership as proof positive of political and economic adulthood with which the 'Any Questions?' panellists were confronted in March 2007. But it is striking that the Irish political class was, apparently, to show very little interest in the economic consequences of this journey from the pound to the euro. After all, very few countries can have experienced three distinct monetary regimes well within a single lifetime: that is, monetary union with one other country; a national currency within an exchange-rate arrangement that could (and did in 1993) experience huge realignments; and a multinational monetary union intended (unlike the arrangement with sterling) to be irrevocable and irreversible.

So how did it all work out?

Figures from the World Bank and International Monetary Fund suggest the following. From 1970 to 1980 – the final decade (almost) that Ireland's currency was tied to sterling – annual growth across those eleven years averaged 4.49 per cent in real, inflation-adjusted terms. From 2001 to 2014, years entirely spent as a member of the single currency, annual growth across those fourteen years averaged just 2.35 per cent.

But it was during the heyday of Ireland's monetary independence, the twenty years from 1981 to 2000, that real GDP growth stood out, at an annual average of 5.4 per cent a year. One might have thought these numbers would have made a case – at the least, one worth discussing – for Ireland to retain its own currency, neither a local version of sterling nor the euro. But if the case were made, it attracted little attention or support.

What was not to be countenanced, apparently, was any official suggestion that the existence of the punt had in any way contributed to the Irish economic miracle that became known as the 'Celtic Tiger', a term first attributed to the British economist Kevin

Gardiner in a report for Morgan Stanley in 1994. This, too, is curious. It is rather as if West Germany's leaders had abjured the notion that the country's post-war economic renaissance had any connection whatever with the existence of the Deutschmark. But an enquiry as to the origins of the 'tiger' economy provides some clue as to why this was so.

Dating the birth of the 'Celtic Tiger' is not straightforward, but many would trace the economic sea-change to the late 1980s and the latter years of the often-controversial prime minister Charles Haughey, whose previous periods in office had been devoid of much in the way of economic success. *The Economist* recalled that 'growing frustration with Ireland's economic stagnation' allowed Haughey to return to power in 1987 'for a third minority term of office'. It added: 'This one, and a coalition government that followed, lasted for five years and, at first, proved remarkably successful.' This was in large part the result of a decision by the opposition Fine Gael party to back all attempts at fiscal reform. 'That allowed the fierce spending and tax cuts that began to transform Ireland from a banana republic into a "Celtic Tiger".'[13]

The change was, indeed, remarkable. But, regardless of the impression given by *The Economist*, it was by no means wholly attributable to the embrace of a Hibernian version of the 'Washington consensus' of tax and spending cuts. Professor Dermot McAleese of Trinity College Dublin, writing in 2000, did indeed credit 'macro-economic stability' with having played a key part in setting the tiger loose: 'New policies in the late 1980s focused on cutting the debt/GDP ratio. The espousal of fiscal rectitude and new consensus economic policies was not in fact new. What was new was the decision to attack the debt by controlling public spending, rather than by increasing taxes.' The proof of the pudding, he said, was in the eating, because for a 'small, open economy' it was far more productive to get a grip on public spending as opposed to raising taxes. 'It created room for tax cuts while simultaneously lowering the debt ratio.'[14]

An easy-to-miss but important phrase here is 'new consensus economic policies', because it referred not only to the market-based consensus in favour of spending restraint and tax cuts, but in addition a broader social consensus. McAleese explains that from the late 1980s, Ireland 'adopted a unique model of wage determination' involving discussion and deal-brokering 'between the social partners'. It is not unique at all, in fact, but it is certainly in sharp contrast to the policies being pursued in the UK. McAleese adds: 'The two key elements were wage restraint in return for income tax cuts and ongoing participation in economic decision-making through social partnership committees. Such a policy is not favoured by economic orthodoxy, but it worked well for both employees and employers.'[15]

While 'economic orthodoxy' may not favour such 'partnership' arrangements, they were common in continental EU countries, not least in Germany, Europe's largest economy. But they were anathema not only to Margaret Thatcher and her successor John Major, but also to their New Labour inheritors. When Gordon Brown as chancellor sought to hold overall public-sector pay increases at no more than the level of the inflation target, he did so not in order to strike up a partnership with the relevant civil-service and other unions but in order to keep the pay bill under control. 'Partnership' with business and the trade unions had been firmly out of fashion in Britain since the end of the 1970s. Once known as 'tripartism' (a good thing), it had since become renamed 'corporatism' (a bad thing).

Irish-style pay policies aligned Ireland firmly with the continental tradition of social democracy, and it seemed to work for the country. As McAleese recorded, national pay deals held down earnings rises as output surged, and 'thus enabled this growth to translate into higher employment and lower unemployment'. By embracing European 'social partnership', Irish policymakers were heading off in a quite different direction from their British counterparts. Furthermore, MacAleese noted that European Union Structural Funds 'gave impetus and direction to Ireland's investment programme'.[16]

The net effect of all this was to banish, for the moment at least, long and painful memories of the lethargic economy of Old Ireland.

It had been only ten years earlier, McAleese recalled, that eminent Irish historian Professor J.J. Lee had mercilessly laid bare the failings of the economy. No other European country, Lee had found, 'had recorded so slow a rate of growth of national income in the twentieth century'. But Lee's analysis ran from Irish independence in 1922 to 1985 – there was no way the professor could possibly know that the best was yet to come, wrote MacAleese: 'Since then, all has changed. The Irish economy has been transformed from the basket case . . . to the shining exemplar of all things economically bright and beautiful of the 1990s.'[17]

Debate may have raged in Britain in the 1990s as to the future direction of policy – towards or away from the euro and a deeper general involvement in the EU, towards a European model of 'stakeholder' capitalism or in the direction of the more bracing 'Anglo-Saxon' model. By contrast, the Irish could congratulate themselves on having chosen an unambiguously European future, and one, moreover, whose fruits were already evident: the construction of new major roads, plans for a light-rail system in Dublin, the launch of an Irish-language television station, and the arrival of software companies and other high-tech employers.

Of course, the time to worry is always the moment at which the great and the good all agree on something. As the funeral rites were being prepared for the punt, the Central Bank of Ireland was, from 1998, setting interest rates not with the needs of the economy in mind but with reference to steering the currency towards the 'irrevocable' rate at which it would be locked into the single currency. On 31 December 1998 this was confirmed as a rate of IRL 0.787564 to the euro.

All the signs at that time were that rates ought to rise: growth had run at 9.08 per cent in 1996 and 10.78 per cent in 1997. Instead, the cost of borrowing was reduced. This was to have knock-on effects for competitiveness in the late 1990s and beyond, as Cormac Lucey was to note many years later: 'Locked into the euro, Ireland's real effective exchange rate (REER) had risen alarmingly since its original conversion rate had been set in the summer of 1998.' Lucey explained that several years of inappropriately low interest rates had proved inflationary and 'had caused Ireland's costs to rise far more than the costs of its Eurozone neighbours'. There is a terrible irony here. Euro membership had been supposed to give Ireland a permanent economic lift, yet the fact was that the circumstances of the country's entry delivered anything but. Or, as Lucey put it, 'Ireland's most important cost measure – the cost at which foreigners buy our goods and services – became incredibly high during the boom.'[18]

All that, however, was in the future in the early days of Ireland's economic miracle, when the tiger's roar appeared to reverberate even on the sports field: the 1990 FIFA World Cup in Italy saw the Republic's team qualify for the competition for the first time, and four years later Ireland was the only one of the home nations to qualify for the tournament being held that year in the United States. 'We're on our way', sang jubilant fans. 'We're on our way to the USA.'

At last, it seemed, the 'young Europeans' were coming into their own.

Raiding parties: The day of the Viking capitalists

The 'Nordic Tiger' soubriquet bestowed on Iceland during its boom years is one link between events there and in Ireland. Dermot McAleese provides another: 'Recently, the Icelandic economist Thorvaldur Gylfason has offered the provocative proposition that with appropriate economic policies and institutions, rapid economic growth is achievable just about anywhere – even in Iceland, one is tempted to add.'[19]

Well, indeed.

But while, as we shall see, there were strong parallels between the boom and bust in both countries, Iceland's journey to 'tiger' status differed in important ways from that of Ireland. Iceland had already, since 1945, adopted two quite distinct socioeconomic models in a period of less than fifty years, and was about to adopt a third.

The first phase was sketched out in a study of Iceland's financial travails by Robert H. Wade and Silla Sigurgeirsdóttir. Initial strong growth, they say, was largely thanks to a number of factors: aid under the Marshall Plan; foreign-exchange earnings from the US/ NATO military base; 'an abundant export commodity, cold-water fish ... and a small, literate, hard-working and ethnically homogeneous population with a strong sense of national identity.' But the market economy was kept in its place, with heavy regulation, along with 'elaborate trade protection and multiple exchange rates'. The authors add: 'Around 1955 about half of imports were subject to quantitative restrictions or rationing.'[20]

This bucolic Arctic autarky was progressively abandoned from 1960 onwards. The exchange rate was unified and trade with the outside world was liberalized, although the government retained a tight grip on the banking system. By the dawn of the 1980s, write Wade and Sigurgeirsdóttir, Iceland's social and economic position had been transformed from one of Europe's poorest countries to one of the wealthiest. 'It established a welfare state in line with the tax-financed Scandinavian model and by the 1980s had attained a level and a distribution of disposable income equal to the Nordic average.'[21]

But despite having dropped anchor in the enviable (to many in the wider world) waters of Scandinavian social democracy, the Icelanders were soon, apparently, restless and keen to move on. As in 1970s Britain, Iceland's intelligentsia included dissidents who openly questioned what they saw as the corporatist consensus. The 1989 fall of the Berlin Wall and the subsequent collapse of the Soviet Union gave impetus to their cause as events appeared to be vindicating the January 1989 declaration of President George H.W. Bush: 'We know what works. Freedom works ... free markets ...'

They were helped also by the fact that fellow Scandinavian countries, notably Sweden, were liberalizing their financial systems. But Iceland was to go very much further. Elected in 1991 at the head of the right-wing Independence Party, Davíð Oddson was to serve as prime minister for fouteen years before taking over as chair of governors of the Central Bank of Iceland. In 2013, Martin Hart-Landsberg looked back at what happened next, beginning with 'an aggressive programme of liberalization and privatization' which, in turn, led to what he calls 'the hyper-expansion of three Icelandic banks': 'Their highly-leveraged growth fuelled massive stock market and housing bubbles, all of which combined to make Iceland's per capita GDP one of the world's highest by the mid-2000s.'[22]

As so often in the history of the EU, rules mandating free movement of capital gave a big push forward to the Icelandic liberalization process. Although not an EU member, the country joined, in 1994, the European Economic Area (EEA), the trade grouping that embraces the EU plus Norway and Liechtenstein. (Switzerland is in a similar position but is not an EEA member.) The conditions for joining the EEA included the removal of obstacles to the movement of capital and labour as well as to trade in goods and services. The two big state-owned banks, Landsbanki and Kaupthing, were privatized in 1998, while a third player, Glitnir, was formed from the merger of some smaller institutions.

To Wade and Sigurgeirsdóttir, this set the scene for Iceland's dramatic entrance onto the world financial scene helped by 'abundant cheap credit (thanks to US loose monetary policy during the 1990s and 2000s) and domestically by strong political backing for the banks'. Ominously, these new banks brought investment and commercial banking under one roof 'so that the former shared the implicit government guarantee of the latter'. Iceland's low sovereign debt helped as well, allowing the banks to bask in favourable judgements from international credit-rating agencies. 'The major shareholders of Landsbanki, Kaupthing, Glitnir and their spin-offs reversed the earlier political dominance of finance: finance now dominated government policy.'[23]

Or, put another way, all the pieces – the newly freed banks, the influx of foreign capital, the strong political backing – were now on the board, so the game could begin. And begin it most certainly did. Magnús Sveinn Helgason identified the central figure in what was to become a compelling national narrative, the 'corporate Viking' whose smash-and-grab tactics recalled the Antipodean 'corporate raiders' of the 1980s. This character was, he wrote, 'the financier who engineered one daring takeover after another: One day buying a British supermarket chain, the next a Swedish real-estate holding company, then turning around to buy a Danish airline. No foreign asset was safe from the leveraged might of these marauding financiers'.[24]

If the Irish had been keen to show the British that their economic miracle arose from a superior, European way of doing things, the Icelanders simply preferred to buy big chunks of their larger neighbour to the south. One of the biggest buyers was Baugur, the Icelandic retail group that took major stakes in the Debenhams and House of Fraser department stores and the toyshop Hamleys, along with holdings in Arcadia (owner of fashion stores Topshop and Dorothy Perkins) and – fittingly – the owner of the supermarket chain Iceland. Baugur's youthful one-time president and chief executive Jón Ásgeir Jóhannesson also found time to take a stake of more than 25 per cent in Aurum Holdings, which owned jewellery shops including Goldsmiths and Mappin & Webb.

Attention turned also to the likelihood that 'the Vikings' would sail their longships up the Thames to the City of London. On 14 October 2004, the *Guardian* reported:

> Icelandic companies were the focus of City takeover speculation yesterday after stockbroker Numis admitted it had turned away a takeover approach, seemingly from an Icelandic bank, while Big Food Group said talks with its Icelandic suitor were continuing. The emergence of the interest of Icelandic bank Landsbanki in Numis follows months of speculation that another City firm, Singer & Friedlander, will receive a takeover bid from Iceland's biggest bank Kaupthing.

The paper added that Icelandic analysts believed the City ought to have seen this coming, despite the relative size of the Icelandic and British economies. One analyst pointed out that Iceland's banking sector had outgrown its small domestic market and the only way to achieve real expansion was to look beyond Iceland's shores.

One alternative was to mount highly geared takeover bids on Iceland's overvalued stock market. In 2007, one of the most famous

'Vikings', Björgólfur Thor Björgólfsson, put $7 billion on the table
to acquire Reykjavik-listed pharmaceutical company Actavis.
Noted *BreakingViews* on 19 December 2014: 'The 12.5 ratio of debt
to earnings before interest, tax, depreciation and amortization is
more than twice the level that worries US bank regulators today.'
BreakingViews added, 'Even by the standards of a frothy, anything-
goes era, Iceland's brief cameo in world finance was odd.'

After the onset of the global financial crisis and the bursting of
the Iceland bubble, 'everybody' had apparently 'always known' that
constructing a giant financial superstructure on the modest foundations of the Icelandic economy was sheer folly. But what was the
view at the time?

Let us look at the International Monetary Fund's Article IV
consultation in 2005, such consultations being the annual health
check to which most IMF members are subjected. The executive
directors 'commended Iceland's recent economic performance on
the back of stability-oriented policies and structural reforms undertaken over the last decade'. These reforms included central bank
independence, the introduction of inflation targeting and a floating
exchange-rate regime, along with the strengthening of financial
supervision, privatization and export diversification. It is harder to
imagine a clearer-cut example of the conventional wisdom of the
1990s and early 2000s which had it that ticking assorted organiza-
tional boxes, such as having an independent central bank and an
inflation target, was synonymous with and proof positive of 'stability'.

To be fair, the Fund went on to remark that that 'more recently'
major investment projects, while necessary for export diversification, 'have contributed to economic volatility and macro-economic
imbalances'. But all this meant was that 'the key challenge' was to
unwind the imbalances and prevent their future recurrence. This
would 'enhance macro-economic stability'. How little 'macro-
economic stability' was available to 'enhance' would become unmis-
takably evident after the crash, as would the limited scope of the
'strengthening of financial supervision praised by the IMF in 2005.

For now, however, the public, by and large, revelled in Iceland's
new era of the 'Viking Capitalists'. As Sveinn Helgason wrote, the

'image of the Saga Age' helped to give legitimacy to the 'the financial plutocrats that emerged in Iceland after the turn of the century'. It added glamour, too: and which besuited business executive would not be flattered at the thought that they were, at heart, axe-swinging warrior chieftains? Nor were those concerned the only ones to be flattered – the nation itself could revel in their reflected glory. Sveinn Helgason writes that the 'Corporate Viking' was presented as the latest embodiment of Iceland's historical tradition and proof that this tradition lived again. 'Finally, after a thousand years, Iceland was again home to "real" Vikings who could strike fear into the hearts of foreigners.'[25]

Furthermore, the good times continued to roll right up to the brink. Casting an eye on the Icelandic scene in 2007, just ahead of the financial crisis, Wade and Sigurgeirsdóttir found Iceland's average income was the fifth highest in the world, riding high at 60 per cent above US levels. Unsurprisingly, perhaps, they found that the 2006 World Database of Happiness ranked Icelanders as the happiest people in the world. They added: 'Reykjavik's shops were laden with luxury goods, its restaurants made London seem cheap, SUVs choked the narrow streets.'[26]

BreakingViews is right to remark on the oddity of Iceland's position as a global financial centre, even by the standards of the 1990s and early 2000s. However, such is the bubble mentality that all but the strongest-minded adjust to the new orthodoxy, whether concurring that 1929 Wall Street had reached a new and permanent plateau of high shares prices, or solemnly agreeing that spiralling indebtedness in the UK in the early 1970s was 'a problem of success', or refusing to enquire too closely into the veracity of alleged sightings of that latest addition to the wildlife of the Arctic, the 'Nordic Tiger'.

And, as with Ireland, Iceland was touted as worthy of emulation beyond its shores. Wade and Sigurgeirsdóttir recall the endorsement of none other than Arthur Laffer, guru of supply-side economics, whose famous 'Laffer curve', drawn on a restaurant napkin, demonstrated that punitive tax rates produced less revenue than lower ones. '[He] declared on a visit to Iceland in November 2007 that fast economic growth with a large trade deficit and ballooning foreign debt were signs of success: "Iceland should be a model to the world," he announced.[27]

Ultimately, the 'Viking Capitalist' was as much an amiable daydream as the 'Celtic Tiger'. In both cases, an unpleasant collision with reality was just round the corner.

All fall down: One banking crisis, two responses

An inflection point is defined by Imperial College London as 'a point where the gradient of the curve stops falling and starts rising, or vice versa'. Adds Imperial's website: 'If you imagine driving along the curve, it's a point where your steering wheel would be in the centre position.'

For that moment, the wheel's central position could give a misleadingly comforting impression of a straight and clear road ahead. So it was in both Iceland and Ireland as the inflection point loomed from boom to bust.

Arwin G. Zeissler, Daisuke Ikeda and Andrew Metrick write that both countries enjoyed prosperous times during the three full years to the end of 2007 'marked by strong economic growth, government surpluses and low unemployment'. As a measure of the two countries' success, GDP growth during those years adjusted for inflation averaged 6 per cent and 5.5 per cent a year in Iceland and Ireland respectively, which was more than twice the 2.6 per cent average growth rate being clocked up by the US economy. Better still: 'Unemployment rates were low from 2005 through 2007, a benefit of the strong global economy at the time. Iceland averaged a remarkably low unemployment rate of 2.6 per cent, and Ireland averaged 4.4 per cent, both below the average unemployment rate of 4.8 per cent in the United States.'[28]

But there was a serpent in this economic paradise – or, to vary the metaphor, each economy harboured a bloated parasitic body. The banking systems in both countries had experienced explosive growth out of all proportion to the size of their economies. Funding such growth far outstripped the deposits of domestic firms and households, and hot money of various sorts was needed to make up the shortfall. In Ireland, the gap between loans and deposits was filled by borrowing on the wholesale market, which was easy enough because, as Ireland was a Eurozone member, its banks could take advantage of the willingness of this market to lend 'in large amounts and at low interest rates'. Much of the money came from foreign lenders. Icelandic banks were in a different position, being both outside the Eurozone and facing an even deeper funding gap than their Irish counterparts. They became increasingly reliant on short-term loans from financial institutions in the US, the Eurozone and Britain. 'However,' write Zeissler, Ikeda and Metrick, 'these wholesale funds were denominated in dollars, pounds and euros, not Icelandic krona, thereby compounding rollover risk with currency risk.'[29]

The major Icelandic banks then sought to broaden their funding base by chasing retail deposits in Europe using highly competitive interest rates. The best-known of these was Landsbanki's online Icesave account, which signed up customers in the UK from 2006 to 2008 and in the Netherlands from spring 2008 until the collapse of the Icelandic banking system in the autumn.

Ballooning credit fed into asset-price bubbles in both countries, expressed in soaring real-estate values and construction activity in Ireland and in a raging stock-market boom in Iceland. In both cases, as in the so-called Lawson Boom in the UK in the late 1980s, the overvalued assets were used as the 'security' for more lending. Thus, Zeissler, Ikeda and Metrick write, Irish banks were heavily exposed to mortgage loans and in lending to property developers 'both of which were collateralised on the underlying real estate'. Icelandic banks did not have that problem to any extent. They had a different vulnerability: 'Iceland's banks often made loans that were collateralised by stock in companies listed on the Icelandic stock exchange.'[30]

The perils of such a self-feeding debt and asset frenzy should have been obvious, but it was not until the extraordinary events of September 2008 that the full scale of the respective economic delusions became obvious. The collapse on the 15th of that month of America's Lehman Brothers investment bank gave the lie to any fondly nurtured hopes that the credit crunch of August 2007 could be filed away under the same category as the 'Black Monday' stock-market plunge of October 1987 – an event generating dramatic headlines but of limited relevance in real-economy terms. As lenders across Britain (Bradford & Bingley), the Benelux countries (Fortis) and Germany (Hypo Real Estate) turned to their governments for support, the spotlight swung to the Irish bank considered at greatest risk of collapse, Anglo Irish.

On 30 September, senior Irish government officials were warned that a failure at Anglo Irish would spark a chain reaction that would deny funding for the other banks. The government responded by introducing a near-blanket guarantee of the liabilities of the country's banks. 'The total amount guaranteed was €375 billion, more than double Ireland's GDP.'[31]

Initially, Iceland appeared to be following a similar course, with a government contribution of €600 million to Glitnir on 29 September in exchange for a 75 per cent stake. But when this, perhaps unsurprisingly, did little to restore confidence in the banking system, events took a different turn.

Capital Economics, the independent research organization, later recalled that a rapid disintegration set in during the autumn of 2008 in terms of overseas investor confidence in Iceland, which 'triggered large-scale capital outflows and a decline in the krona of over 40 per cent in trade-weighted terms.'[32] Inflation rocketed to nearly 20 per cent and the economy dived into recession.

In terms of policy, rather than bail out these stricken institutions, the Reykjavik authorities split each of the three major banks into a 'good' and 'bad' bank, the difference between most such exercises elsewhere in the world and the Icelandic version being that the wheat was not separated from the chaff on the basis of asset quality but, essentially, in terms of nationality. Thus domestic assets and deposits were transferred into the 'good' – or 'new', in Icelandic terminology – banks, while foreign assets, deposits and liabilities stayed with the 'bad – or 'old' – banks. Domestic assets exceeded liabilities; thus, each of the new banks was solvent. None of the old banks was, therefore they all filed for bankruptcy. 'This action did not endear Iceland to foreign creditors.'[33]

That's one way of putting it. The Icelandic crash and the official response to it left a large number of foreign depositors in Icesave and other accounts facing the loss of all their money. Hart-Landsberg listed some of the losers, which included 300,000 people and institutions including the universities of Oxford and Cambridge, the Metropolitan Police and 116 local governments in the UK. He added: 'In the Netherlands, more than 125,000 people opened accounts. Kaupthing [had] followed by establishing Kaupthing Edge in 2007 in Germany and several other European countries.'[34]

On 8 October 2008, the British authorities retaliated, using powers available under the Anti-terrorism, Crime and Security Act 2001 to freeze Icelandic funds in the UK in order to help defray some of the £2.4 billion bill expected to be presented to British taxpayers to compensate individual Icesave customers. But no less a body than the IMF was to approve Iceland's decision to let the 'old' banks fail, albeit while also calling for deposit guarantees to be honoured across national frontiers. A team arrived in Reykjavik in October to offer a $2.1 billion loan to stabilize the krona. Not only did it approve the letting go of the 'old' banks, it also approved the temporary imposition of capital controls, for many years anathema to the Fund. Iceland was granted a second loan from its fellow Nordic countries – Denmark, Finland, Norway and Sweden – worth $2.5 billion.

What was happening in Ireland while Iceland was flouting economic orthodoxy and (largely) getting away with it?

Not only were the Dublin authorities underwriting their lenders but, again in contrast to Iceland, they held off nationalizing their banks until being forced, in January 2009, to take Anglo Irish into public ownership and to provide capital for all important banking institutions. Ireland, self-evidently, did not have the option of devaluing its currency, and its bank guarantees were to prove extraordinarily costly for the Irish taxpayer.

Having hung on without asking for bailout funds, Ireland followed Iceland almost two years to the month later. In November 2010, it received €45 billion from the European Union and €22.5 billion from the IMF. An additional €17.5 billion was made available by the country's own pension reserve fund and the UK offered a bilateral loan of up to £3.25 billion. According to Zeissler, Ikeda and Metrick, 'The funds were to be used as follows: €35 billion to support the banking system and €50 billion to finance general government operations.'[35]

Aftermath and a reckoning

Such sharply divergent policy responses in two comparable, although far from identical, economies have inevitably prompted discussion, debate and sometimes fierce argument over which had proved the right path to follow. One such public spat involved the eminent and vocal economist Paul Krugman, who stated on 3 July 2012: 'I was alerted to a remarkably stupid attack on me over the subject of Iceland from the Council on Foreign Relations.'[36] For its part, the council had written that, once subjected to serious scrutiny, Krugman's Icelandic 'miracle story collapses'.

A temperate and unbiased view is thus not easy to come by. Perhaps, then, it is best to try to start by seeking an analysis from a viewpoint in which any biases are evenly distributed.

Britain's Institute of Economic Affairs, the venerable free-market think tank, can probably be assumed to be equally unenthusiastic about, on the one hand, defaulting on bank debt and inflating the currency and, on the other, subjection to the strictures of the European Union's bailout requirements, not to mention the assumption of a very large amount of moral hazard through the issue of blanket guarantees to banks.

On 25 October 2013, it published an assessment of the two countries' approaches: 'When Iceland pursued the inflationary option, its recession seemed muted and short-lived. It bottomed out quickly and nominal income surpassed the boom-time high by early 2011. The idea was that exports were promoted by the depreciation of the Icelandic krona, and this was what spurred on the quick recovery.' No such outcome for Ireland, which 'slowly ground to a halt'. There was no way a member in a currency union could inflate or devalue its way back to competitiveness and growth. The public debts run up by the bank bailouts were, in essence, a millstone round the country's neck.[37]

But, adds the assessment, the passage of time has altered the story somewhat, in that high levels of inflation in Iceland wiped out savings and has meant that nominal GDP is a poor measure of comparison because Ireland's numbers, being calculated in euros, can be seen to have fallen much less steeply than those in Iceland. It goes on: 'The fall from grace for Icelanders felt worse than it appeared to outsiders owing to this loss in purchasing power and wealth ... Outright deflation swept the Emerald Isle as prices fell ... [but] as prices fell, regular Irish citizens saw their cost of living fall and what savings they had increased in purchasing power.'

All that said, the bailout of the financial system lumbered Ireland with huge borrowings, with a public debt-to-GDP ratio well over 100 per cent. Iceland, too, has a vast government debt 'but it is at least not being directed at paying off debts to keep an insolvent financial sector afloat'; rather, resources are being used in 'a way that does not promote a bloated and unnecessary banking system'.[38]

When the IEA talks in these terms we can assume the banking system in question is indeed very bloated and largely unnecessary. We can also wonder at any lingering view on the left that the euro's inherently 'progressive' nature makes it greatly superior to 'narrow nationalistic' monetary regimes. The Iceland vs Ireland debate is about more than the relative merits in a crisis of different arrangements for currency denominations and interest-rate policies. It even goes beyond the question of whether ordinary people should bear huge burdens in order to bail out the follies of the banking and financial sectors. The tale of two crises goes to the heart of whether an economic system should be arranged in the interests of working people or whether it should be organized so as to defend the interests of the holders of wealth.

We have saved the most telling comparison until last. According to the OECD, the unemployment rate in Ireland is 11.1 per cent of the workforce. Iceland's unemployment rate is 4.9 per cent.

Some success, as Ernest Hemingway might have put it. And some failure.

Indeed, recent strong economic growth in Ireland does not seem to have impressed the voters, who used the 2016 election to administer condign punishment to the coalition partners, Fine Gael and Labour. Reported Derek Mooney in the *Guardian* on 28 February 2016: 'For them, the recovery is something happening in parts of Dublin. It is no coincidence that these are the areas where the swing against Fine Gael was weakest.'

And by the spring of 2016, there were signs that Ireland may be forced to relive the boom–bust experience all over again, starting with inappropriately loose monetary conditions. Strong growth in Ireland coincided with further monetary stimulus from the European Central Bank in early March in an attempt to pep up the sluggish Eurozone economy.

Things were rather different in Iceland, which was able to tailor its monetary policy to its own needs. On 16 March, the European Economics Update reported that Iceland's central bank had decided to keep its key interest rates unchanged for the third meeting in a row, citing low global inflation and a strengthening currency. 'But with inflationary pressures building and the economy growing strongly, more rate hikes are just around the corner.'[39]

A last word: those on the left still squeamish about abandoning such an instrument of international cooperation as the euro in favour of 'monetary nationalism' may care to revisit the words of John Maynard Keynes in 1933, as relevant now as they were then: 'Ideas, knowledge, art, hospitality, travel – these are the things which should of their nature be international. But let goods be homespun whenever it is reasonably and conveniently possible; and, above all, *let finance be primarily national* [our emphasis].'[40]

In our next chapter, we remain in the North Atlantic but look at the euro story from a very different perspective – that of the high drama surrounding Britain's eventual, but by no means preordained, decision to remain outside the single currency.

CHAPTER 6

A BULLET DODGED

How Gordon Brown, Ed Balls and the man in the white coat saved Britain from a euro nightmare

Minister, Britain has had the same foreign policy objective for at least the last five hundred years: to create a disunited Europe. In that cause we have fought with the Dutch against the Spanish, with the Germans against the French, with the French and the Italians against the Germans and with the French against the Germans and Italians. Divide and rule, you see. Why should we change now, when it's worked so well?

Sir Humphrey Appleby in *Yes Minister*

Dawn was breaking on the morning of 8 June 2001 as the private jet carrying Tony Blair and his entourage touched down at Stansted Airport in Essex. The prime minister had made the same short journey south from his Sedgefield constituency on a similar night a little more than four years earlier – the night when he had led Labour not just to victory, but to a bigger landslide than Clement Attlee had managed in 1945.

Aides remarked on how distracted the prime minister looked during the flight; how, despite making history as the first Labour leader to secure two full consecutive terms in office, he appeared downcast as he stepped into the car that would take him to a victory party at London's Millbank. Arriving at 5.30 a.m., the prime minister went through the motions of celebrating a victory over

William Hague's Conservatives in which Labour had won 412 of the 659 seats being contested, only six fewer than in 1997 but on a much lower turnout. For Blair, the election campaign had lacked the excitement of his first as leader; those heady days in the last few weeks of John Major's premiership, when it was clear Labour was returning to power for the first time in eighteen years. Even worse, he had found dealing with Gordon Brown more difficult than ever.

Blair's relationship with his chancellor had changed, and not for the better, since the time when they were seen as the coming men during Labour's wilderness years of the 1980s. While it had originally been assumed that Brown was the more likely of the pair to clamber to the top of what Disraeli called the greasy pole, it was Blair who had been elected leader after John Smith's death in 1994. Brown had stepped down to give his friend a clear run at the top job, but there were some in the party who thought a lot of resentment would have been avoided had he put his name forward for a contest. Legend had it that the two men had come up with a deal while at the Granita restaurant on Upper Street, Islington, close to Blair's North London home: Brown would stand to one side provided he was eventually given the chance to be prime minister and, in the meantime, would hold sway over domestic policy.

It was an arrangement Blair had come to regret during his first term. He was, he knew, beholden to his old friend. The strength of the economy had been the bedrock of his second successive victory, because, for once, a Labour government had avoided being blown off course by a sterling crisis midway through a parliament. There had been no devaluation, no run on the pound, no need to impose spending cuts in the second half of the parliament, and no eventual defeat. Instead, Brown had been praised for giving the Bank of England control over the setting of interest rates and for keeping a tight rein on the public finances during Labour's first two years in power. Yet, for months Blair's closest friends and the officials at 10 Downing Street had been telling him that, after the anticipated second election victory, he ought to move his chancellor to another job, just as Margaret Thatcher had taken advantage of her landslide in 1983 to reshuffle Sir Geoffrey Howe from the Treasury to the Foreign Office.

Rumours that Blair was thinking about moving Brown had been swirling round Westminster and Fleet Street in the months leading up to the general election, and these reports had inevitably reached the chancellor. This had soured the already strained relations between the prime minister and his next-door neighbour. A few weeks prior to Blair's journey back to Downing Street, he had spoken with Peter Mandelson about Brown: "'He's out of control,'" Tony said . . . "He's been out of control for weeks." He said that Gordon had been contributing next to nothing to the campaign planning, except to launch assaults on Tony's lack of "vision" and the government's lack of purpose. "I have no illusions any more," he said. "He could come for me – and he would do, probably, if he got the chance."[1]

Mandelson had been lobbying hard for Brown to be shipped out of the Treasury, but he was not the only one. All the people Blair trusted – Jonathan Powell, Sally Morgan, Alastair Campbell – had been making a similar case. While acknowledging the political risk involved, they argued that in order to leave a lasting legacy, the prime minister needed to remove the roadblock represented by Brown. That, they said, was particularly true if Blair wished to take Britain into the single currency, where the economic tests for entry set by the Treasury had so far trumped what Blair saw as the in-arguable political case for joining monetary union.

Blair stepped through the door of 10 Downing Street to be greeted by Secretary of the Cabinet Sir Richard Wilson, Britain's most senior civil servant. As if reading the prime minister's mind, Wilson said: 'You are now at the peak of your power. You may never again be as strong as you are now.'[2]

His mind made up, Blair asked for Brown to come over from the Treasury, where the chancellor was already back at work. While he was waiting, the prime minister thought back with fondness to the days when as shadow ministers in the late 1980s, the Brown–Blair double act had raised morale by roughing up Conservative ministers. Yet, it had surely been obvious to the Labour faithful at the

Millbank party that the two men were like John Lennon and Paul McCartney following the break-up of The Beatles: estranged partners who no longer had anything to say to each other.

Even now, Blair had his doubts. How could he be thinking of sacking Labour's most successful chancellor? What would happen if, instead of taking the Foreign Office, Brown retired to the backbenches where he could plot revenge? Wasn't it an axiom of British politics that prime ministers who lost their chancellors in acrimonious circumstances didn't last much longer themselves?

These doubts were banished when Brown entered the room. This was not the time for small talk; this was the time for the terse approach that Attlee favoured when he was wielding the ministerial axe. 'Gordon, I want you to move. I know that you have not done anything wrong and that this election victory is as much yours as mine. But I need to make changes. So I want you and Robin to swap jobs. He becomes chancellor, you get a stint at the Foreign Office that will stand you in good stead for when you take over here.'

Brown said nothing other than that he wanted time to think about it, turned on his heels and left. Blair wondered whether Brown would go outside into Downing Street and announce to the waiting reporters that he was leaving government. But, after speaking to his closest advisers, Brown bowed to Blair's wish. Robin Cook became chancellor with orders from Blair to make sure the five economic tests for euro entry were passed and that a referendum to replace the pound with the single currency would be fought before the next election.

The above, of course, never happened, although the account is not entirely fictional. Blair certainly toyed with the idea of moving Brown to the Foreign Office. He took soundings from the people he trusted and many of them thought he should take the gamble of having an embittered former chancellor causing trouble from the backbenches. He used similar words when he gave an unsuspecting Cook his marching orders. Ultimately, though, the prime minister was not prepared to take the risk. His bond with Brown, though strained, was still strong. He admired his old friend and, to an extent, was in awe of his intellect. He kept Brown where he was and sacked his foreign secretary instead. Cook's replacement was Jack Straw, who had campaigned for Britain to leave the Common Market in the 1975 referendum and who was a sceptic of long standing. Blair's explanation was that Straw would carry more weight with the public once the new foreign secretary had been won round to the case for joining monetary union. He never was.

In this chapter, we follow the reversal of fortune for those determined to take Britain into the single currency from the apparent inevitability of UK euro membership at the turn of the century to its deep unlikelihood by the time Blair left office in 2007. And we posit a fascinating 'what if?'

Fantasy politics

Virtual history is a growing academic discipline, to which the question 'What if Tony Blair had sacked Gordon Brown as chancellor in 2001?' is worth adding. The thesis goes as follows: with Brown out of the way, a more biddable chancellor would have been less dogmatic about the economic tests. Blair, who thought joining the euro was Britain's destiny, would have been able to make a political case for entry at a time when the opposition was demoralized by a second big defeat and distracted by a leadership contest following Hague's resignation on the morning after the 2001 election. Indeed, the supporters of Britain's entry into the single currency had made precisely the same case in the summer of 1997 in the wake of Blair's first landslide. In a TV programme made to mark Blair's departure as prime minister in 2007, Mandelson said: 'He should have gone into government and very early held a referendum on the principle not the timing . . . If he had won the argument when he was strong enough to do so, he would have been better off.'[3]

The message to Blair, that he now had a second opportunity to hold a referendum that would allow entry at a later date, was made by a cross-party group of political heavyweights from Mandelson and Charles Clarke on the centre-left to Michael Heseltine and Kenneth Clarke on the centre-right, taking in Liberal Democrats such as Paddy Ashdown on the way. The Yes camp could count on the support of grandees sitting on the boards of multinational companies: men such as David Simon of BP, Niall FitzGerald of Unilever and Colin Marshall of British Airways liked to give the impression that business was overwhelmingly behind joining the single currency, although this was something of an exaggeration. As with the economics profession, business was divided over the issue.

Most trade unions were broadly in favour, although those in the public sector were in general markedly less enthusiastic than their brethren in manufacturing industry – the former feared EU-mandated spending cuts, while the latter looked forward to a stable currency platform for exports. In December 2001, on the eve of the introduction of euro notes and coins, John Monks, general secretary of the Trades Union Congress, said in his new year's message that it would be 'disastrous' if the government failed to hold a referendum on the single currency, adding: 'If the decision is put off again, the international community will conclude (probably rightly) that New Labour simply hasn't got the bottle to face down the Eurosceptics, and that will have serious economic and political consequences.'[4]

The Europe minister, Peter Hain, took to the airwaves on 1 January 2002 to tell Radio 4's 'Today' programme: 'I doubt that in the end it is possible to run a sort of parallel currency economy.' During the period that led up to the Treasury assessment of the economic tests, there were repeated, and often lurid warnings, of how terrible life would be for Britain if it insisted on keeping the pound. Kenneth Clarke wrote in the *Independent* on 10 May 2003 that the economy would be damaged if the UK stayed out too long, while Mandelson told readers of the *Sunday Mirror* on 18 May 2003 that failure to join would mean 'progressive economic isolation'.

There was also a concerted campaign by an influential group of centre-left media commentators to get Britain into the euro. The late Hugo Young wrote in the *Guardian* on 6 April 2000 that remaining outside monetary union would mean the loss of jobs. David Aaronovitch, writing in the *Independent* on 13 February

1998, compared David Owen (who was setting up an anti-euro think tank on the left) to Oswald Mosley and Enoch Powell. The *Observer*'s Andrew Rawnsley described the No camp in unflattering terms: 'On the pro-Euro side, a grand coalition of business, the unions and the substantial, sane, front-rank political figures. On the other side, a menagerie of has-beens, never-have-beens and loony tunes with only two things in common: their hostility to Europe and their unpopularity in Britain.'[5]

Brown's insistence that the tests be rigorous is now seen as one of the best decisions he made as chancellor, even by his sworn political enemies, of whom there are plenty. The euro has proved to be exactly the job-destroying, recession-creating, undemocratic monster the doubters always warned it would be. But this was not the received wisdom on the mainstream left at the time, when to suggest that the euro would be supercharged monetarism – Thatcherism with knobs on – was deemed unseemly.

People who liked the euro were civilized, supported the arts, mingled together for a glass of champagne in the Crush Room at the Royal Opera House, and holidayed in Tuscany or the Dordogne. People who didn't like the euro preferred sliced white to ciabatta, couldn't tell a burgundy from a claret, watched game shows on commercial television and went to work in white vans decorated with the flag of St George. It doesn't take that much of a leap of faith to imagine what might have happened had Blair decided to cross the Rubicon in June 2001 . . .

Blair has shunted Brown off to the Foreign Office and replaced him with Cook. An early date has been set for a referendum, on the eve of which the Treasury announces that, after due consideration, the five tests have been passed. During the short referendum campaign the prime minister says that economists will always have different views about whether the UK is ready for monetary union, but that he is sure the economy is as convergent as was Greece, Italy or France when they joined.

Most of the opponents of euro membership come from the political right, with the Conservative Party under its new leader, Iain Duncan Smith, campaigning strongly for a No vote. There is also a much smaller cadre of people on the left opposed to membership. This group says that it is far from clear that the euro is a successful single currency or ever will be; that the Treasury's five tests have not been met; that monetary union will only work if it is accompanied by some form of political union, including a centralized budget and tax-raising powers; and that Britain should only join if political union is acceptable to the British public.

The prime minister brushes aside these objections. There is no possibility, Blair says, of monetary union being a stepping stone to full political union. But Britain will be relegated to the second division of world powers if it turns its back on the euro. At an eve-of-poll rally, the prime minister says that it is the UK's ineluctable destiny to join. The vote is closer than the polls have suggested, but Britain decides to join the euro by a 55 per cent to 45 per cent majority.

Once the referendum is won, the first problem is how to manage the transition from the pound to the euro. The most important part of this process is to fix the right level for the pound to join monetary union, with Blair insistent that the government must avoid the mistakes of the ERM, when sterling was shackled to the German mark at an excessively high rate of DM 2.95. This proves challenging for Cook.

Sterling has been overvalued in the early 2000s, with hot money attracted into London by a combination of relatively high interest rates and a prolonged period of strong growth. The UK government is rightly fearful that joining the euro at the wrong rate will penalize British manufacturers, but the twelve existing members of the single currency express concerns that too cheap a rate for sterling entry will hand an added competitive advantage to the UK's strong financial services sector.

Despite attempts by the new governor of the Bank of England, Mervyn King, to drive down the level of the pound, when the time comes for the euro to be adopted it is clear that the exchange rate is too high, just as it was when Britain joined the Exchange Rate Mechanism a decade and a half earlier. That, say Britain's new partners in the single currency, is the penalty to be paid for failing to join from the outset.

Stage two of the process is the bubble phase. Having ceded the right to conduct its own monetary policy, the UK has to accept the interest rate the European Central Bank sets for the Eurozone as a whole. As one of the larger members of the club, Britain carries some weight at the discussions in Frankfurt, but monetary policy proves to be far too loose for a country already in the early stages of a housing boom and where the balance of trade is deteriorating year by year.

From the vantage point of the Foreign Office, Brown points out that part of the preparatory work he had commissioned as part of the 'five tests' process had involved assessing what would have happened had Britain joined with the first wave of countries in 1999. The answer provided by the Treasury, Brown says, is that in the first year, 2000, growth would have potentially been 2 percentage points higher at 5.5 per cent, but inflation would also have been significantly higher because the UK economy would not have been capable of meeting such strong demand. In the second year, growth would have been 1.75 points lower than it actually was. Inflation would have been significantly higher, reaching 4.5 per cent by the end of 2000, as the result of interest rates being too low.

The key passage in the assessment, Brown says, is the statement that 'if the UK had joined EMU in 1999, it would not have remained on a path of stability. Instead, it would have repeated the economic policy mistakes of the past and suffered as a result.'[6] Contrast this with Labour's actual record since it came to power – that, he says, is what we are now putting at risk.

Brown, though, is seen as yesterday's man. His detractors portray him as Labour's Edward Heath, an embittered soul who bore a grudge for decades after being ousted as Conservative leader by Margaret Thatcher. The former chancellor is derided for saying that interest rates are too low, because for a while the economy booms. But gradually it becomes clear that the Treasury was right to have misgivings. It becomes easy to borrow money at low interest rates and, as in Spain and Ireland, a spectacular bubble develops in the housing market. Even outside the euro, in the early 2000s, the

UK's housing market was hot. Once inside, it's like the Wild West. The newspapers are full of stories about house prices rising by 5 per cent a month in the more desirable parts of the country. The third major housing market boom since the late 1970s proves to be the biggest of the lot.

That means that when the crash comes in 2007 it is a spectacular one. The financial markets implode, the banks stop lending and cheap credit dries up. The housing market collapses, unemployment rises, tax receipts shrivel and the government's budget deficit goes through the roof. Outside the euro, the Bank of England was able to act as the lender of last resort to support ailing UK banks. The ECB has no such role and the fear that banks will go bust means investors demand a high premium for financing borrowing by the UK government. Speculation that the UK may leave the euro, as it had left the European Exchange Rate Mechanism in 1992, means bond yields rise, first to 5 per cent, then to 6 per cent. When they hit 7 per cent, Blair has no choice but to ask for help from the troika – the International Monetary Fund, the ECB and the EU.

Severe conditions are attached to the loan, the biggest the IMF has ever organized, including deep cuts in welfare and pensions and wage reductions across the public sector. Deprived of the safety valve of currency depreciation, Britain has no choice but to do what Spain, Greece, Ireland and Portugal are doing and drive down domestic costs to make the economy more competitive.

Unlike in Spain, Greece, Ireland and Portugal, however, there is no deep attachment in Britain to Europe as a political concept. Far from it: stripped of its economic rationale, support for the euro evaporates and the build-up to the general election of 2010 is marked by street protests even more widespread and angry than the poll tax riots of 1990. The Conservative Party in opposition goes into the campaign pledging a referendum on whether Britain should leave the euro and wins by a landslide. The number of Labour MPs falls to under a hundred, its worst performance since the 1930s. Nigel Farage's UK Independence Party (UKIP) makes spectacular gains.

In the referendum that follows the election, the vote is over-whelmingly in favour of exit. The financial markets respond by selling the bonds of any other Eurozone country struggling to cope with the rigours of austerity programmes demanded by the European Commission in Brussels and the ECB in Frankfurt. By then, this means pretty much every country apart from a hard core that includes Germany, Austria, the Netherlands and Finland.

The market turbulence caused by Britain's exit proves terminal for the euro. Bond yields rise sharply across the single currency as investors realize they have underpriced the risks of a country leaving the club. Outside the euro, life is not exactly a bed of roses for the UK; indeed, for a while it is extremely tough. But after a deep and painful recession, economic recovery begins.

Second thoughts

Nowadays, there are still some enthusiasts for UK membership of the single currency, but they are harder to spot and much more guarded in their support. Not all those who were urging Blair on between 1997 and 2003 have given up the fight. The *Observer* columnist Will Hutton, for example, maintains that Brown's deci-sion not to join led to the creation of an economic 'doomsday machine' that exacerbated the deep recession of 2008–09 and made it impossible for Labour to win a fourth term in office. Provided entry to the euro could have been at a lower exchange rate, Hutton believes, growth would have been better balanced and the financial excesses of the bubble years avoided.[7]

This is an argument that deserves a fair hearing, not least because the slump of 2008–09 was the longest and deepest Britain had suffered since the early 1920s. What's more, the recovery that followed was slow, faltering and based on the same housing-led, debt-fuelled model that led to the original boom–bust in the economy. Could life really have been much worse had Britain joined the single currency some time in the first half of the 2000s?

Hutton's case rests on a number of assumptions: that a refer-endum could only have been won had it been obvious that joining was a 'good deal', with the pound entering at a competitive rate; that there would have been reform of the euro's structure, rules and governance to accommodate Britain's interests; that the European Central Bank would have been turned into something akin to the US Federal Reserve so that it had more scope for fiscal and monetary activism; and that in return for making the ECB less conservative in its outlook, Germany would have insisted on the EU banking system being more conservatively managed. It is hard to disagree with Simon Wren-Lewis, professor of economic policy at the University of Oxford, when he says that the Hutton argument relies on 'a lot of wishful thinking'.[8]

Danny Alexander was the press spokesman for the Britain in Europe pressure group that lobbied for the UK to join the single currency in the early 2000s. Alexander's failure to make a convincing enough case for the euro proved no bar to him becoming a Liberal Democrat MP, and he joined the coalition government in 2010 as chief secretary to the Treasury. Interviewed on the Andrew Marr show in November 2011, during one of the many episodes of the Greek crisis, Alexander said he had only been in favour of joining the euro if the economic conditions were right, which they had not been, and that he was glad of the flexibility that staying outside monetary union had afforded. Suffice it to say that this was not the impression he gave when he was a spin doctor for Britain in Europe.

Alexander's recantation was, in a sense, curious. He was a senior member of a coalition dedicated to cutting public spending in order to balance the UK's books – the same remedy that Germany believed was the cure for the profligate countries of the Eurozone. In the Labour Party between 2010 and 2015, there was no such confusion, since the party leader, Ed Miliband, and the shadow chancellor, Ed Balls, had both been part of the Brown team at the Treasury that had rejected the euro.

The disillusionment with what was once called The Project started to set in on the left quite quickly, as soon as it was clear that the UK's economic performance was superior to that of the Eurozone. The estrangement became even more obvious when the Eurozone sovereign debt crisis embroiled Greece, Ireland, Portugal,

Spain, Italy and Cyprus. Any chance of a reconciliation was lost once the hardliners in the Eurozone imposed a Carthaginian peace on Greece in the summer of 2015 for its temerity to ask for some respite from an austerity programme that was crippling its economy. For the first time in many years, it became quite cool on the left to be not just against the single currency but to voice doubts about the European Union itself. Nor was this just the hard left, which had always viewed the search for ever closer union as an attempt to make Europe cushier for capitalists. Disgust at the way Greece had been treated fostered a leftist movement in favour of leaving the EU, which was dubbed Lexit.

In the early 2000s, the olive groves of Tuscany were alive with members of the UK intelligentsia bemoaning the failure of the Blair government to be more positive about Europe. Being positive about Europe was testing at a time when the Greek economy had shrunk by more than 25 per cent in five years and youth unemployment in Spain was above 50 per cent. The sales pitch for the euro when it was a live issue for the UK between 1997 and 2003 was: 'Join the single currency and have higher living standards.' It was not: 'Join the single currency and find out what the Great Depression was like.'

Fortunately, Britain did not choose to try the full *Grapes of Wrath* experience, but it is easy to see how it could have ended up in the same situation as Ireland, Portugal or Greece. Mounting a defence of the euro has become more difficult for those who see themselves as progressives and most have not bothered to try. Public opposition to joining the euro is now so strong that opinion pollsters have long ceased asking voters whether they want to adopt the single currency instead of the pound.

Blair's own biographer, Anthony Seldon, believes events since 2003 have proved Brown right. As he noted: 'The euro was a clear Brown win, and one on which he was unequivocally on the right side. Many in Number 10 as well as the FCO thought that Britain would lose influence in Europe if it did not join the single currency and that joining the euro was the litmus test of whether we would be considered to be good Europeans.'⁹ But Britain has not missed out on a European golden age. All three chancellors since the decision was taken not to join have been thankful that the UK has enjoyed the freedom to manage its own affairs. There has been no more talk of the UK standing on the dockside watching as the ship headed out to sea since it became clear that the boat in question was the *Titanic*.

Even at the height of euro enthusiasm polls showed no more than one in three voters planning to vote Yes in a referendum on giving up the pound. There is little evidence that the existing members of the Eurozone would have been happy to see the UK government drive down the level of the pound before entry, since that would have eroded their trade surplus in manufactured goods and handed a competitive advantage to Britain's services sector, which was already running a hefty surplus of exports over imports. There is even less evidence that the Germans would have rubber-stamped a UK proposal to turn the ECB into a clone of the Fed. The idea that Germany would have insisted on tougher banking regulations that would have softened the impact of the 2007–08 financial crisis is undercut by the fact that German banks were among the least conservative in the years before the meltdown. Other than that, the Hutton thesis is absolutely watertight.

Spain and Ireland were both founder members of the Eurozone and had colossal boom–busts in their housing markets as a consequence. The economist Maurice Obstfeld (now the economic counsellor for the IMF) wrote a paper in 2013 for the European Commission explaining what had gone wrong in parts of the Eurozone. The ability to move capital across borders allowed banks to increase the size of their balance sheets, making it harder for national governments to provide credible guarantees if something went wrong. The erroneous assumption that countries in the Eurozone would press ahead with structural reforms compressed the interest rates on government bonds, because it was thought that Greece was as creditworthy as Germany. Banks from Germany and other northern countries decided to bet heavily on speculative investments in countries such as Greece and Spain. Finally, the official cost of borrowing fell when countries joined the euro. As Obstfeld notes, 'lower nominal interest rates and easy credit access helped to boost demand and inflation and to depress real interest rates [interest rates adjusted for inflation], with destabilizing effects, in peripheral euro zone economies. Domestic credit expanded rapidly compared to historical levels.'[10]

Being outside the euro did not spare Britain a housing roller-coaster ride of its own, but there were two reasons why it was not as painful as in Spain or Ireland: on the way up, interest rates were more suited to the UK's own needs, and on the way down, there were alternatives to the savage adjustment programmes demanded of Eurozone countries that ran into difficulties.

Interest rates were cut more quickly and more deeply than they were in the Eurozone. Just as importantly, the UK's floating exchange rate meant the pound was able to fall, making exports cheaper. Between the middle of 2007 and early 2009, the exchange rate of the pound adjusted for inflation depreciated by 25 per cent. Over the same period, Spain's real exchange rate increased because it was unable to devalue and it had higher inflation than the Eurozone average. Paul Krugman noted that the comparison showed how 'Britain effortlessly achieved a real depreciation that, if it's possible at all, will take years and years of mass unemployment in Spain.'[11]

Britain had had its own experience of the sort of treatment meted out to Spain and Ireland, but that was in the period immediately after the First World War. Since sterling came off the gold standard in 1931, governments of both left and right had devalued the pound rather than inflict the more painful method of adjustment known as internal devaluation, which requires squeezing the economy so that wages and inflation come down. This provides the same sort of competitive boost supplied by currency depreciation. The difference is that internal devaluation is much more protracted and tends to lead to slower growth and deflation, both of which make it more difficult for a country with high debts to put its public finances back in order.

Britain's experiment with internal devaluation came in the early 1920s, when the government responded to a loss of competiveness in an orthodox manner that would have pleased the European Commission and the German finance ministry. It imposed what the IMF calls 'severe fiscal austerity and tight monetary policy'. Spending was cut and the higher tax levels introduced during the First World War were maintained. The high interest rates were designed to drive the pound back up to its pre-war gold standard parity of $4.76 against the US dollar.

Unsurprisingly, the UK's economic performance was just as poor as those of the crisis-affected Eurozone countries since 2008. Growth in the interwar years was weak and a long way below the average for developed countries. Unemployment was high even before the onset of the Great Depression in the 1930s and deflation was common. The level of economic output was barely any higher in 1938 than it had been in 1918. Export performance, courtesy of the overvalued exchange rate, was especially weak. 'If the policies pursued had successfully reduced debt and restored British growth and prosperity, the short-term costs perhaps would have been acceptable,' according to the IMF. 'Unfortunately, they did not. In fact, the policies had the opposite effect: British prosperity was hampered by the dual pursuit of pre-war parity and fiscal austerity.'[12]

Other countries took a more constructive approach, with European neighbours enhancing their competitiveness through exchange-rate devaluation, with negative knock-on effects for British exporters. The IMF added: 'Furthermore, managing the exchange rate forced the Bank of England to maintain high interest rates, which increased the burden of the national debt and generally constrained economic activity – further undermining tax receipts.'

What's more, it didn't work. The debt-to-GDP ratio continued to rise to 170 per cent in 1930 and 190 per cent in 1933, and it was not until 1990 that it returned to its pre-First World War level. After the Second World War, a different approach to debt reduction was tried.

This period has its own special place in the history of the Labour Party. It is the era when the decision to put Britain back on the gold standard in 1925 prompted the wage cuts that led to the General Strike a year later. It is the era when the Treasury's insistence that the budget had to be balanced through cuts in unemployment benefit despite the deepening slump in 1931 broke the minority Ramsay MacDonald government and split the party. For the left, it is the era of the dole queue, extreme poverty and the Jarrow March.

Loading the gun

The scars left by this period of internal deflation proved deep and long-lasting. To this day, the Labour Party pantheon of villains has included those, such as Churchill and Philip Snowden, deemed responsible for attacks on the working class during the period between the two world wars. But Labour also likes to see itself as the party of modernity, a movement that looks to the future and not just the past.

Europe was as synonymous with modernity for Blair as public ownership was for Clement Attlee in 1945 and science and technology was for Harold Wilson in 1964. This pro-European tide had been a long time coming in. Labour was sceptical of the early post-war attempts at closer European integration and the Attlee government had refused to be bounced into joining the European Coal and Steel Community, the embryonic plan for integration drawn up by Jean Monnet and presented to the then foreign secretary Ernest Bevin as a *fait accompli* in 1950. Bevin had made his views clear in a paper presented to cabinet in October 1949: 'We must remain, as we have always been in the past, different in character from other European nations and fundamentally incapable of wholehearted integration with them.' For at least two more decades, the Conservatives could rightly claim to be the more positive of the two main parties when it came to Europe. It was a Conservative prime minister, Harold Macmillan, who made the first application to join the Common Market at a time when the Labour leader, Hugh Gaitskell, was arguing that he was against membership if it meant the end of '1,000 years of history'. In 2003, Gaitskell would have been considered a Little Englander.

Labour launched its own thwarted bid to join the Common Market in 1967, but the party remained split over Europe even after the Conservative prime minister Edward Heath finally secured membership in 1973 on the basis of a parliamentary vote rather than a referendum.

Heath lost office in 1974, and Wilson said Labour would hold a plebiscite after his government had renegotiated the terms of membership. Tony Benn's diaries for 1973–76 cover the period leading up to the June 1975 referendum when the cabinet was split over whether the UK should leave. For Benn:

> This is the most important constitutional document ever put before a Labour Cabinet. Our whole political history is contained within this paper. It recommends a reversal of hundreds of years of history which have progressively widened the power of the people over their governors.
>
> Now great chunks are to be handed to the Commission. I can think of no body of men outside the Kremlin who have so much power without a shred of accountability for what they do.

Benn predicted that Britain would effectively be governed by a European coalition government 'that we cannot change, dedicated to a capitalist or market economy theology'.[13]

Benn and the other anti-marketeers, including Michael Foot and Barbara Castle, were on the losing side by sixteen votes to seven on that occasion, but by the early 1980s, when the left had wrested control of the party, Labour's manifesto included a commitment to leave the EU. However, under three successive leaders, Neil Kinnock, John Smith and Tony Blair, Labour moved to a more pro-European stance. Like Blair, Brown was a modernizer, and as shadow trade and industry spokesman in 1990 he fully supported the decision to take Britain into the Exchange Rate Mechanism.

By the late 1990s, however, Brown's attitude had shifted. He was not opposed to the single currency on principle (although the Bennite rump of the Labour Party did hold that view), but his support was conditional. The chancellor approached the single currency in an empirical rather than ideological manner. If the euro worked and it could be proved that Britain could live with its strictures, then he was in favour. Otherwise, he was not.

There were a number of reasons for this change of heart. One was that Brown had been scarred by Britain's ill-fated two-year membership of the ERM. By the time of Black Wednesday in September 1992 Brown was shadow chancellor and it was Labour policy to remain within the ERM right up to the moment that the policy collapsed. In the twenty months between Black Wednesday and the death of John Smith, Brown's star waned as that of his friend, Tony Blair, waxed.

A second reason was that Brown believed that the reforms he had made as chancellor after Labour's 1997 election victory had given Britain a better system for conducting monetary and fiscal policy than was available by joining the euro. Brown's view was that his independent Bank of England had less of a deflationary bias than the European Central Bank, and that his rules for running the public finances provided more flexibility than was available under the Eurozone's Stability and Growth Pact.

A third reason was that Brown was being counselled by an official who was instinctively far more sceptical about the euro than he was. Ed Balls was a twenty-seven-year-old leader writer on the *Financial Times* when he went to work for Brown as a special adviser. Balls did not share his paper's enthusiasm for the single currency, and two years earlier, shortly after Britain's exit from the ERM, he had written a paper for the Fabian Society outlining his misgivings.

In this paper, Balls made the classic left-of-centre argument against monetary union. It was all well and good, he said, supporters of monetary union saying that handing the setting of interest rates to the European Central Bank would prevent meddling by national politicians. There were times, though, when it was useful to have monetary freedom, such as was the case in the early 1990s when Britain was in recession but Germany was experiencing its post-reunification boom.

The core countries of Europe could live with a single currency, but Balls predicted there were would be problems for the southern

European countries and the UK, because they were out of sync with the core countries. The Maastricht Treaty paving the way for monetary union implied 'that all European countries should first link their exchange rates and monetary policies together, eschewing devaluation, and then join the single currency when they meet the convergence criteria'. With unerring accuracy, Balls predicted what would happen next. 'The result is that the southern, poorer countries are likely to suffer more frequent swings in output and employment in EMU.'

To be sustainable, he added, gains from monetary union had to outweigh the pain; and the pain – higher unemployment and slow growth in certain regions and countries – had to be small and short-lived enough that voters would find them politically acceptable. The US had mechanisms in place to ensure that this was the case; a cultural homogeneity and a single language that fostered labour migration from poor to rich states; and a sizeable budget that could move resources in the opposite direction. Europe did not, and was unlikely to get them for some time. Balls concluded that it was a mistake to let politics run ahead of politics:

> In short, monetary union, in the manner and timetable envisaged in the treaty, is an economically and politically misconceived project. Imposing the same monetary policy on the whole of Europe, without automatic fiscal stabilisers, would mean persistent regional growth and unemployment differentials within the Community, with all the political and social dislocation that brings. Already, Europe is plagued by right-wing nationalism and opposition to the European project as a result of the slow growth and high unemployment that the inflexible version of the ERM has brought.[14]

Balls was hugely influential on Brown's thinking on every subject from independence for the Bank of England to tax credits for the working poor. On monetary union, his advice was pivotal.

Anybody who spoke to Balls during the period when euro membership was a live issue was left in no doubt about his misgivings concerning premature UK entry. Brown's chief economic adviser argued that Britain's twentieth-century history was littered with examples of bad economic decisions being taken for political reasons. This was true of the decision to go back on the gold standard in 1925, the reluctance to devalue in 1945 and 1964, and the ill-timed embrace of the Exchange Rate Mechanism in 1990.

This argument was crystalized in the speech Balls made in Oxford in late 2002. He said the ERM decision had been taken at a time of weakness, with the timing dictated by politics and with no comprehensive assessment of the economics ever made. Balls said that since 1997 Labour had avoided the 'historic mistake ... of setting a political timetable for entry, and then anchoring the government's credibility in the decision coming out a particular way, thereby prejudging the economic assessment.'[15]

The message was that, with Brown at the Treasury, the economic assessment currently being conducted would be thorough and rigorous. The chancellor refused to give what he called a 'running commentary' on the five tests, but it was clear to those in contact with Brown and his team that the assessment would not be positive. The Treasury, from the top down, was against Britain joining the euro.

Enter the man in the white coat

The Treasury official put in charge of conducting the assessment was the cycling enthusiast Dave Ramsden, who was given a team of forty and a £5 million budget for the in-depth analysis. This involved a report backed up by eighteen separate studies covering issues such as the theory of optimal currency areas and the state of the UK housing market. Ramsden's job was to look at each of the five tests that Brown said in 1997 had to be passed before the UK could contemplate joining. By late 2002, around the time Balls was making his Oxford speech, this work was being finalized.

Of the five tests, the first was by far the most important. The Treasury wanted to know whether there was lasting convergence between the UK and the Eurozone. This meant looking at whether economic cycles were in sync, whether the structures of the econo-mies were compatible, and whether the UK could live comfortably with Eurozone interest rates on a permanent basis.

The second test ascertained whether the UK had the flexibility to cope, if things went wrong, without the tools it would be giving up in order to join monetary union. Test number three involved whether the euro would be good for investment. The fourth test was designed to ensure that EMU Membership would not impair the City of London's dominance. Finally, the Treasury wanted to know whether joining EMU would be good for growth, jobs and prosperity.

The conclusion of Ramsden's team was that only one of the five tests – the fourth, regarding benefits to the City – had been passed. There had been progress towards greater convergence with the Eurozone but the Treasury was not convinced that the UK could live with Eurozone interest rates permanently. Similarly, it said more work was needed to enable the UK to cope with economic shocks that might stem from its lack of convergence. If the first two tests were not passed it was impossible to show that membership of the euro would boost investment or be good for growth, jobs and prosperity. So tests four and five were also failed.

Even so, anyone who has read the 246-page *UK Membership of the Single Currency: An Assessment of the Five Economic Tests* published in June 2003 could see how a different conclusion could have been drawn. For test five, which looked at growth, stability and employment, the Treasury found that membership of the single currency could 'significantly' raise UK output and lead to a perma-nent increase in jobs. National income might increase by between 5 per cent and 9 per cent over thirty years, or around 0.25 per cent a year. This, though, would only happen once 'sustainable and durable' convergence had been achieved.

It was a similar story with the investment test. Brown's officials thought it was possible that businesses would invest more if they knew that the exchange rate was not going to keep gyrating wildly, but they would only do so if the convergence and flexibility tests were passed. 'EMU entry at this stage would lead to greater macroeconomic instability in the UK which would be damaging for domestic investment', the assessment concluded.

Brown was quite proud that the economy, under his steward-ship, had become more productive and more agile, so the flexibility test posed one or two problems for the Treasury, which could hardly say that the UK was too inflexible to join the euro. Instead, it noted that flexibility had improved since 1997 due to reforms introduced by the Labour government but still was not flexible enough. Brown's team also expressed doubts – rightly, as it turned out – about the Eurozone's lack of a fiscal policy regime that would help countries to smooth out the ups and downs of the economic cycle.

That left the big test: had the UK achieved a suitable level of convergence with the Eurozone? The Treasury concluded that it hadn't and, once again, events have shown that it made the right judgment. Yet, the assessment also noted that the UK was more aligned with the Eurozone than some members of the single currency had achieved in the run-up to the launch of monetary union in 1999 and 'remains more convergent than a number of EMU countries today'. With a different chancellor, a case might have been made that the convergence test had been passed, and that as a result the investment and growth, stability and output tests had also been passed, and that the UK was now sufficiently flexible to cope with giving up the pound. Truly, this was a bullet dodged.

The Treasury findings were relayed to the prime minister in a series of ninety-minute seminars conducted by Ramsden in early 2003, during which the official was dubbed 'the man in the white coat' by a bored and frustrated Blair. Until late on in the process, a prime minister who fronted a rock band at Oxford and who once named the Fender Stratocaster as the symbol of the twentieth century ignored the mood music that had been coming out of the Treasury at a volume appropriate for a Led Zeppelin reunion concert. By the time he finally accepted that he could not prevail upon his chancellor to 'fix the tests', it was far too late.

Having considered sacking Brown in order to smooth the path to EMU entry, Blair played his final card: give me the euro and I will give you the job you have always wanted. According to one of his biographers, Brown turned the offer down flat. 'Given his ambition to be premier, Brown's response was strikingly robust whenever Blair dangled the keys to Number 10 in return for the Treasury saying the five tests had been passed. He would always say: "History will never forgive us for having that conversation: I'm not going to do it."'[16]

Brown made some minor concessions when he formally announced the results of the tests in the House of Commons in June 2003, but the battle had been fought and won months earlier.

Those in favour of joining the euro were furious. Hugo Young said in the *Guardian* that Brown's statement was 'an epitaph on six years of timidity, deception and failure'. In a sign of his disappointment with a prime minister he thought he could influence, Young compared Blair unfavourably with Margaret Thatcher:

> Mrs Thatcher spent her time taking Britain deeper into Europe, a process that climaxed with the Single European Act, while talking the British people ever further out. It was a disastrous failure of statesmanship, deepening the angst of a divided nation. Tony Blair goes on talking us further in. But he acts at decisive moments – the currency, the convention – in ways that tend to leave Britain outside the mainstream. If this continues, his could be an even more damaging betrayal of leadership than Mrs Thatcher's.[17]

Young's loathing of Thatcher was well documented, so for him, this was the ultimate insult. A whole generation of pro-Europeans thought they had been let down by a prime minister who was instinctively on their side, but who had baulked when it was time to make a big decision.

The euro and Iraq: A contrast

Rumours quickly circulated among the supporters of the euro that Brown's opposition to The Project had itself been political. The chancellor's economic objections were simply a smokescreen to hide his true motivation: to defy and frustrate the prime minister's will at every turn. Balls, it was said, had come up with the five tests in the back of a New York City taxicab.

This line of attack was both false and unworthy. Firstly, the charge of dashing off the five tests on the spur of the moment hardly squared with the careful study Balls had made of monetary union and Britain's approach to it, dating back to the days when he was fresh out of Oxford. Ramsden is adamant that there was no question of the five tests being made up on the hoof.[18]

Secondly, whatever their origin, the UK's five tests were clearly superior to the convergence criteria laid down in the Maastricht Treaty. Ramsden says that the UK tests looked at the things that really mattered, namely whether the UK would be able to live comfortably within the Eurozone in both good times and bad. Subsequent developments have, he says, borne out the decision not to join, particularly since many of the developments in the Eurozone have been 'unwelcome'.

It is accepted in the Treasury that the five tests did not pay enough attention to the risks posed by the UK's large financial sector or by the build-up of private and public debt. There was only one short paragraph on financial stability in the euro assessment report, and Ramsden admits that 'It wasn't given the attention it deserved.' But it is not as if the financial crash was spotted by countries inside the Eurozone either, and as events subsequently proved in countries from Ireland to Spain, and from Greece to Germany, membership of the single currency was no guarantee that banks were going to behave prudently. A decade on from the five tests, Ramsden said that they were an example of how policymaking is supposed to work. 'I don't think the five tests were window dressing. Officials advise and ministers decide.'[19]

Simon Wren-Lewis, who wrote one of the eighteen supporting papers and who has been a consistent critic of the economic policies pursued by George Osborne since 2010, says the exercise was exactly what it purported to be: an attempt by civil servants to give the best advice they could to politicians. 'What marks it out for me was the extent to which those civil servants involved academics, and placed academic work at the centre of their analysis. The merits or otherwise of the euro did divide macroeconomists, but there was no attempt to just consult those who agreed with some predefined view.' Although the question of Britain's membership of the euro generated strong opinions, Wren-Lewis says the Treasury assessment was not fundamentally ideological. Brown was a chancellor who had a very strong respect for ideas and needed to marshal a strong enough case to convince the prime minister. 'The decision was based on the best analysis that macroeconomics at the time could provide. It is a shame that this way of making economic decisions now looks like the exception rather than the rule.'[20] Finally, the claim that Balls dashed the tests off while driving through Midtown Manhattan says more about the people making the accusation than it does about Brown's then special adviser.

In his essay 'The Lion and the Unicorn', George Orwell wrote that England was 'perhaps the only great country whose intellectuals are ashamed of their own country'. Never did this judgment seem more apposite than during the debate over whether Britain should join the euro. It was taken as read that joining the euro was better than sticking with the pound, simply because Europe was so self-evidently superior to Britain in every way.

Blair, whatever the pro-euro side believed, was not a fully signed-up member of this camp. He was a pragmatist who knew the limits of his own power. Opposition to joining the euro was strong even in the first five years of Blair's premiership, when he was politically dominant, and it was the one issue that could have reinvigorated an enfeebled Conservative Party. He would have liked to have taken Britain into the euro, but even the most pro-euro speeches from Blair between 1997 and 2003 always contained the caveat that the economics had to be right. He disliked the term 'five tests' and preferred to say Britain would join when the 'economic conditions' were right, but he never believed that politics should be allowed to trump economics completely. Had Brown said the tests were inconclusive, as Blair hoped he would, the prime minister might have taken the gamble and called a referendum. But he was never prepared to overrule his chancellor once the decision had been taken in 2001 not to move Brown out of the Treasury.

'The euro saw Blair at his most enigmatic,' says Seldon. 'Private memos for his inner circle from 2001 and 2002 stress the importance he gave to entry in his second term. He told the euro enthusiasts in Number 10, several of whom held key positions, how important it was for him. "Tony Blair was completely up for this," said [Peter] Hyman. "He realised it was going to be the battle of his second term." '[21] Actually, as Seldon makes clear, the prime minister had other battles to fight. In late 2002 and early 2003, Blair only had a certain amount of political capital and he could spend it either on the euro or Iraq. There was never any real question that he would choose the latter.

During the same period that Ramsden was beavering away on the five tests in the Treasury, Blair had to make up his mind about whether Britain should join the United States in the attempt to topple Saddam Hussein. There was no Brown to obstruct him when it came to this decision: on this matter, Blair was fully in charge and acting as his own foreign secretary. Curiously, those on the left who castigate Blair for his 'failure of statesmanship' over the euro rarely, if ever, praise the success of his statesmanship over Iraq.

Had the Treasury not been in charge of the process, the assumption must be that Blair would have been as cavalier in putting together a case for joining the euro as he was in finding a reason for going to war with Iraq. Brown said there was no constitutional bar to British membership of the single currency, and there would be benefits from joining a successful single currency. But the case for entry had to be 'clear and unambiguous', which meant a 'comprehensive and rigorous' assessment of the Treasury's five economic tests. The contrast with the decision to invade Iraq could hardly be more stark. Seldon, Blair's biographer, notes that in the autumn of 2002, MI6 and GCHQ had little evidence that Saddam Hussein had weapons of mass destruction, but were instructed by the prime minister to go away and find some, which they duly did.

As a small digression, it is perhaps worth speculating on what might have happened had Blair moved Brown to the Foreign Office in June 2001. Would Brown have gone along with the so-called 'dodgy dossier' put together by MI6 and GCHQ? Might he have slowed down the march to war in early 2003, or stopped it altogether? What is certain is that Blair was thwarted in his European ambitions by the Treasury's five tests in a way that he was not thwarted by the Foreign Office over Iraq.

It is worth noting also that, in 2002–03, in the run up to and aftermath of the invasion of Iraq in March, there were fears among Eurosceptics that Blair would use the momentum and goodwill generated by the 'inevitable' success of British forces to convince the public that he made all the big calls correctly, whether Iraq or the euro. Here is Stephen Glover, writing in the *Daily Mail* on 15 April 2003:

> Will membership of the euro be the child of the war? . . . I'm terrified I may be right . . . Imagine what [Tony Blair] is thinking. He is saying to himself that if he can take Britain to war, against the wishes not only of the Labour party but also of France, Germany and Russia, he can surely take Britain into the euro. He would be less than human if he did not think he is touched by political genius . . . Mr Blair the successful war leader will be still more determined to leave his mark, and confirm his status as a prime minister who changed the course of British history.

After the Falklands, the Gulf War, Kosovo, Sierra Leone and Afghanistan (at that time), few doubted that British forces would triumph.

As authors of books that have exposed the structural weaknesses of the UK economy, we would be the last to say that life outside the euro has been an unalloyed success for the UK. That, though, is not the issue. The question that matters is whether life would have been better or worse had Britain adopted the single currency in 2003 or shortly thereafter. The answer to that question is that Britain would have been a more extreme version of Ireland or Spain.

In our view, it would have saved a lot of economic pain had other countries, such as Italy, Spain and France, used the Treasury's five tests to assess whether the case for giving up the lira, the peseta and the franc was 'clear and unambiguous'. The only way in which Britain joining the euro would have been a good idea is that the single currency would have collapsed by now. That is not just because the financial shocks from a crisis in the UK, the second biggest economy in Europe, would have been far greater than those that emanated from Greece, Portugal, Ireland or Cyprus. Neither would it have been simply the difficulty in putting together a bailout package for a country the size of Britain. It is also because no government would have been able to impose Greek-style austerity at the behest of the German finance ministry. Given the choice put to Greece – stay or walk – Britain would have walked. Once it had become clear that there was, after all, a way out of the burning building, the financial markets would have demanded a ruinously high premium for buying the government bonds of other vulnerable-looking countries. The euro would have unravelled fast.

To its credit, the UK Treasury understood that the single currency was a bad idea whose time had come. Brown and Balls and the man in the white coat deserve credit for a decision that looked sound at the time and has looked even sounder as the years have passed. This was a narrow escape, a bullet dodged. The moment in June 2003 when Britain rightly chose not to join the euro marked the high point of enthusiasm for Europe on the left, because in the years since it has become clear that the price for staying inside monetary union can involve nugatory growth, permanently high unemployment, falling wages, reduced pensions and public spending cuts. None of which has traditionally been considered left-wing.

From a country that had a fortunate escape from the travails of single-currency membership, our next chapter takes us to the other side of Europe, to a nation that has experienced the full brunt of the euro crisis for more than five years: Greece.

CHAPTER 7

THE SISYPHUS EFFECT

Greece's tormented euro-odyssey

Alexis: 'You've got everything except one thing: madness! A man needs a little madness, or else . . .'
Basil: 'Or else?'
Alexis: '. . . he never dares cut the rope and be free.'

Zorba the Greek

To the Greek people, 2016 looked likely to prove another Unhappy New Year. More than five years into a seemingly interminable crisis, the country's woes showed no sign of coming to an end.

On 14 January, Gerry Rice, director of the International Monetary Fund's Communications Department, told a press conference: 'Greece's pension system is unaffordable. As it stands the contributions are not sufficient to finance the generous level of benefits requiring transfers of the state of close to 10 per cent of GDP each year.' For good measure, he added 'the vulnerable banking sector [and] the structural impediments to growth' to Greece's list of woes.[1]

The previous month, Prime Minister Alexis Tsipras had insisted that the IMF should keep out of Greece's affairs, and that the country's third bailout since 2010 could be handled entirely within the Eurozone. Perhaps ironically, this chimed with the critics of the

Fund's involvement with previous bailouts, on the grounds that the IMF ought not to be lending to developed economies within the European Union. 'By any standards, the entanglement with the Eurozone crisis is a whopper of a screw-up,' declared Jeremy Warner in the *Daily Telegraph*, adding that 'heads must roll'. Nor was there any doubt as to whose head should be first on the chopping block: 'If this were any normal organization, the IMF's managing director, Christine Lagarde, would be forced to resign and someone with less of a vested interest in propping up the folie de grandeur of European monetary union installed in her place.'[2]

At his press conference, Gerry Rice was confronted with Mr Tsipras's reluctance to countenance IMF involvement in the third bailout. To the question, 'The prime minister and his ministers ask you many times to leave Greece and the Greek problem. Why do you insist to stay?' Rice replied: 'Maybe just as a first order of business. Just to remind you, Greece has requested a programme from the IMF.'

Indeed it had. Having perhaps remembered this, the Greek government executed a swift U-turn. The following day's edition of the London financial paper *City AM* reported that Jeroen Dijsselbloem, the Dutch finance minister who doubled as president of the Eurogroup of Eurozone finance ministers, had spoken to his Greek opposite number Euclid Tsakalotos who 'confirmed to me that the Greek government accepts that the IMF needs to be part of the process.'[3]

To someone returning to Earth after a twelve-month space voyage, this may have seemed a monumental cave-in of the sort that prompts ministerial resignations and puts a question mark over the future of governments. But after a year of Mr Tsipras's prime ministership, this was pretty much par for the course. Outright defiance of the country's creditors and EU partners followed by acquiescence followed in turn by another 'last stand' had become something of a pattern since Mr Tsipras had taken office on 26 January 2015.

Another theme of this period was the sometimes confusing rationales for these 'last stands'. Thus, elbowing the Fund out of the third bailout arrangements made little sense given that, on the topic of debt relief, the IMF was closer to the Greek position than were the country's European creditors.

But we are getting ahead of ourselves. The core point is that, in 2015 and 2016, the Hellenic Republic, a Balkan nation with a population of just 11 million, provided the narrow stage on which all the left's fantasies about the euro were to be played out to their tragic conclusion.

The first fantasy was that the single currency was a progressive project that would deliver benign economic and social outcomes, especially for the EU's poorer members, such as Greece.

The second fantasy held that the austerity regimes imposed on those countries, including Greece, that had sought bailouts could be alleviated provided voters gave a democratic mandate to an anti-austerity government.

The third fantasy, emerging after the collapse of the second, was that it would be possible to achieve the same result through belligerent confrontation and a diplomatic policy apparently predicated on the notion that cultivating the continent's political leaders would allow Athens to bypass the 'troika' of creditors – the European Commission, European Central Bank and the IMF – by appealing to people who, unlike the technocrats of Brussels, Frankfurt and Washington, had some grasp of the realities of electoral politics..

Above all, there was the overarching piece of wishful thinking that dominated Tsipras and his colleagues' first six months in office: that it was possible not only to stay in the single-currency bloc while demanding an end to the rigours that, in Greece's case, accompanied it, and not only to demand such alleviation successfully, but to do so *while making it quite clear that Greece had no intention of leaving the Eurozone.*

This high-stakes poker game, it seemed, could be won despite the only high-value card being thrown away from the start.

When all these illusions were brutally despatched by the march of events, all that was left for Tsipras was to claim, implausibly, that submitting to harsher terms than had originally been on the table was somehow an achievement or, as he put it, 'a very important legacy'.

To imagine Greece's leaders in 2015 as having been in the grip of a serious delusion would at least go some way towards explaining the extraordinary series of manoeuvres of that time: the defaulting on a payment to the IMF, the first such act of delinquency by a developed nation; the holding of a referendum on a package from the troika that was no longer on offer; the response to the vote supporting the government's rejection of this now-defunct package – sacking the finance minister who had been the most visible symbol of official Greek defiance in the face of its creditors and appointing someone more emollient; and the aforementioned acquiescence to harsher demands from creditors.

Others have different, less charitable, explanations, as we shall see. But to give credit where it is due, the Syriza approach, bizarre though it may seem, has won adherents, with Podemos in Spain demanding sweeping changes to economic governance while ruling out Spanish exit from the Eurozone, and Portugal's left-wing parties allowed to take office only after giving pledges of good euro-behaviour.

To some, this is merely one symptom of the much-discussed 'crisis of the left', with social democrats and socialists not only unable to offer a coherent economic critique and an accompanying programme for action, but also being hopelessly isolated from ordinary working people, preferring to make what there is of policy at each other's dinner parties rather than in trade union meetings or mass-movement gatherings.

Such a dearth of either understanding or practical proposals led perhaps inevitably to the absurdist antics pioneered by Syriza, apparently based on the notion that the powers that be in the Eurozone are susceptible to bellowing confrontations (in Greece's case, laced with frequent references to wartime German atrocities), vague appeals to an embryonic, indeed nonexistent, pan-European anti-austerity coalition, and *ad misericordiam* arguments stressing the 'hurt' and 'humiliation' being suffered by those populations that were subjected to the austerity programmes.

On 21 December, after a very strong showing in the Spanish general election, Podemos received a fraternal tweet from former

Greek finance minister Yanis Varoufakis full of the sort of fiery but vague words in which the new Eurozone insurgents seemed to specialize: Podemos, like Syriza, is not committed to leaving the euro.

Portugal's incoming socialist prime minister António Costa had already set the bar high in terms of overblown and incoherent rhetoric, being reported thus by the *Financial Times* as he took office on 24 November 2015: 'In what Mr Costa describes as the fall of "a Berlin Wall", the PS [Socialist Party] has signed separate agreements on supporting an anti-austerity government with the BE [the radical Left Bloc], the PCP [Communist Party] and the pro-communist Greens, parties that were implacable opponents until less than two months ago.' But while the accords were signed and Mr Costa pledged to 'turn the page on austerity', some had the poor taste to point out that Portugal's President Aníbal Cavaco Silva had appointed Costa, whose party was not the largest single political force after the October election, on the understanding that his administration would meet Portugal's commitments to the Eurozone in full.

Defiance hand-in-hand with acquiescence. Tsipras's apprentices had, it seemed, learned well from the Greek sorcerer.

In this chapter, we will look at the background of the Greek crisis, at its often-troubled relationship with its fellow members of the European Union, and at the doomed attempt by the country's left to alleviate the sufferings imposed by euro membership while refusing to contemplate what became known as Grexit.

The problem child: Greece and Europe, 1974–95

Great was the excitement among believers in scriptural prophecy when, on 1 January 1981, Greece joined the European Community. For those convinced that the apocalyptic events foretold in the Book of Revelation were coming to pass, this was an important piece of evidence.

Why? The thinking was as follows. The 'end times' would be marked by the recreation of the State of Israel and the return of the

Roman Empire. The Community fulfilled this latter role. A 'beast' with ten horns would emerge from the sea, said creature standing for this revived empire. And with Greece's accession, the EC now boasted ten members.

Four and a half years later, Spain and Portugal spoilt the picture by taking the membership total to twelve. That said, Greece's arrival in the EC club was indeed highly significant, although not for the reasons suggested by any students of Scripture.

To begin with, Greece was the first member of the club to have had recent experience of dictatorship. The existing nine members had all been functioning democracies since the immediate post-war period, whereas Greece had been ruled by a military junta – 'the Colonels' – from April 1967 to July 1974. Furthermore, while all existing Community members were, by definition, in the front line of the Cold War, Greece, uniquely, was quite likely to become embroiled in a 'hot war' with Turkey over the divided island of Cyprus, possibly dragging the rest of the Community into a deeply unwelcome confrontation with Ankara.

Then there was the economic background to Greek accession. The original 'Six' had come together in 1957, as the post-war boom was hitting its stride. Britain, Denmark and Ireland came aboard in 1973, just as that boom was entering its final giddy phase. By contrast, Greece was joining at the tail end of the second deep global recession in seven years. Most importantly, Greece – in contrast with all the existing members – was a strikingly poor country by European standards. Hitherto, the Community had been a group of nations with more points of similarity than difference, in particular more points of economic similarity. That was now to change.

The European Commission dug its heels in on Greek membership, proposing in January 1976 a ten-year accession period for the country. But the Council of Ministers, for the first time in its history, unanimously overruled the Commission's view.[4] In part, the ministers felt obliged to honour implied pledges to the Greeks that sticking with democracy would earn the reward of Community membership. But some saw a Cold War motive behind Greek accession, with membership a way of fastening the country's allegiance to the western alliance. However, those who see the hand of Washington in every such manoeuvre would, on this occasion, be mistaken. A State Department paper of 15 December 1975, the month before the Commission's failed attempt to delay Greece's membership, was less than enthusiastic, for US strategic reasons. There was a risk, it said, that Greece's accession could 'accelerate the loosening of ties with the US without providing anything viable and effective to replace them'. In other words, a European quasi-alliance of the Community type may give Greek politicians the justification they needed to wind down their links with the US. Furthermore, the State Department detected a quite different party with an ulterior motive in this question: 'France – most eager of the European Community partners to draw Southern Europe into the Community's orbit – would be pleased to become a major if not the chief military arms supplier and external political influence in the region.'[5]

Such suspicions would have been fanned by the strong support for Greek membership voiced by Valéry Giscard d'Estaing, the president of France. By 2012, he regretted this support. In a joint interview with the former German chancellor Helmut Kohl, he said: 'Greece is basically an Oriental country. Helmut, I recall that you expressed scepticism before Greece was accepted into the European Community in 1981. You were wiser than me.'[6]

At the time, however, the accession of Greece was seen as a way of rolling out the welcome mat for the two other former dictatorships that, in the mid-1970s, had emerged as fledgling democracies: Portugal and Spain. As Eirini Karamouzi states:

> While Giscard and others may say, with hindsight, that accepting Greece into the EEC was a mistake, at the time, in those particular geopolitical circumstances, it was a sound and politically justified decision that profoundly transformed the *finalité politique* of enlargement. Placing the blame for Greece's difficulties today on its accession to the EEC, without immersing ourselves in the history and geopolitical dynamics, is a dangerously easy conclusion to draw.[7]

As Greece prepared for its January 1981 accession to the Community, the country's position on the fault lines of Mediterranean geopolitics was an ever-present factor, not least with regard to Cyprus, an island divided between an internationally recognized ethnically Greek republic and a smaller, largely unrecognized ethnically Turkish zone with a separate government. In Washington, there were hopes that Greece's European aspirations could be turned to the West's advantage in terms of getting Athens to cajole the Greek Cypriots into agreeing a deal with the Turks.

A White House meeting on 10 February 1977 included the following exchange between Cyrus Vance, President Carter's secretary of state, and Clark Clifford, the president's special emissary to Greece, Turkey and Cyprus:

> Secretary Vance: 'It will be important to work with the Nine [the existing Community member states]. The Nine have leverage with Greece, so that will be an important piece of the puzzle.'
> Mr Clifford: 'Yes, but we cannot use their leverage with Turkey, and that is where we need it.'[8]

By 30 August 1978, however, all seemed set fair for the 1976 approval in principle for Greek membership to turn into membership in practice, according to a memorandum prepared by the Central Intelligence Agency, which noted that issues of the timing of Greek membership had been resolved and everyone was committed to Greece joining in 1981. Friction over agriculture and free movement of workers was unlikely to prove a major stumbling block given Greek desperation to get into the club: 'the unstated Greek desire for membership at almost any price and the Community's sympathy for [the Greek prime minister Kostas] Karamanlis make it unlikely these negotiations would go off the rails.'[9]

But Community (and later European Union) membership would not prove any sort of miracle cure for the problems of the Greek economy, at least not to start with. As was noted in a paper given at a conference in Athens in December 2000, the economy performed very poorly over the quarter-century from 1970 to 1995, during which Greece was the poorest country in the European Union. Key to this underperformance was a fall in 'multifactor productivity', economist-speak for the efficiency of the economy. Real GDP growth, the paper's authors note, slowed to 1.5 per cent per annum on average between 1973 and 1995. From the middle of the 1970s, governments began to clock up 'large and sustained' budget deficits and loose monetary policy allowed for a sharp rise in inflation, in particular wage inflation, which 'led to a squeeze of profit margins and a weakening of investment incentives'. Nor was there anything inevitable about this: 'For the twenty years up to 1973, Greece enjoyed high growth and low inflation.'[10]

Greek membership of the EC, later the EU, was from the start marked by allegations of corruption, inefficiency and a chaotic public administration in alliance with a ruthlessly efficient approach to milking the country's European partners for as much cash as possible. Central to this, in the imagination of some of the country's many critics, were the 'phantom olive groves', the allegedly non-existent holdings attracting, quite improperly, Community subsidies for olive production. In the 1980s, it emerged that such fraud was made very much easier by the fact that there was no proper land registry in Greece.

To the extent that the data are reliable, Barry Bosworth and Tryphon Kollintzas feel able to attribute the economic stagnation of period between 1973 and 1995 to a breakdown of macroeconomic policy linked with microeconomic weaknesses, including a rigid labour market, declining competitiveness in terms of exports, and subsidies to inefficient enterprises. After noting that Greece enjoyed high growth and low inflation for the two decades preceding 1973, they add: 'and for the 20 years thereafter the economy stagnated and inflation became high and persistent.' They also suggest that the move from military dictatorship to democratic rule may explain the marked deterioration in economic conditions.

For the post-1989 generation, accustomed to the view that democracy and well-functioning free markets go hand in hand, it may seem odd even to imply that a period of military dictatorship could be some sort of golden economic age and that the return to civilian, constitutional rule put a spanner in the works. But the economic and other benefits of democracy can be harvested only when that democracy is functioning in a healthy manner. For Greece, this was far from being the case.

Instead, a spoils system arose in which the two main parties, New Democracy (ND) and the Panhellenic Socialist Movement (PASOK), representing the centre-right and centre-left respectively, established networks of patronage and what has been called 'clientelism', a state of affairs in which conceptions of the common good and civic duty were inevitably downgraded. ND and PASOK took turns in office, leading to 'political polarization and after each governmental change to massive allocation of favours to the party's clientele'.[11] Greatly exacerbating this tendency to patronage was the marked increase in the size and scope of the Greek state in the first quarter-century or more after the return to civilian rule. This led to the creation of a bloated public sector whose employees were essentially subservient to the political parties.

Against this background, Greece's woeful economic performance is easier to understand. Bosworth and Kollintzas map Greece's development against that of three other European countries – Ireland, Portugal and Spain – that were at a similar stage of performance in the early 1960s. Writing in March 2001, the authors could not know that all four countries would require bailouts in the wake of the 2007–08 financial crisis and would be bracketed together in the inelegant acronym PIGS. They note that between 1960 and 1996, Greece compared fairly well to the other three, but this finding is flattered by the strong pre-1973 growth period. Since then, Greece has had the lowest rate of increase in output per worker, and its multifactor productivity – the key measure of economic efficiency – has been negative. Ireland has moved up to the EU average in terms of output per worker with Spain only slightly below the average, but both Greece and Portugal have failed to narrow the gap after 1973. They sum up:

> The macroeconomic environment clearly collapsed in Greece in the latter part of the 1970s and remained in disarray

throughout the 1980s. The general government budget balance switched from an average surplus equal to one per cent of GDP in the 1960s to steadily increasing deficits after the 1973 oil-price shock. These deficits averaged 9 per cent of GDP in the 1980s and peaked at 16 per cent in 1990.[12]

Indeed, the real size of the budget deficit was hidden by the fact that Greek banks were required to lend money to the public sector.

To us today, living at a time when the European Commission and other EU public bodies routinely issue instructions (with varying degrees of effectiveness) to member countries on topics ranging from public finances to the treatment of refugees, it seems extraordinary that this Rake's Progress was allowed to continue unchecked. To which there are two answers.

The first is that the authority of the EU institutions was more circumscribed in the 1980s and for most of the 1990s than it became subsequently. This was particularly the case in the years prior to the launching of the euro which gave the EU an expanded remit over the economic policies of the governments of those countries that had joined the single currency.

The second is rather more straightforward: Greece did not really matter. In 1981, Greece's accession year, its economy amounted to about 1.9 per cent of the GDP of the then ten members of the Community.[13] Until the 2007 accession of Romania and Bulgaria, Greece was separated from the rest of the EU not, as was the case for both Britain and Ireland, simply by a relatively narrow patch of sea, but by both a narrow patch of sea *and* by a great chunk of the Balkans.

Out of sight, out of mind. This was the country we later learned was considered 'Oriental' by Giscard d'Estaing. In that light, Greece's strange practices were no big deal. Its heart was not in Europe but in the mysterious East. Like many locations in the developing world, it could be a great place to go on holiday but you would not wish to live there.

There was one further reason not to worry about Greece. Come the mid-1990s, it seemed finally that the country was mending its ways.

Working out (maybe): Greece gets into shape for the euro

Hard though it is to recall now, there was a period when Greece seemed set to shake off decades of underachievement and embark on a period of much more rapid expansion. Economic reforms in the late 1990s were thought to have set the stage, and an encouraging precedent was at hand in Ireland, a country whose example it was hoped Greece would follow. Greece, in other words, should imitate the action of the Celtic Tiger, although in deference to the magnificent stone creatures that guard the gate to the ancient city of Mycenae, perhaps its hoped-for pace-setting status should have earned it the description the 'Balkan Lion'.

With the lure of early – although not 'first-wave' – membership of the single currency providing a powerful incentive, Greece set about getting into shape from 1995 onwards. In 2001, Bosworth and Kollintzas noted approvingly that inflation had been reduced from double digits to a rate of less than a 3 per cent, the fiscal deficit had been cut from 12 per cent of GDP in 1990–95 to below 2 per cent in 1999, with a projected surplus by 2001, and interest rates had been converging towards the European norm. These gains had translated into an improved growth performance 'at least as compared to the performance of the prior quarter-century', and they concluded: 'Thus, by most standards, Greece has met the criteria for admission to the Eurozone and is scheduled to become a participant beginning in 2001.'[14]

The European Commission's 'convergence report' on Greece was published on 3 May 2000. A decision that was to prove so fateful was, inevitably, couched in the lifeless prose of multinational bureaucracy, the gist of which was that in the year ending March, inflation was at 2 per cent and the long-term interest rate was 6.4 per cent, an acceptable level; there was no longer an 'excessive' budget deficit; and Greece had been a member of the Exchange Rate Mechanism during the previous two years and had not devalued the drachma.

But there were those who saw this verdict as having a significance that went well beyond the economic. Bernhard Herz and Angelos Kotios took this wider view:

> In the early 1990s '. . . it became fashionable to portray Greece
> as an awkward partner or indeed a black sheep in the European
> Union' because of its economic mismanagement and frequently
> non-cooperative spirit in political matters. Greek admission to
> the Eurozone indicates that after a long process of democratiza-
> tion and economic reforms Greece has become – in economic
> and political terms – a country like any other member of the
> European Union. Greece is finally coming home to Europe.[15]

It would be some years before the truth about Greece's 'homecoming' began to emerge, a truth that would cast serious doubt on
the extent to which it had become 'like any other member of the
European Union'. On 15 November 2004, the BBC reported that
Greece had admitted it joined the euro on the basis of figures
suggesting the budget deficit to be much lower than it really was; it
had claimed a false figure for its 1999 deficit in order to qualify. '"It
has been proven that Greece's budget deficit never fell below 3%
since 1999," finance minister George Alogoskoufis admitted on
Monday.' By then, Athens had staged the 2004 Olympics, defying
all predictions of disaster and pre-event rumours of unfinished
venues, and putting on a Summer Games that compared favour-
ably, to say the least, with those staged in Atlanta eight years earlier.
The mood of self-confidence was not, at first, much dented by the
disclosures about the fancy accounting that had allowed Greece
into the single currency. And, as the BBC noted: 'Greece's membership of the single currency would not, however, be questioned.'

Nor, apparently, was the country alone in the supposedly elite
euro club, as the BBC report made clear: 'Katinka Barysch, chief
economist at the Centre for European reform, said the announcement would not be a surprise for Brussels insiders. "Quite a few
member states did something similar because of the political
imperative to join the euro as soon as possible. Greece has just gone
a bit further."'[16]

In hindsight, however, this was a straw in the wind. It was also
an invitation to examine just how successful the much-touted
reforms of the late 1990s had proved in reality. At the turn of the

millennium, Greece was caught up in the modernization programme of Kostas Simitis, the PASOK premier from January 1996 to March 2004. All seemed to be set fair for success, with a reasonably positive climate both politically and economically. Greece was ready to join the EMU and preparations for the 2004 Olympic Games were under way.

But there was one huge failure among the successes: pension reform. Large-scale demonstrations in Athens had for a long time pushed the plans off track. Surrounding this was a flotilla of smaller failures: on reforms to transport, the higher education system, health and the labour market. 'The endless list of ill-fated reforms shows firstly the limited degree of success of Simitis' modernization project and secondly, the effectiveness and power acquired by party and organized interest groups.'[17]

That said, euro membership certainly worked its magic in terms of allowing Greece to borrow at low cost, as investors ignored both the uncertain economic outlook and the country's erratic credit history. Apparently believing that EMU had ironed out the risks of lending in the Eurozone, markets allowed yields on Greek government debt to fall to match those for some of the most creditworthy countries in Europe, such as Germany. 'And that scenario persisted up until the eve of the financial crisis and Great Recession.'[18]

On 14 September 2004, the International Monetary Fund published the result of its Article IV consultation with Greece. On the surface, the Hellenic success story was rolling on under the Mediterranean sunshine, with 'several years of robust economic growth' in contrast with economies elsewhere, in Europe and further afield. Jobs and real earnings had both risen substantially. 'This enviable performance was capped last month by the successful completion of the Olympic Games.'[19] However, clouds were starting to gather on the horizon. The IMF noted that 'some of the factors that have propelled the economy forward, notably the stimulus from joining the euro area, are beginning to wane', concluding that the outlook for the future was uncertain.

By now, even the patchy reform efforts of the Simitis administration had proved too much for its critics and nowhere near far-reaching enough for the majority of citizens who felt both that the government had failed to improve their lives and that their relationship with the state and public services had deteriorated.[20]

ND was returned to power for the first time in eleven years in a landslide victory in March 2004. The IMF had some advice for the incoming prime minister Kostas Karamanlis and his freshly minted ministers, calling for an economic strategy that would bring the benefits of growth to all sections of Greek society.

The problems identified by the Fund included deteriorating competitiveness as a result of rising inflation and wage costs and the need for urgent fiscal consolidation. The Article IV report rather assumed that this consolidation would not only take place but could itself pose a problem for the economy it that it 'will sap consumer demand'.

The IMF needn't have worried on that score.

The New Democracy government had talked the talk on major reform – and even appeared to enjoy public backing for it – but walking the walk was to prove a challenge too far. The public sector continued to balloon while revenues declined and the deficit headed for 15 per cent of gross domestic product in 2009.[21]

Quite how revenues were declining at a time of economic growth takes us to an absolutely central feature of the looming Greek crisis. Even in the good years of high growth and the international prestige accruing from the successful homecoming of the Olympic Games to their ancient birthplace, there was a cancer gnawing at the vitals of the Balkan Lion: tax-dodging.

This was a problem with a very long history. On 25 February 2015, the *Wall Street Journal* reported that Greeks had long been averse to paying their dues to the state, an attitude dating back to the centuries-long Ottoman occupation, during which time non-payment was seen as a sign of patriotism. 'Today, that distrust is focused on the government, which many Greeks see as corrupt, inefficient and unreliable.'

The *WSJ* added that by the end of 2014, Greeks owed their government about €76 billion in unpaid taxes accrued over the decades, mostly since 2009, and that only €9 billion could ever be recovered. 'Billions more in taxes are owed on never-reported revenue from Greece's vast underground economy, which was estimated before the crisis to equal more than a quarter of the country's gross domestic product.'[22]

In the run-up to the crisis, Greece's traditional reluctance to pay taxes was on full display. On one estimate, the underground economy amounted to 27.5 per cent of GDP in the years 1997–2007, larger than in any other EU country; the VAT tax gap in 2006 was 30 per cent, against an EU average of 12 per cent; and tax debt as a share of annual net tax revenue was 72.2 per cent in 2011, against an OECD average of 12.3 per cent.[23]

Despite this, as late as 2009 the IMF was adopting measured tones in discussing the issue. That year's Article IV consultation report suggested that tax-dodging could be combatted by spreading the tax burden more fairly, 'by broadening tax bases by phasing out exemptions and deductions' and by ensuring that both the self-employed and the 'informal sector' paid their way, while also bringing excise duties up to the average for the Eurozone.

But right up until the threat of national bankruptcy loomed, the special characteristics of Greek society militated against decisive action. In retrospect, some believe the first ten years of the current century was a lost decade for Greece, during which a window of opportunity to introduce reforms was ignored and the country was left highly vulnerable when the financial crisis put the world economy into cardiac shock.[24]

Nor is there any certainty that even the very worrying numbers for tax-dodging in Greece come close to disclosing the real picture. Estimates show that farming and self-employed incomes account for the majority of tax-dodging, with underreporting of all incomes in 2006 leading to a 27.8 per cent tax gap. But there are suggestions that, in order to appear 'consistent', tax-dodging individuals may have underreported their earnings to quite separate income surveys. In other words, the tax base is larger than it may appear, making the shortfall larger.[25]

Once the crisis was under way, the Greek state resorted in 2011 to collecting property taxes by adding them to electricity bills, the thinking apparently being that this made them virtually impossible to dodge. The measure was repealed at the end of 2013, with a new, more conventional property tax taking effect the following year.

In the period immediately after the 9 August 2007 credit crunch, there were warnings that Greece was especially vulnerable in light of the aforementioned deficits and its exposure as a trading nation to the global recession that many now saw as an inevitable purgative after the years of easy money and bank-prompted speculation.

However, there was little preparation or warning in Greece regarding economic risks. On the contrary, complacency bred by high levels of political apathy and distrust of political leaders made Greece perhaps one of the worst-equipped countries in the face of the oncoming storm. A cocktail of 'clientelism', cynicism about politics and low levels of civic engagement was to prove a witches' brew.[26]

Summer's end: The storm breaks

The Greek debt crisis – to use the universal umbrella term – can be dated to 4 October 2009. Before that day, the country's problems were pretty much of a piece with those of the rest of the developed world: a recession induced by the cardiac shock delivered to advanced economies by the near-collapse of the banking system and a scramble among ministers and officials to put in place institutional structures better able both to prevent a repeat performance and, should that objective not be achieved, to contain the damage. After that day, Greece became a case apart, a subject of horrified fascination as its population suffered under the various austerity measures imposed in a bid to stem the crisis and as its leaders desperately tried to avoid either default or departure from the Eurozone.

To the European left, the initial focus was not on the euro but on two interlinked features of the crisis: the grand-scale tax-dodging and influence-buying by a super-rich elite that had brought Greece to this miserable state of affairs; and the savage cuts demanded by its creditors, which ensured that ordinary people paid the price for the looting and betrayal of Greece by plutocrats and corrupt politicians.

This analysis ignored the fact that tax-dodging was endemic at most levels of Greek society and that a reluctance to hand over money to public authorities in any circumstances extended to widespread free-riding on the Athens metro system. Nevertheless, the sense that a decadent and incestuous political and business class was largely to blame for the crisis was pervasive, reaching far beyond leftist circles.

Recalling a visit to the theatre in Greece in 2009, Chris Blackhurst described a general scramble for seats – for some, not others. The well-dressed and wealthy in the first few rows wandered in at the last minute, gold jewellery on show, a clear case of them and us. He added:

> Now [in 2010] Greece is torn apart, with rioters protesting against the austerity measures agreed as the price to be paid for the EU and IMF's . . . bailout; three workers lie dead after their bank was petrol-bombed. Much of the anger, I suspect, is directed against the sort of people I saw that night. Ordinary folk and public-sector workers feel they are being made to suffer through spending cuts and higher taxes, while the rich continue to enjoy the profits of corruption and evade tax.[27]

Leftist anger at tax-dodging plutocrats and at the austerity measures imposed on ordinary people to pay for their errors found a focus in the Greek protests in Syntagma Square in Athens. This key battle-ground was bracketed with uprisings in the Arab world, violence in the French ghettoes and a student riot in London as evidence that, as the then BBC correspondent Paul Mason put it in a famous blog-post on 5 February 2011, 'it's kicking off everywhere'. Only later, when the turbulence of the early 2010s died down – whether temporarily or not – did the spotlight swing on to the central role in Greece's agonies of euro membership.

On 4 October 2009, PASOK was returned to power in parliamentary elections. Sixteen days later, the new government announced that the deficit was expected to hit an astronomical 12.5 per cent of GDP. It had been previously put at 6 per cent, another example of a weakness for fancy accounting in official Greek circles. Ten-year bond yields, which had been within touching distance of those in Germany, at about 5 per cent, took off like a rocket, topping 30 per cent. Greece faced being shut out of international bond markets by credit-rating downgrades.

Often forgotten now is that Greece's parliament voted for two austerity packages, in February and March 2010 respectively, before Prime Minister George Papandreou formally applied for a bailout in April and what was to become known as the troika came into existence. In May, €110 billion was advanced to Greece as the government unveiled the third austerity package.

This was of a different order from its two predecessors, imposing salary cuts, privatizations, the shutting of thousands of municipal bodies, pension reductions and VAT rises. It was aimed at saving €38 billion by the end of 2012. Rioting and a general strike greeted the measures, which were nevertheless passed by the Greek parliament.

At this time, Greece had just crawled out of a recession that had lasted seven quarters, with a return to growth in the second quarter of 2010. The third austerity programme put a stop to all that, and the economy slumped once more. There was to be no return to growth until the last quarter of 2014, by which time 25 per cent of the economy had quite simply been destroyed. Unemployment was running at about 25 per cent, rising to perhaps 50 per cent among young people.

Harsh medicine indeed. But was it working? The bailouts certainly brought some temporary relief to the debt load, but the collapse of GDP had the inevitable effect that the debt-to-GDP ratio has continued to rise.

A second rescue package was put together in March 2012, worth €165 billion. That Greece needed the money was perhaps unsurprising, given that the conditions attached to the first loan had helped to create a Depression-era economic environment that could only reduce the revenue available to the country's debt-laden government.

Indeed, this time round there was much greater scepticism as to the efficacy of another bailout, given that it too was conditional on reforms including privatization of public assets. But some took a more cynical view of the troika's apparent generosity, believing it to have been inspired by a very different motive. The view of the *New York Times* on 14 March 2012 was that many believed the sheer burden of Greece's debt made it impossible ever to get the country back on a growth track. But European governments preferred a second bailout to a chaotic default. Furthermore, the paper suggested, there may have been a second motive: 'The aid also gives European officials breathing room to try to shore up other vulnerable, and bigger, economies like Spain and Italy.'

The second bailout came alongside 'haircuts' for the private-sector holders of €206 billion in Greek bonds. But as yet there was no sign of the 'expansionary contraction' under which a fiscal squeeze was supposed to release resources for a resurgence of private-sector business activity.

In the November prior to the second bailout, Mr Papandreou had resigned in the face of criticism of his handling of the crisis and the possibility that parliament would fail to introduce the new austerity measures attached to the March agreement. In a last throw of the dice, he had suggested putting the package to a referendum, a highly unusual step in a country whose only legitimate post-war plebiscite had been on whether to retain the monarchy after the ousting of the junta in 1974 (King Constantine II came off worst, and had to content himself with being a Prince of Denmark, which, indeed, he is).

The referendum idea was withdrawn, but some sort of precedent had been set that would be followed before too long.

Another consequence of the Papandreou resignation was the creation by his successor Lucas Papademos, a former vice-president of the ECB, of a government of national unity including PASOK, New Democracy and an ND spin-off, the right-wing populist LAOS. Some doubtless saw this development with mighty relief after the years of crisis. Others took a different view.

'After four days of bargains and scheming behind closed doors, the pillars of the Greek political system have produced a "national unity government" – a term which isn't a misnomer if one excludes from the "nation" the various left parties, currently polling the same as or above the leading conservatives, and a majority of Greek citizens.[28] Whether one agrees with this analysis or not, it is incontestable that all the main parties were now on the same side, implementing what seemed an endless series of austerity measures. That may not have mattered had there been a widespread resolve in Greece, however mistakenly, to bite the austerity bullet and work through the crisis. But that was far from being the mood of twenty-first-century Greece. As Lyrintzsis puts it, the clientelism and patronage that had dominated Greek politics after the fall of the junta continued to foment distrust and alienation against the Greek political class and a 'widespread attitude that the system could be used to extract personal or collective favours and spoils'.[29]

Furthermore, all those years of Community/EU membership had done little to fix the institutional and underlying economic malaise in Greece. The lack of a land registry that we mentioned earlier had still not been remedied many years later. As the *New York Times* reported on 26 May 2013, the age of satellite imagery and computerized records had passed Greece by: 'Greece's land transaction records are still held in ledgers, logged by last names.' And this despite the Greece's having taken $100 million from the EU to build a modern land-ownership recording system.

By this point, the failure to establish a properly functioning register of property ownership was having an impact far beyond the fraudulent accessing of EU subsidies. It was hampering the privatization programme agreed on by Greece with the troika, given that the difficulties in establishing 'good title' made it hard to identify state assets, and it was a huge obstacle to the collection of property taxes.

But even in the turmoil of the Eurozone financial crisis, there were some for whom the fictional olive groves remained a priceless image of an indolent, dishonest country. In March 2010, as then Prime Minister George Papandreou was due to visit Berlin, the German newspaper *Bild* published an open letter:

You are in Germany, a country very different from yours. Here no-one has to pay thousands of euros in 'special gratuities' to secure a bed in a hospital. Germany has high debt but pays it off as we wake in the morning and work all day. Our petrol stations have cash registers, taxi drivers give receipts and farmers don't swindle EU subsidies with millions of non-existent olive trees.[30]

Much of this was unfair, as Greece was not alone in the EU in terms of public and private corruption. It even had some competition when it came to olive-related fraud – Spanish growers were fingered by *The Economist* on 28 June 2001 for passing off oil from trees planted since 1998, which did not qualify for an EU subsidy, as oil from trees planted before that date, which did qualify. But the country was particularly prone to the effects of a combination of clientelist politics and a weak state.

The ramshackle nature of much of the Greek public sector did not only affect the proper registration of land. Bosworth and Kollintzas write that there are 'significant reservations about the quality of the economic data for Greece', adding that there is only limited historical data about individual industries 'and with the recent revisions in the national accounts, information for the pre-1988 period has become even more questionable'.[31]

Putting all this together – the coalition of the 'respectable' parties, the above-mentioned alienation from conventional politics, the dire state of the Greek economy, the chronic unemployment and pay reductions giving rise to homelessness and hunger (on 10 February 2012 the *Guardian* reported that 20,000 Greeks had lost the roofs over their heads and that the Greek Orthodox Church was feeding 250,000 people a day) – the rise of Syriza ought to have come as little surprise.

The name of the game theorist: Enter Varoufakis

Radio 4's 'Profile' slot on 22 February 2015 was given over to Yanis Varoufakis, finance minister in the newly-formed Greek government led by the left-wing Syriza party. Syriza had triumphed in the

25 January elections, ousting the coalition of PASOK and ND. It was a remarkable performance for a party that was only founded in 2004, and was testimony to the salience of the anti-austerity rhetoric and personal charisma of its leader, Alexis Tsipras.

Lacking an overall majority, Syriza went into coalition with the Independent Greeks party, a right-wing populist grouping. Installed in office, Tsipras despatched Varoufakis on a tour of European capitals to build support for Greek demands for an end to austerity – what Tsipras called 'bailout barbarity' and Varoufakis described as 'fiscal waterboarding'. With his leather jacket, untucked shirt and shaven head, Varoufakis was a bird of exotic plumage in the drab ranks of besuited European finance ministers and an obvious choice for the 'Profile' programme.

Presenter Mark Coles told listeners that Varoufakis had described himself as 'an erratic Marxist', that he had a quarter of a million Twitter followers and that he saw himself as 'testing the limits of game theory', this last a reference to his specialist subject, the study of conflict and cooperation among decision-makers. A contributory report from Athens for the programme ran thus: '"He's one of us," says his local greengrocer . . . "These days because of his travel commitments we don't see him very often, but he used to pass by a lot and his wife and their maid come and shop here."'

'Their maid'? Ah, *that* sort of erratic Marxist.

The employment of domestic staff was, however, the least of the causes for concern about the strategy being pursued by Varoufakis and his boss, the new prime minister Alexis Tsipras. At the time of Syriza's victory, Greece was negotiating for a final tranche of bailout funds worth €7.2 billion, vital if the country were to meet a heavy schedule of debt repayments in the coming months. This money was conditional on agreeing further austerity measures with the troika including more spending reductions and additional pension reforms.

An early counter-offer by Athens included one proposal that would actually have cost more money, a scheme to help people whose homes were worth less than the value of their mortgages. Aside from this early skirmishing, Syriza executed a mini U-turn, getting a four-month extension to the bailout agreement in return for agreeing to stick *pro tem* to the general outlines of the deal agreed by the government's predecessors.

Perhaps nettled by having had to make this concession on 2 March, Tsipras appeared on the 11th to threaten to seize German assets in Greece in compensation for the death and destruction wrought during the Second World War. The German government confined itself to saying that it had honoured all its reparation commitments to Greece.

While Varoufakis met fellow finance ministers, Tsipras schmoozed both US administration officials and Russia's Vladimir Putin. None of this moved Greece any nearer to a deal on releasing the €7.2 billion, nor was it likely to, given that the Syriza-led government was no less committed than its predecessors to remaining a member of the single-currency bloc. Proposals went to and fro, with the Greek government unable to make the very painful concessions demanded by the troika without utterly betraying its election commitments.

However, if Tsipras and his colleagues refused to play the only card that could have given the troika a concrete incentive to make significant compromises – a credible threat to leave the euro – they reached instead one of lower value but, still, some significance: partial default.

On 6 May, Greece had managed to swerve its way round one default by making a €200 million debt repayment to the IMF, and made a second, two days later, of €750 million. The pace of events quickened noticeably. Come 24 May, Athens was threatening to default on €1.6 billion of debt repayments to the IMF due by the end of June. A torrid early summer was in prospect, with the IMF walking out of talks with Greece on 11 June citing Greek refusal to compromise on pension and labour-market reforms. On the 18th, talks broke down between Greece and Eurozone finance ministers; they were revived, only to break down again on the 25th.

On 26 June, Greece stunned the other eighteen Eurozone members by announcing a referendum to be held on 5 July on the terms on offer for the last €7.2 billion. Given the second bailout deal, of which the €7.2 billion was part, would expire on 30 June, the Greeks would be in the bizarre position of voting on an offer that had ceased to be available. By now, the criticisms of Syriza's strategy were increasing in volume, with John Hulsman in *City AM*'s 2 July edition offering the following thoughts: 'Never underestimate the ability of the over-rated Greek prime minister (and his even more feted-for-no-reason henchman Yanis Varoufakis) to get things wrong. By all accounts, it was the Greek finance minister who convinced Tsipras to head down the road of the plebiscite gambit in the first place. Varoufakis may be in the business of game theory, but no-one has said he is any good at it.'

The ECB turned off support for Greece's banks so the government imposed capital controls, closing bank branches and limiting cash-machine withdrawals to €60 a day. On 30 June, Greece became the first developed country to default on an IMF loan repayment.

Tsipras, who had campaigned for a No vote, achieved a stunning victory on 5 July. More than 60 per cent of voters agreed with him, despite threats from elsewhere in the Eurozone that doing so would mean a return to the drachma.

The next four days resembled less a Greek drama than a performance of the theatre of the absurd. On 6 July, Varoufakis resigned at Tsipras's request; on the 8th, European leaders gave Athens a new deadline of 12 July to agree to what were slightly harsher terms than had been on offer previously; and on 9 July, Greece caved in.

Talks then began on a third bailout, with the government agreeing the conditions in principle later in July. On 16 July, Reuters reported that Greece has accepted reforms including significant pension adjustments, increases to value-added taxes, an overhaul of its collective bargaining system, measures to liberalize its economy, and tight limits on public spending in exchange for an €86 billion bailout.

By this stage, the troika was dictating legislation to give effect to the new austerity measures. It all sounded rather like more of the same 'bailout barbarity', but it cleared the Greek parliament on 14 August.

The morning after: Legacy of a grand gesture

So what had it all been for?

On 13 July 2015, Tsipras declared: 'We earned our popular sovereignty. We sent a message of democracy, a message of dignity throughout Europe and the world.'[32] It could, of course, be argued that the first eight months of his government achieved precisely the reverse of all these listed items, showing that there was little room for popular sovereignty, democracy or dignity inside the Eurozone.

In the immediate term, it did Tsipras little harm. The 20 September election returned Syriza with enough seats again to lead a coalition and for Tsipras to remain as prime minister. Some were less forgiving than those who returned Syriza to power. Writing in the *Guardian* on 25 January 2016, the anniversary of Syriza's first victory, Costas Lapavitsas said: 'A year on, the Syriza party is faithfully implementing the austerity policies that it once decried. It has been purged of its left wing and Tsipras has jettisoned his radicalism to stay in power at all costs.' He concluded: 'Syriza failed not because austerity is invincible, nor because radical change is impossible, but because, disastrously, it was unwilling and unprepared to put up a direct challenge to the euro.'[33]

To be fair, there was some fight left in Syriza but, as we saw at the beginning of the chapter, it expressed itself bizarrely, in telling the IMF to mind its own business when, uniquely among the troika, the IMF was pressing for the sort of debt relief that Syriza itself was seeking: substantial debt relief rather than minor fiddling with maturity dates.

Syriza now faced ridicule from all sides. 'You cannot be Syriza!' declared *Private Eye* magazine in early 2015, punning 'Syriza' and 'serious', and maybe Syriza wasn't. Writing for the *Spectator* on 22 December 2015, Brendan O'Neill suggested Spain's Podemos was essentially a gaggle of academics with little real-life experience, declaring: 'Syriza's leading lights were nabbed from universities, especially British ones . . . No amount of swooning over "revolutionary" Varoufakis can disguise the fact he's a politics lecturer in a leather jacket.'

Rather than faculty, however, perhaps Syriza had more in common with the students. It certainly displayed an undergraduate relish for gestures, such as Tsipras making his first port of call on gaining the premiership the shrine at Kaisariani to people murdered by the Nazis, a pointed dig at Greece's largest national creditor. German forces behaved abominably in wartime Greece – the country's death toll was well over half a million out of a population of less than 7.5 million[34] – but they behaved abominably in many places. It is hard to avoid the thought that if the State of Israel can have good relations with the Federal Republic of Germany, anyone can.

Then there were the suggestions, at the start of the first Syriza-led government, of moves to separate the state from the Greek Orthodox Church. It is rather as if, upon taking office in March 1974 in the middle of the most serious economic crisis since the war, Britain's Harold Wilson had found time to look at the disestablishment of the Church of England.

Doubtless it is coincidental that Syriza threw in the towel in early July, about the time many universities break for the summer. But it is hard not to envisage the Syriza phenomenon as an extended picket of faculty buildings that was fun during days of sunshine and hot summer nights but which inevitably ran its course, with the kids going their separate ways leaving the grown-ups in charge – as, in truth, they always had been.

Costas Lapavitsas draws the one conclusion that Syriza was determined to avoid – that the only alternative to austerity is to confront EMU and that 'for smaller countries this means preparing to exit'. It was, he said, 'the only positive lesson from the Syriza debacle'.[35] We agree. Keeping Greece in the euro meant, in effect, accepting the German critique of the Greek economy and people as in sore need of abrasive structural reform. The Syriza governments can be seen as colossal exercises in trying to avoid an unavoidable truth, that the only way to achieve their objectives was to head for the exit. These exercises in delusion have not ended well.

From Greece it is but a short journey, geographically, to our next destination, but a large one in terms of economic difference as we visit a Eurozone member whose problems could threaten the whole EMU project: Italy.

CHAPTER 8

THE ITALIAN JOB

Uh-uh. I know what you're thinking. 'Did he fire six shots or only five?' Well to tell you the truth in all this excitement I've kind of lost track myself. But being this is a .44 Magnum, the most powerful handgun in the world and would blow your head clean off, you've got to ask yourself one question: 'Do I feel lucky?' Well do you, punk?

Clint Eastwood as Harry Callahan in *Dirty Harry*

It was a terrifying sight for the citizens of Rome huddled behind the city walls. An army of Visigoths under the command of Alaric was laying siege to a metropolis that for four centuries had been the capital of an empire that stretched from Hadrian's Wall in the north to the deserts of North Africa in the south, and from the Pillars of Hercules in the west to Mesopotamia in the east. The zenith of Rome's glory had long since passed and, in the first decade of the fifth century, troops – many of them mercenaries – were recalled from far-flung provinces such as Britain to defend the city, leaving those outposts defenceless against the tribes moving west from central Europe. It was, though, a futile gesture. Alaric had been causing mayhem in northern Italy for years without any significant opposition and by 410 was ready to take the biggest prize of all. Rome was weak and its citizens were soft, lazy and frightened.

Alaric made his demands abundantly clear: buy me off or I'll lay waste to your city. The emperor Honorius and the Senate did what beleaguered politicians have done ever since: they played for time in the hope that something would turn up. As the days wore on, it became clear that no reinforcements were going to sail along the Tiber or march up the Appian Way. Realizing that he was being played along, Alaric lost patience and sacked the city. Rome's empire in the east, with Constantinople as its capital, lasted for a further thousand years, but in the west it fell apart.

There was a curious echo of this episode some 1,601 years later, when politicians in Rome again found themselves on the receiving end of the tactics deployed by Alaric. This time Rome's adversaries were not long-haired tribesmen from beyond the Rhine but a pair of central bankers; the urbane Jean-Claude Trichet, president of the European Central Bank, and the man who was about to replace him, the Goldman Sachs alumnus Mario Draghi. Ironically, one of the latter-day Alarics was himself an Italian.

As we shall show in this chapter, Italy has played a curious role in the story of the euro. Italians were instrumental in creating the single currency and yet Italy has been one of the countries that has struggled most with its disciplines. Draghi's time at the ECB has been spent trying to make monetary union work. This chapter, therefore, has three themes. It will look at how Italy, the third-biggest economy in the Eurozone, has fared. It illustrates how Italian intellectuals have been so pivotal. And it takes the story of the single currency from the financial crisis and global recession of 2007–09 to the period of maximum danger in 2012, when the euro was fighting for its life.

Trichet and Draghi had no armies to call upon, but they had no need of them because the economic and financial weapons in their arsenal were as potent and as menacing as an army of Visigoths. Rome was at the mercy of the marauding hordes of the global financial markets and help was available – at a price. The view from the ECB's headquarters in Frankfurt in the summer of 2011 had changed little since the Germanic tribes looked across the Danube and the Rhine in the early fifth century: Rome was corrupt, idle, vulnerable and ripe for the picking. Trichet and Draghi did not want to sack Rome, they wanted to cleanse it of its rottenness; and they were prepared to use their financial clout to do so.

In truth, since the start of the Eurozone's debt crisis the ECB had used the same scorched-earth tactics against all governments in need of assistance even when they showed a willingness to bend the knee to Frankfurt. There could scarcely have been a more contrite nation than Ireland after its housing bubble left its banks facing ruin, but when the government in Dublin said bondholders should accept a share of the losses resulting from the wild speculation, the response from Trichet was blunt: unless Irish taxpayers would foot the bill for the banks – which initially amounted to €64 billion or one-third of the Republic's GDP – the ECB would cut off financial support.[1]

Italy was, however, both quantitatively and qualitatively different from Ireland. It was not just that Italy was a large enough economy to have twice outstripped the UK during the past thirty years, first in 1987 and again in 2009. Nor was it simply that Europe lacked the financial heft to bail out a country where the national debt was comfortably bigger than that of Greece, Ireland and Portugal combined. There were two other factors at play. The first was a fear in Brussels and Frankfurt that the crisis would work its way up through Italy to threaten the core of the Eurozone itself, just as the Allied armies had fought their way up the peninsula during the Second World War. The second was a feeling that the crisis presented a once-in-a-lifetime opportunity that had to be exploited. Italy's economy was in bad shape; its prime minister, Silvio Berlusconi, was tainted by scandal and, thanks to his well-publicized 'bunga bunga' sex parties, was seen as a buffoonish modern-day Nero. Getting rid of Berlusconi would pave the way for a new, more pliable government in Rome that would impose root-and-branch economic reforms. What was needed was a silent coup to make an example of the third biggest economy in the Eurozone. No time was wasted. Within three months the coup had taken place. First, however, there needs to be an explanation of how Italy came to be so vulnerable. What was it that led to a minatory missive from two central bankers in Frankfurt?

In search of lost times

For fourteen centuries after the fall of Rome, Italy was divided. It was not until the *Risorgimento* or 'rising again' of the mid-nineteenth century that the country was once more united. The intervening period had seen the peninsula repeatedly invaded, the Visigoths being followed by the Huns, the Ostrogoths, the Franks, the Normans, the Habsburgs of Spain, the Habsburgs of Austria and the French armies of Napoleon.

Forging an Italian state involved fusing together what had been up until then two completely different economic entities: the Kingdom of the Two Sicilies in the south and Piedmont in the north. Italy to the south of Rome was much more backward and more rural than the country to the north of the new capital. There were fewer roads, fewer railway lines, and far higher levels of illiteracy. In its way, the enforced unification of Italy by Garibaldi and Cavour in the years up to 1861 prefigured the creation of the Eurozone a little less than a century and a half later, with the pronounced gulf in economic performance between a prosperous core and a struggling periphery.

At the time monetary union was launched in 1999, Italians harboured the belief that Turin and Milan formed the bottom tip of a crescent of prosperity that curved up through Switzerland, Lyon and Paris and on to the Netherlands and the western Länder of Germany. There was some truth in this assessment. Milan certainly had more in common with Munich than it did with Messina in Sicily, not least the network of small family businesses that were the bedrock of the manufacturing sectors in both Italy and Germany. Southern Italy remained backward and poor, but was supported by a non-stop injection of public money provided by taxpayers in the richer half of the country. This was one of the two ways in which Italy as a nation state differed from the Eurozone: Rome was in control of a budgetary mechanism that could redistribute money around the country, whereas the Eurozone had no such mechanism. The second difference was that a common language meant the peasant farmers of the *Mezzogiorno* could leave their small-holdings and find work in the car plants of Turin.

The Italians were deluding themselves when they imagined that, without the encumbrance of the Mezzogiorno, they could compete on an equal footing with Germany. Italy's economic strength was illusory. Initially it was based on the availability of cheap labour from the south. When these workers became union-ized and politicized, a series of short-lived governments sought to buy off trouble by increasing state spending. They also responded by breaking up established firms and shifting production to small companies and cottage industries, where employers could enlist family members, including children and juveniles, as well as casual and part-time labour. This led to an expansion of the informal or black economy, which, together with higher public spending, led to a deterioration in the public finances.

The small plants lacked the resources to innovate and the lack of technological advance proved costly as Italy from the 1960s onwards faced increasing competition from the cheap producers of the developing world and from the more advanced parts of Europe. Governments in Rome found the temptation to boost export competitiveness by devaluing the lira irresistible. In the last three decades of the twentieth century, Italy had problems with indus-trial militancy, political corruption, economic inefficiency and fiscal sustainability. Yet, somehow, it continued to grow and remained both cohesive and relatively content.

Italy's intellectuals, however, were unhappy with muddling through. As in Britain after the loss of empire, the unhappiness manifested itself in a hankering after the days when the country was the hub of the civilized world. For a century and a half after unification, Italy had manifested a curious mix of national self-assertiveness and an inferiority complex, best illustrated by the period between the two world wars when the failure to secure the expected gains from the Treaty of Versailles fostered Italy's belief that it was not being accorded the respect it deserved, creating a climate in which Mussolini's aggressive nationalism could flourish. Although it was never expressed as such, Il Duce's recipe for keeping Italy on the gold standard – a 20 per cent wage cut in 1927 – was precisely the sort of measure championed by the troika for countries that found it tough to stick to the disciplines of monetary union. Mussolini succeeded, by brute force, in taming Italy's militant trade unions but only at the expense of his expansionary foreign policy, since the decision to remain on the gold standard after every other country except France resulted in slow growth and less money available for military spending. Italian fascism was an extreme example of what Perry Anderson describes as 'an overwhelming sense of the gap between past glory and present misery, among its educated elites'.[2] Ancient Rome loomed large in the national consciousness, particularly the sense that the dissolution of the empire had seen a relapse into barbarity and a retreat from civilization.

The sense of yearning was made all the more acute by the role of the Italian city states in the emergence of Europe from what became known as the Dark Ages and into the modern world. This included Venice's status as the staging post for trade with Asia, the origins of modern banking in Lombardy, and, most especially, by the roles played by Florence, Milan and Rome in the artistic, scientific and political changes that coalesced in the Renaissance of the fifteenth and sixteenth centuries. The modern world has been shaped by repeated waves of technological advance, typically associated with cultural shifts, and the first of these had its roots in the work of Da Vinci, Galileo, Michelangelo and Machiavelli. 'From Dante onwards,' says Anderson, 'there developed a tradition of intellectuals with an acute sense of their calling to recover and transmit the high culture of classical antiquity, and imbued with the conviction that the country could be put to rights only by the impress of revivifying ideas, of which only they could be the artificers, on fallen realities.'[3]

What the Italian intellectual class wanted was a return to the Europe of the late Middle Ages, when Rome was the centre of Christendom, the writ of the pope held sway across a patchwork of small princedoms, and the Catholic Church was a unifying force. They saw the move towards ever closer union as a return to Europe as it existed before the system of modern nation states had been established by the Treaty of Westphalia, signed at the end of the

Thirty Years War in 1648. Brussels would be the new Rome, the European ideal would be the new Catholicism; there would be one overarching ideology that would hold sway over a collection of relatively weak princedoms. The ECB would take on the role once played by the Vatican in a modern version of the Holy Roman Empire in which Italy could feel it was playing an important role. That was particularly the case when one of its own, Draghi, was handed the imperial crown in 2011.

What have the Romans ever done for us?

It should, therefore, come as no surprise that Italy and Italians have been important in the development of Europe over the past sixty years. Tommaso Padoa-Schioppa was the intellectual force behind the creation of the euro, providing the economic argument to bolster the political case for monetary union. In a seminal paper in 1982,[4] Padoa-Schioppa said that for a group of nations such as the European Union it was impossible simultaneously to enjoy capital mobility, free trade, fixed exchange rates and independent monetary policies. The case for creating a single European market free from restrictions on the movement of money and goods was made by another Italian, Paolo Cecchini in his 1988 report, so that by the late 1980s the choice was between member states of the European Union keeping control of their own monetary policies and a fixed exchange rate. Padoa-Schioppa said that by creating a single currency and a European Central Bank it would be possible for Europe to have free trade within its own borders, free movement of capital and a fixed exchange rate. In return, they would have to give up control of their own monetary policy.

Padoa-Schioppa's arguments helped shape the Delors Report of 1989, which in turn led to the Maastricht Treaty of 1991. Giulio Andreotti, then Italy's prime minister, gave monetary union a political push forward by outwitting Margaret Thatcher at the Rome summit in October 1990, an event that indirectly led to the downfall of the longest-serving British prime minister of the twentieth century a month later. Romano Prodi was prime minister during the period when Italy was employing Enron-style tactics in order to qualify for monetary union and was rewarded by becoming the next president of the European Commission in 1999.

When the European Union was looking for academic justification for the austerity measures imposed on member states during and after the financial crisis of 2007–09, it was to the Bocconi Boys that they turned. This was not the name of a branch of the mafia, but graduates of a business school attached to the private Bocconi University in Milan who developed the theory of expansionary fiscal contraction.

A study comparing budget cuts in Denmark and Ireland in the 1980s by Francesco Giavazzi and Marco Pagano concluded that fiscal contractions could be good for growth, especially if accompanied by an easing of monetary policy delivered through interest-rate cuts and a lower exchange rate.[5] This paved the way for the work of two other Bocconi Boys. In terms of their influence on the expansionary fiscal contraction debate, Alberto Alesina and Silvia Ardagna (strictly speaking a Bocconi Girl) were Lennon and McCartney to Giavazzi and Pagano's Everly Brothers. They took the earlier findings, expanded them, removed the caveats, and published at precisely the time when the European policy elite was looking for a counter to the fundamental Keynesian belief that governments should run budget deficits to support growth during a recession. It was to Keynes that finance ministers had turned during the winter of 2008–09, when the collapse of industrial production and the shrinking of world trade was as acute as in the early stages of the Great Depression, but as soon as recession bottomed out in the spring of 2009, some governments (most notably in Berlin), the ECB and the European Commission believed it was time to end deficit financing and take action to stop national debts from ballooning.

Alesina and Ardagna's 'Large Changes in Fiscal Policy: Taxes Versus Spending'[6] was not the snappiest of titles, but in terms of impact it was the equivalent of the 1967 release of The Beatles' *Sgt. Pepper's Lonely Hearts Club Band*. Trichet took to quoting from the paper in his speeches; the analysis was incorporated into the ECB's monthly bulletin in June 2010; and it was central to the way in which George Osborne approached deficit reduction in the UK. Alesina presented a simplified version of his paper to EU finance ministers in April 2010, in which he said that those governments that believed they could spend and borrow their way back to prosperity were wrong. There was, he said, no alternative to budgetary rigour and he cited twenty-six examples where countries that had tried expansionary fiscal contraction had grown faster than countries that had not been so determined to put their public finances in order. Alesina's case was that consumers and businesses would look to the future and envisage a time when the elimination of the budget deficit and a reduction in debt ratios would result in lower taxes and lower interest rates. That would make them more confident, thereby leading to higher spending and increased investment. It was important, Alesina and Ardagna said, that the repair job on the public finances should be carried out not through tax increases but through public spending cuts, which should be focused on reducing the generosity of welfare states.

At the meeting of finance ministers, Alesina said they should not fear the political consequences of slashing social payments in the middle of a slump, because they would be rewarded rather than punished for their boldness. Cutting was both unavoidable and fair because 'the rhetoric about the immense social cost of fiscal adjustment is blown out of proportion and is often used strategically by certain groups, not necessarily the most disadvantaged, to protect themselves'.

Rather like some of the tracks on *Sgt. Pepper*, 'Large Changes in Fiscal Policy' is now a bit dated. It has been rubbished by economists at the International Monetary Fund for its methodology and been found wanting when put to an empirical test. The Eurozone did not grow more rapidly when it experimented with expansionary fiscal contracting; the confidence fairy (as Paul Krugman puts it) did not arrive on the scene to boost consumer confidence and what Keynes called the animal spirits of entrepreneurs, the willingness to take risks. Instead, the Eurozone stumbled from recession to slow growth to recession again, and high levels of unemployment became entrenched.

The one country hailed as a success story for expansionary fiscal contraction – Latvia – was a strange sort of triumph. Critics of the Alesina and Ardagna thesis would not dispute that it is possible for a country to make itself more competitive through a policy of mass unemployment and wage cuts; merely that devaluation of the currency – eschewed by Latvia – is a quicker and more humane method of achieving the same result. Latvia's 'success' has been a lost decade in terms of living standards and a lost generation of young workers who have emigrated overseas in search of jobs.

As for the idea that Eurozone politicians would be fêted by their electorates for taking the axe to budget deficits, all that can be said is that the graveyard for European leaders who have tried to put the theory into practice has become rather crowded. But this is from the perspective of 2016. In 2010, those running the Eurozone were as smitten by 'Large Changes in Fiscal Policy' as a blissed-out hippy in a San Francisco flophouse listening to 'A Day in the Life' during the Summer of Love. All of which explains the letter Berlusconi received from Trichet and Draghi in August 2011. The missive was supposed to remain secret, although that was always a naïve hope on the part of the ECB, given the explosive contents of the correspondence.

The postman knocks

It had been a difficult summer for the Eurozone. Spooked by the prospect of inflation, Trichet had raised interest rates not once but twice in the first seven months of 2011, choking off a weak recovery and pushing the Eurozone back into recession. To make matters worse, the opportunity to ring-fence Europe's sovereign debt crisis by dealing decisively with Greece's problems had been spurned. As has been shown, Ireland became the second Eurozone country to need a bailout in late 2010; Portugal became the third in May 2011. Unsurprisingly, financial markets scanned the Eurozone to see whether any other countries might need help. Equally unsurprisingly, they saw Italy as a likely candidate.

Since the phrase 'sick man of Europe' was coined by Tsar Nicholas I of Russia to describe the Ottoman Empire in the 1850s, many countries had found themselves given that unwanted soubriquet. It was conferred upon Britain during the 1970s and Germany in the early 2000s when unemployment reached levels not seen since the last days of the Weimar Republic. There are so many current candidates, from France to Finland, that there is a good case for saying that the real sick man of Europe is the Eurozone itself, but in terms of being a persistent laggard no country can really compete with Italy, where incomes per head in 2016 were no higher than they were when the single currency was launched in 1999.

Italy's low birth rate belies its reputation as a nation of red-hot Latin lovers; it ranks 207th out of 230 countries in births. The population has been ageing, with 20 per cent already aged over sixty-five, and it would currently be declining too were it not for inward migration. There was a period between the signing of the Treaty of Rome in 1957 and the first oil price shock in 1973 when Italy's growth rate was higher than the average for the rich-country members of the Organisation for Economic Co-operation and Development, but inflation had always been a problem even in the era of Fellini's *La Dolce Vita*. In the 1970s and 1980s, inflation was double the OECD average and Italian goods only remained competitive on global markets through regular devaluations of the lira. This option was closed off when Italy joined the single currency, and the late 1990s and 2000s saw the country's high concentration of small- and medium-sized companies under threat from cheaper Asian rivals. That was especially true of one of Italy's specialisms: textiles and clothing.

In the fifteen years since the creation of the euro, Italy has suffered as many recessions as it had in the previous forty. Unemployment has doubled since the start of the global financial crisis and would be even higher were it not for Italy's labour laws. The state has provided cash payments so that firms keep workers on the payroll even if there has been no work for them to do and, until 2015, it was hard for companies with more than fifteen employees to make staff redundant. With an ageing population, no Italian government has an incentive to reduce the generosity of the pension system, preferring to let the public finances take the strain. At 90 per cent of GDP, Italy's national debt was high by Eurozone standards when monetary union was launched in 1999, but this was not deemed to be a problem either by the European Commission, which bent the rules of the Maastricht Treaty to allow Italy to join monetary union, or by the financial markets. But by the summer of 2011 there was plenty of concern about Italian public debt, even though the debt ratio was not markedly higher than it had been in 1999.

The reason for the alarm bells in the financial markets was not just that Italy had weak growth. Nor was it the surrender of the devaluation option. These factors were important but had been known about since the late 1990s. The real issue was that the crisis in Greece had changed perceptions about whether the Eurozone would survive. For as long as the assumption held that a country would stick to the single currency through thick and thin, and that the ECB would act as a genuine lender of last resort to a country that ran into trouble, Italy's national debt was of no importance. It mattered a lot once it became clear that the ECB was different from the US Federal Reserve or the Bank of England, because even a slim chance of euro exit raised the prospect of a debt default.

As a result, investors demanded insurance for holding Italian government bonds. They received it in the form of higher bond yields, the interest payments that the government had to pay for the money it was borrowing. Italy was different from Ireland or Spain, two Eurozone countries that had run into difficulties as a result of excessive private-sector debt that fuelled housing and construction booms. As Mark Blyth notes, Italy was more like Portugal in that it had an ageing population, weak growth prospects and high public-sector debt.[7] An indication of the scale of Italy's debt problem is that, after the US and Japan, it has the third biggest bond market in the world.

Throughout the summer of 2011, interest rates rose sharply, with the mood noticeably darkening after the second of the two ECB interest rate increases in July. Bond yields rose to more than 6 per cent and for the first time in more than a year were higher than those in Spain, where boom had turned to bust.

It was then that Trichet and Draghi made their move. Their letter said that help was available to Italy on certain conditions. It stressed that the state of Italy's economy made 'bold and immediate' action essential, with an end-of-September deadline for enacting a series of reforms. The ECB insisted that there be a 'major overhaul of the public administration'; 'large-scale privatizations'; a reduction in the cost of public employees by making it easier to hire and fire and 'if necessary by reducing wages'; reform of the collective bargaining system; less generous pensions; and changes to the law to tighten control of the budget.

This was, indeed, the approach once adopted by Alaric the Visigoth. It also smacked of the tactics favoured by the Sicilian Mafia or the Neapolitan Camorra when choosing targets for protection rackets: 'Nice little economy you've got here, Silvio. It would be a shame if something happened to it.'

Giulio Tremonti, then Italy's finance minister, later commented that in August 2011, the government in Rome received two threatening letters: one was from a terrorist group, the other was from the ECB. 'The one from the ECB was worse,' Tremonti said, only half-joking.

Italy caved in, or at least gave the impression that it was doing so. A letter was sent to the ECB in Frankfurt two days later promising economic reforms and stronger action to reduce its budget deficit. Trichet was mollified and ordered that the ECB should make a public show of buying Italian bonds. Interest rates duly fell, but only for a while because, rather like the Roman Senate in 410 AD, Berlusconi was really only playing for time. He let it be known that he had no intention of passing laws that would penalize Italian pensioners.

Had he bothered to study his Roman history, Berlusconi would have known what would happen next. The ECB stopped buying Italian bonds and did nothing as interest rates rose to even higher levels than in August. Standard & Poor's duly downgraded Italy's credit rating.

But there was more to come. If the decision to stop buying Italian bonds was the equivalent of the horse's head in the bed in

The Godfather, what happened next was the equivalent of a Mafia drive-by shooting, minus the bullet-riddled limousine and the blood-splattered corpse.

Trichet and Draghi phoned Berlusconi to impress upon him the importance of keeping his promises (pay the protection). This was followed by a call from the president of the European Council, Herman Van Rompuy, who said that if the Italian prime minister didn't start taking the crisis more seriously 'we are all in trouble'. What Van Rompuy meant was that Berlusconi would be in trouble if he did not fall into line with the ECB's demands. The German chancellor Angela Merkel, the 'Godmother' in this story, then took a hand. Merkel's dislike of Berlusconi's policies was only matched by her dislike of his personality, so she took it upon herself to orchestrate a change of government. The German chancellor phoned the octogenarian Italian president, Giorgio Napolitano, and told him that she wasn't quite sure Berlusconi was up to the job of pushing through the reforms Italy needed.[8]

Napolitano, a long-standing member of Italy's Communist Party, noted that Berlusconi's parliamentary majority was wafer thin, and promised to see what he could do. Merkel expressed gratitude but was not prepared to leave matters there. In collaboration with Nicolas Sarkozy, she humiliated Berlusconi at an EU summit by giving him three days to come up with a package of reforms – reforms that were more than cosmetic. The pressure was ratcheted up still further at a disastrous summit gathering of the Group of Twenty club of developed and developing nations in Cannes a week later. Here, most of the attention was on Prime Minister George Papandreou, who a few days earlier had announced that he would hold a referendum on the terms of Greece's second bailout from the ECB/European Commission/IMF troika. Papandreou was told that if the plebiscite went ahead, Greece could forget about getting any more financial help, and that the question should be changed to ask Greek voters whether or not they wanted to stay in the euro.

Faced with a revolt at home, Papandreou was gone within a week, but so was Berlusconi, hastened on his way by a less than helpful suggestion from Germany at the Cannes meeting that Italy might like to apply for a line of credit from the IMF. Quite reasonably, Berlusconi made the point that Italy had for years been able to rely on domestic savers to buy government bonds and that the suggestion that IMF help might be needed would give the financial markets even more reason to be concerned about Italy, leading to bond yields rising still further. The Italian prime minister did not grasp that this was precisely what Merkel had in mind. Barack Obama backed Berlusconi and said Europe should think about using its reserves held at the IMF to construct a bigger war chest with which to fight speculative attacks on the euro. The summit broke up in disarray but Merkel had her scalp. She had engineered a situation in which Berlusconi was friendless at home, increasingly isolated in Europe, and impotent to deal with a financial assault that threatened to make his country's debts unpayable. Within four days, he was (politically speaking) sleeping with the fishes, and was replaced by someone Merkel found much more amenable.

Cannon to right of them, cannon to left of them

Italy's new prime minister, Mario Monti, ticked all the boxes. He was a former European commissioner, which meant his loyalty to the 'project' was unshakeable. Like Draghi, he had worked for Goldman Sachs, so could be relied upon to have orthodox economic views. Best of all, though, he was a technocrat rather than a politician. Far from being an impediment, the fact that Monti was not an MP was seen as a positive advantage; he was appointed to the job by Napolitano after being made a senator for life but without the inconvenience of having to ask any actual Italian voters for their support. As Stephen Foley put it, seen from a traditional left-of-centre perspective, this episode could be considered something less than an unalloyed victory:

> The accession of Mario Monti to the Italian prime ministership is remarkable for more reasons than it is possible to count. By replacing the scandal-surfing Silvio Berlusconi, Italy has

dislodged the undislodgeable. By imposing rule by unelected technocrats, it has suspended the normal rules of democracy, and maybe democracy itself. And by putting a senior adviser at Goldman Sachs in charge of a Western nation, it has taken to a new height the political power of an investment bank that you might have thought was prohibitively politically toxic.[9]

Italy now had its dream team: one Mario running the Italian government in Rome, the other at the head of the ECB in Frankfurt. Between them, Monti and Draghi would remove the stain on Italy's reputation from the Berlusconi years, sort out the country's economic problems, and end the threat to the euro from the financial markets. Things were, however, going to get a lot worse for the single currency – and for Italy – before they got better.

To understand why that was, the clock needs to be turned back to the start of the financial crisis, which began in August 2007. The root cause of the problem was the US housing market, where a collapse in house prices revealed that a large number of Americans were living in homes worth far less than they had paid for them and lacked the means to keep up the mortgage payments. There was *Schadenfreude* in European capitals at the idea that the Anglo-Saxon model of capitalism had been found wanting – rather ill-advised revelling in the misfortune of others, as it transpired. It soon became apparent that banks had convinced themselves that the US housing market was a one-way bet and had bought vast quantities of financial contracts – known as derivatives – that magnified their original bets. Banks did not know how exposed they or their rivals were to subprime debt, and most of them did not have sufficient capital to cover their losses when they started to appear.

European banks were just as heavily mired in potential subprime losses as their US counterparts. It was a French bank, BNP Paribas, that hoisted the first distress signal on 9 August 2007 when it suspended trading on three of its hedge funds due to subprime losses. The first central bank to respond to the SOS was the ECB, which made almost €100 billion available to European banks the following day. The display of urgency was, however, not repeated. The eight years between the creation of the euro and the onset of the subprime crisis underlined one of the left's critiques of monetary union, namely that a one-size-fits-all interest rate and the lack of exchange-rate flexibility would suit no member state. The years that followed highlighted all their other misgivings: the ECB's conservatism; the belief that keeping inflation below 2 per cent took precedence at all times; the sluggishness of the European political system; the flouting of democracy; and the open attempts to use the crisis to impose neoliberal structural reforms.

For more than a year after August 2007, the view that this was simply an Anglo-Saxon problem seemed to have some justification. The first two banks to run into serious trouble were the UK's Northern Rock and the American investment bank Bear Stearns. The collapse of a second US investment bank, Lehman Brothers, in September 2008 took the crisis to a new and far more dangerous level. There were immediate contagion effects throughout the entire global banking system, which prompted Sarkozy to call for all Eurozone countries to pool resources to create a €300 billion bank rescue fund. Sarkozy's plan did not find favour with Merkel, as the French president made clear when giving an account of his talks with the German chancellor at a European summit in early October 2008: '*Elle a dit: chacun sa merde*' (a loose translation of which is: Everyone should deal with their own shit).

Merkel quickly relented when it became clear that, with the collapse a few days later of Hypo Real Estate, she had her own steaming pile of ordure to take care of. With Germany now backing the idea, Europe announced a package of loan guarantees and bank recapitalizations six times as big as the fund Sarkozy had originally proposed.

Despite the common pot, there was to be no one-size-fits-all approach to bailouts – each country was told to sort out its own problems in its own way.

This episode set a template for the next eighteen months, the crucial phase of the crisis. The Lehman bankruptcy set off a chain reaction through the financial system in which banks refused to lend to each other and stopped providing credit to individuals and companies. The initial response from central banks was to cut interest rates in the hope that this would discourage saving and make it cheaper borrow. By Christmas 2008, the Federal Reserve had pegged US official interest rates at an all-time low of 0–0.25 per cent. The Bank of England had followed in the Fed's wake, reducing its bank rate from 5 per cent at the time of the Lehman bankruptcy to 2 per cent by the end of the year. This was as low as interest rates had been in the Bank's history, but further reductions followed in early 2009, taking UK borrowing costs to 0.5 per cent in March. The ECB also relaxed monetary policy, but much more slowly and over a much longer period. The ECB's benchmark interest rate was cut from 4.25 per cent to 2.5 per cent by the end of 2008 but it was not until May 2013 that they were cut to 0.5 per cent to match the UK. In the meantime, under Trichet the ECB had raised interest rates on the grounds that rising global oil prices posed a threat to inflation.

By late 2008, the Fed and the Bank of England had concluded that interest rates on their own would be insufficient to stave off a second Great Depression. Their next move was to dust off an idea that Keynes had championed in the 1930s: buying up bonds and exchanging them for cash. This initiative, known as quantitative easing, was designed to have two stimulative effects. Firstly, the central banks hoped that the new cash would find its way into circulation and thereby compensate for the shrinking of the money supply caused by the unwillingness or inability of banks to lend. Secondly, central banks only directly control official – or short-term – interest rates. The bond markets set long-term interest rates: higher bond prices are associated with lower interest rates and vice versa. Under the laws of economics, central bank action to buy bonds would limit supply, resulting in higher bond prices and lower interest rates.

Quantitative easing was not, however, to everybody's taste. Germany was instinctively wary of anything that smacked of printing money, and it didn't really matter that the presses on this occasion were electronic. In Berlin, the feeling was that QE meant countries could finance their deficits through the creation of increasingly worthless cash rather than by taking the tough decisions necessary to cure their structural economic problems. Central banks should resist the siren's lure of so-called 'unconventional monetary policy' because failure to do so would risk the return of an economic blight that the Germans thought they had banished for ever: hyperinflation. Trichet was also lukewarm about QE, insisting that the ECB would only consider starting a bond-buying programme once Eurozone member countries admitted they had been profligate and announced measures to reform their economies and cut their deficits.

There was a third way in which central banks could help revive economic growth: by providing incentives for commercial banks to start lending again. The Bank of England came to the conclusion by the summer of 2012 that even record-low interest rates and QE were not leading to an increase in lending because banks were hoarding the cash. The response was a scheme called Funding for Lending, under which commercial banks could borrow from the Bank of England at generously low rates provided the funds were recycled into loans to businesses or to home-buyers. This proved to be a pivotal moment for the UK: within six months the economy's growth rate had accelerated, albeit as a result of most of the additional funds fuelling house purchases rather than loans for business investment.

The US also found ways to encourage banks to resume lending. The Federal Reserve did not just buy Treasury bonds; by agreeing to buy up a range of loss-making asset-backed securities it helped clean up the balance sheets of the commercial banks. Risks of insolvency following the chastening experience of Lehman Brothers were removed by a willingness to use the federal budget to recapitalize banks, while the Federal Deposit Insurance Corporation did its part by closing down or restructuring banks.

It would be wrong to imagine that the ECB did nothing while all this was going on. It pumped funds into banks through its balances on TARGET2, the Eurozone's interbank cross-border payment system. This procedure ensured financial institutions did not run out of day-to-day cash but had the perverse effect of keeping alive a host of zombie banks.

TARGET2 was needed because banks in the core countries such as Germany and France had lent large sums to faster-growing countries in the periphery, such as Spain and Greece, in the years before the crisis. When the storm broke, the German and French banks demanded their money back, thus threatening a wave of bank failures. The solution was for central banks in the core countries to lend money to central banks on the troubled periphery of the Eurozone. The funds were then passed on to the troubled commercial banks in the periphery countries, which then completed the circle by repaying their debts to the German and French private banks. In one way, TARGET2 was a success, because it prevented a wave of defaults; what it didn't do was replicate the methods deployed in the UK and the US to channel funds to banks that were sound. As Yves Smith noted:

> Despite many criticisms, the expansion of the Target 2 balances in 2011–12 was appropriate because it prevented disorderly defaults and panic and, hence, maintained financial stability. But that balance sheet expansion provided no monetary stimulus and, importantly, it was only in part a liquidity operation. Because the expansion was not followed by aggressively closing down or restructuring banks – while inflicting losses on their creditors – the breathing space gained was misused to provide extended regulatory forbearance to weak and insolvent banks.[10]

Throughout the crisis, therefore, the ECB's response tended to be too little, too late. None of the major central banks covered themselves in glory in the years running up to the crisis; all of them were guilty of complacency and a failure to spot the threat posed by an out of control financial system. But once the long boom came to an end, there was a clear distinction between the Federal Reserve and the Bank of England, which showed a willingness to experiment and to dispense with ideas that were not working, and the ECB, which, by never acting until it was forced, ensured that it was always running to catch up.

The same criticism applies to the way in which the European Commission, the Council of Ministers and the ECB approached the need to help countries in difficulty. Much pain would have been avoided had help been provided to Greece rapidly in late 2009 or early 2010. The fact that it was not owed something to Europe's cumbersome political structure. In the US, action in a financial emergency can be taken with the agreement of three people: the president, the secretary of the Treasury and the chairman of the Federal Reserve Board. In the Eurozone, there tends to be a prolonged round of horse-trading between nineteen member states before anything happens, leading to indecision and a tendency to look for a solution that 'kicks the can down the road'.

This, though, is far from the whole story. The real failure of the Eurozone during its existential crisis was not institutional but ideological. There was an assumption that member states had found themselves in trouble through the profligacy of their governments when, with the exception of Greece, the problems were caused by an excess of private borrowing. There was an insistence, courtesy of Alesina and Ardagna, on pre-Keynesian fiscal policies that turned the clock back to the early 1930s. Since the Great Depression, it had been accepted in most finance ministries that in a recession there would be a drop in tax revenues as a result of lower profits, fewer people working and weaker consumer spending, and a rise in spending as unemployment pay and other welfare benefits increased. Budget deficits would rise in the short term, but seeking to prevent this happening through tax increases or spending cuts would suck still more demand out of the economy, making the recession worse and so putting additional pressure on the public finances. The one part of the world that had difficulty grasping this fairly simple concept was the Eurozone, which decided that in exchange for its bailout, Greece should aggressively tighten fiscal policy. Six years later, Greece has had two more bailouts and its national debt as a share of GDP has risen from 115 per cent in 2009 to 200 per cent. As blunders go, this might be considered the economic equivalent of the Charge of the Light Brigade, except that Lord Raglan did not need a second or third attack on the Russian guns to work out that the plan was suicidal.

Feeling the heat

The mess that confronted Monti and Draghi when they took up their new jobs in the autumn of 2011 can be illustrated by the increasingly gloomy tone of the IMF in the Washington organization's half-yearly *World Economic Outlook* (WEO). In April 2011, the month in which Trichet decided to take pre-emptive action against inflation, the IMF was predicting solid growth in the Eurozone of 1.6 per cent and expressed guarded confidence that the worst might be over. Italy was expected to grow by 1.1 per cent in 2011 and by 1.3 per cent in 2012, in both cases half a percentage point below that of the Eurozone. By September, the IMF was growing a little concerned. As its economic counsellor Olivier Blanchard noted:

> Markets have clearly become more sceptical about the ability of many countries to stabilise their public debt. For some time, their worries were mostly limited to a few small countries on the periphery of Europe. As time has passed, and as growth prospects have dimmed, their worries have extended to more European countries and to countries beyond Europe – from Japan to the United States. Worries about sovereigns have translated into worries about the banks holding these sovereign bonds, mainly in Europe. These worries have led to a partial freeze of financial flows, with banks keeping high levels of liquidity and tightening lending. Fear of the unknown is high. Stock prices have fallen.[11]

This was a tactful way of saying that the Eurozone authorities had managed to do the opposite of what Franklin Roosevelt achieved when he became US president in the depths of the Great Depression. FDR's great success was to tell Americans that they had nothing to fear but fear itself and to back up his words with action. The Eurozone authorities had turned what could have been a localized problem into a systemic crisis, creating fear where there had previously been none. By the time of its April 2012 *World Economic Outlook*, the message from the Fund was even more alarmist, with Blanchard leading off by recognizing that, 'Soon after the September 2011 *World Economic Outlook* went to press, the euro area went through another acute crisis.'[12] Growth in the Eurozone in 2011 was now put at 1.4 per cent rather than 1.6 per cent, with the economy now expected to contract by 0.3 per cent in 2012. For Italy, which had been forced to accept a €70 billion austerity package as the price of receiving help from the ECB, the news was even grimmer. Growth of 0.4 per cent in 2011 was to be followed by a 1.9 per cent drop in GDP in 2012. The IMF made the correct but otiose observation that 'fiscal policy will weigh increasingly heavily on activity' in the Eurozone.

A similar view was taken by Standard & Poor's, which in January 2012 warned as it cut the credit rating of nine Eurozone countries, including France, Italy and Spain, that fiscal austerity alone 'risks becoming self-defeating'. The ratings agency showed none of the IMF's discretion as it took European policymakers to task for failing to take sufficient action to address fully the systemic stresses in the Eurozone. These stresses included a credit crunch, an increase in the interest rates an increasing number of Eurozone countries had to pay in the bond markets, a simultaneous attempt by both governments and consumers to tighten their belts, weakening growth prospects and, finally, 'an open and prolonged dispute among European policymakers over the proper approach to address challenges'.[13] In a commendable show of Gallic sangfroid, France's finance minister François Baroin said it was not good news but not a 'catastrophe' either, presumably because the list of S&P's concerns did not include the re-emergence in Europe of the bubonic plague.

By this point, alarm bells were starting to clang in the minds of those on the left who had previously been strong supporters of the single currency. They had been happy to accept the view of Sarkozy and Merkel that the crisis involved the hated Anglo-Saxons getting their comeuppance, but it was a bit of a worry that the US had recovered the ground lost in the recession of 2008–09 and had falling unemployment while the Eurozone was in the middle of a double-dip recession and had an unemployment rate in excess of 10 per cent. Nor was it especially comforting that the European Commission and the ECB seemed to be pursuing economic policies that had always been anathema to those who considered themselves progressive: wage cuts, pension reductions, and making it easier for workers to be fired. Had they not known in their heart of hearts that monetary union was a glorious left-wing project, these progressives might have wondered whether European policymakers were repeatedly allowing the Eurozone economy to teeter towards the edge of the precipice so that they could force through unpopular reforms on benighted governments. This, of course, was precisely what was happening. Mark Weisbrot notes that countries were left with no choice but to enact reforms that their voters would never have backed: 'Such "reforms" as raising the retirement age (in Italy, Greece, and Spain) or making it easier for employers to fire workers (in Spain and Italy) are among the numerous examples of the European authorities taking advantage of the situation to partially dismantle or remake the welfare state and economic structure in the borrowing countries that are more to their liking, and more neo-liberal.'[14] In other words, there was method in the madness.

Draghi, despite his subsequent reputation for saving the euro from collapse, played his part in this dangerous game of chicken. In his honeymoon period after becoming ECB president, he wisely reversed Trichet's interest-rate increases and said the need to take out insurance against deflation as well as inflation would justify an intensification of 'support for the European economy'. There were, inevitably, strings attached: the quid pro quo was that political leaders took 'more radical steps to enforce spending discipline among members'.

Help for Eurozone banks came in the form of long-term refinancing operations (LTROs), which injected emergency liquidity – or working capital – into banks that were running short of cash. But for all his deftness, Draghi was still mopping up after the last crisis and, once again, the ECB was left playing catch-up. The financial markets looked at the Eurozone and saw weak growth, high unemployment, pro-cyclical fiscal policies that threatened to make growth and unemployment worse, and a central bank that, unlike the Federal Reserve and the Bank of England, was unwilling to act as a lender of last resort. They saw LTROs, channelling money to banks in the hope that they would buy sovereign bonds, as a very poor substitute to the ECB doing the job itself. Unsurprisingly, the mood soured during the first half of 2012, and the situation was acute in Draghi's own country, where the positive response to the replacement of Berlusconi by Monti was short-lived. By July 2012, Italy had to pay investors more than 7 per cent to buy bonds with a ten-year maturity, a crippling expense for a country where the debt-to-GDP ratio was nudging 100 per cent. Spain's bond yields were even higher, but Italy – larger, and with a stronger anti-euro political movement – was the real concern.

Three little words

On 26 July 2012, Draghi arrived for an investment conference held amid the splendour of Lancaster House in London. Sir Mervyn King, the governor of the Bank of England, was also among the speakers, but it was Draghi who made the headlines.

There was little indication of what was to come when the president of the ECB began his talk with a somewhat whimsical comparison of the euro to a bumblebee. It was a mystery of nature, Draghi said, that the bumblebee flew, but it did. He went on to say that the euro was 'much, much stronger' than people acknowledged and – warming to his own rhetoric – asserted that great strides had been made in the past six months. It took some time for Draghi to reach the point, but when he did, three words would suffice.

When people talk about the fragility of the euro and the increasing fragility of the euro, and perhaps the crisis of the euro, very often non-euro area member states or leaders, under-estimate the amount of political capital that is being invested in the euro. And so we view this, and I do not think we are unbi-ased observers, we think the euro is irreversible. And it's not an empty word now, because I preceded saying exactly what actions have been made, are being made to make it irreversible.

But there is another message I want to tell you. Within our mandate, the ECB is ready to do whatever it takes to preserve the euro. And believe me, it will be enough.[15]

Financial markets got the message. 'Whatever it takes' meant the ECB was going to act like a regular central bank with a lender-of-last-resort facility. It was going to wade into the markets with its inexhaustible firepower and blow away the speculators in the way that Clint Eastwood dispatched the armed robber in *Dirty Harry*. It was a couple of weeks before Draghi announced how he would deploy the ECB's equivalent of a .44 Magnum – Outright Monetary Transactions – but it didn't matter. Italian and Spanish bond yields started to fall as soon as the three words were uttered, and they carried on falling. And, like Dirty Harry, Draghi never needed to fire his gun. The threat that the ECB would act was quite sufficient.

Before assessing the success of 'whatever it takes', it is worth asking why the ECB finally stirred itself into acting as a lender of last resort in the summer of 2012. In part, it was because Europe was under pressure from the Obama administration to sort itself out. In part, it was because of the changing political dynamic of the Eurozone: François Hollande had just been elected French presi-dent on an anti-austerity ticket. In part, it was because technocrats such as Monti in Italy had to be rewarded for their willingness to reform. These, though, were of relatively minor importance. What really made a difference was that Draghi was able to isolate German opposition to Outright Monetary Transactions, arguing that the parlous state of Italy meant the euro itself was in danger. Jens Weidmann, the president of the Bundesbank, put up a rearguard action, choosing an appropriate metaphor, Goethe's *Faust*, to make his point. In the tragedy, Mephistopheles persuades the Holy

Roman Emperor to solve his economic woes by printing paper money backed not by bullion but by gold yet to be mined. The emperor finds the need to return again and again to the printing press and runaway inflation results.

Draghi was not soft on inflation; nor had he suddenly decided that it was wrong-headed to force structural adjustment programmes on countries in need of financial help. It was, however, clear to him when he made his Lancaster House speech that the costs of continuing to put the frighteners on Italy and Spain vastly outweighed the potential benefits.

So was 'whatever it takes' a success? In one way, certainly, because at a stroke Draghi removed the threat that the monetary union would break up as a result of financial pressure. All central bank governors know they can change sentiment with the right word or phrase, but Draghi is a cut above the rest when it comes to manipulating the markets.

Yet, seen in the round, it was merely a partial success, another example of a stopgap solution to a chronic problem. Put simply, what had been a financial crisis in the years running up to July 2012 became an economic and, eventually, a political crisis. 'Whatever it takes' did not, as we shall show, lead to markedly stronger growth in the Eurozone, and there was a slide towards deflation, despite repeated warnings from the ECB that there was no threat of a period of falling prices. Economic stagnation begat political unrest in the form of support for parties of both left and right: Podemos in Spain, the True Finns in Finland, Syriza in Greece, the Front National in France.

As for Italy today, the good news is that the economy has started to grow again. The bad news is that GDP is almost 10 per cent lower than it was before the start of the financial crisis, unemployment has doubled to more than 12 per cent, and debt as a share of national income has risen to more than 130 per cent. Italian banks, many of which are small and undercapitalized, are vulnerable to new European rules that require private investors to take a share of the losses in the event of a failure. Italy is a classic example of a country that should never have surrendered the freedom to devalue its currency, and now finds itself being pressured into reforms that would be difficult even if the economy were growing, but are impossible with growth continuing to disappoint.

This was not quite what was envisaged back in 1999. Italy has got rid of Berlusconi and remained in the euro but it has not flourished since giving up the lira. It would perhaps share the shock expressed by the crook Charlie Croker in the film that gives this chapter its name when his explosives expert blows up a van: 'You were only supposed to blow the bloody doors off!'

The result of blowing off more than the doors has been Beppe Grillo's making. Grillo is a stand-up comedian who founded the Five Star Movement, which espouses an iconoclastic blend of euro-scepticism, anti-austerity, anti-immigration and neoliberal populism. This is proving more attractive than the approach favoured by the traditional left: subservience to the right-wing doctrines promulgated by the ECB and the European Commission. Grillo has repeatedly said that there will come a time when a politician will 'hold up a copy of the EMU treaty, declare it null and void, and the debt null and void right along with it. That politician will be elected.'

As we show in our penultimate chapter, those responsible for monetary union are aware of the threat and have taken increasingly desperate measures to revive the Eurozone economy. Why? Because they can see the barbarians massing at the gates.

CHAPTER 9

KICKING THE CAN

The Eurozone's never-ending crisis

*'My dear young friend,' said Mr Micawber ... 'At present, and
until something turns up (which I am, I may say, hourly
expecting), I have nothing to bestow but advice.'*

Charles Dickens, *David Copperfield*

Ditchley Park is a country estate nestled in the English Cotswolds.
Opened in 1720, the year of the South Sea Bubble crisis, it was used
on occasion by Winston Churchill during the Second World War
when the prime minister's residence, Chequers, was considered too
dangerous due of the threat of aerial attack.

In recent years, Ditchley has become the setting for high-
powered conferences that bring together politicians, civil servants,
academics and journalists to mull over hot topics in their field of
expertise. The British have a phrase for these sort of events: a gathering of 'the great and the good'. One such conclave was held over
two days in early November 2015, organized by the Centre for
European Reform, a think tank that sees itself as being pro-
European but not uncritically so. There were fifty participants,
including a brace of former European commissioners, the chief
economist at the German finance ministry, the IMF official responsible for Greece's structural adjustment programme, and two
former deputy governors of the Bank of England. Some of those in

attendance, such as Ed Balls, the former Labour shadow chancellor, and the LSE academic Paul De Grauwe have already featured in this book. At the end of a traumatic year for Europe, the theme of the conference was: Has the euro been a failure?

The choice of title for the conference was itself telling, given that the CER had been in favour of Britain joining the single currency when the debate was raging in the years from 1997 to 2003. For many years after the launch of monetary union, it was an article of faith in polite Ditchley-type circles that the single currency had been a notable achievement, with any problems put down to teething troubles that would be resolved after an inevitable bedding-down period. Not even the onset of the deepest and longest recession since the 1930s could dent this rosy view of the euro, hailed as a 'remarkable success' by Jean-Claude Trichet when he stepped down as president of the ECB in 2011.

Ditchley events are run on a Chatham House basis, which means that there is a record kept of what has been said, but not who said it. Anonymity is considered vital so that participants can speak candidly, as they appear to have done on this occasion. Had Trichet been on the guest list for Ditchley, he might have brought with him some of his breezy optimism. As it was, the official account of the conference showed that it was a sombre affair. 'There was broad consensus that the euro had been a disappointment,' it records:

> the currency union's economic performance was very poor, and rather than bringing EU member-states together and fostering a closer sense of unity and common identity, the euro had divided countries and eroded confidence in the EU. While only a few participants thought it possible or advisable to dismantle the eurozone, there was broad pessimism over the ability of the eurozone political elite to sell the needed integrationist steps to their increasingly disillusioned electorates.[1]

This summary is interesting on a number of levels: for its candour; for its recognition that the euro has been corrosive of European unity rather than a glue binding countries together; for the acceptance that a gulf had opened up between the 'political elite' and their 'increasingly disillusioned electorates'; but most especially for the recognition that a break-up of the single currency was no longer unthinkable but rather a possibility that had to be taken into account. Two of the five sessions were devoted to the economic and political consequences of dismantling monetary union. To return to the first chapter of this book, it was finally recognized that the euro might, after all, be similar to New Coke, and there was discussion about how it might be taken off the shelves.

All things considered, it is unsurprising that a possible euro break-up was now being contemplated. It is not just that Greece came within a whisker of becoming the first country to leave (or being asked to leave) the single currency. Rather, it is that the relentlessly poor performance of the Eurozone has become so obvious that it can no longer be ignored, even by those who would consider themselves ardent supporters of the European Union.

As one of the Ditchley panellists noted, the Eurozone economy was barely any bigger in 2015 than it had been when the so-called Great Recession started in 2008. The contrast with countries such as the United States and the UK, which were not in the euro, was marked. Unemployment averaged 11 per cent in the nineteen countries using the single currency, which was double the rate for those EU countries that retained control over their own interest rates and exchange rates, and four or five times as high in countries such as Spain and Greece.

What's more, this participant continued, there had been a faulty analysis both of what had gone wrong in the Eurozone and what was needed to restore growth. The gap between the Eurozone and other better performing countries could not be explained by 'supply-side deficiencies' but was the result of a classic example of boom turning to bust. Excessive demand in the upswing of the early 2000s had turned into a dearth of demand in the downswing that began in 2007. Cutting wages, reducing the value of pensions and shrinking the size of welfare states – the sort of supply-side remedies favoured by the Eurozone – had led to even weaker demand. Eurozone policymakers had administered the wrong medicine.

Equally unsurprisingly, there was still little appetite for breaking up the euro. This reflects the unwillingness to accept – even in the face of the available evidence – that monetary union has been an experiment that has gone disastrously wrong; the desire not to squander the political capital that has been invested in the euro project, and valid concerns that dismantling would involve serious costs. Since the crisis, the dominant (German) view has been that the problems of the Eurozone had all been caused by economic mismanagement, industrial incompetence and an unwillingness to face up to the need for reform, rather than a lack of macroeconomic freedom. Put simply, there is nothing inherently wrong with monetary union, and a break-up would be a case of throwing the baby out with the bathwater, causing 'devastating financial dislocation' without addressing the real issues.

The German argument was well aired at Ditchley. It did not, however, go unchallenged, with the view expressed that there would be financial instability if the Eurozone continued to struggle, because weak growth and low inflation would lead to debt write-downs. To be sure, a break-up would be messy but so would be a continuation of the status quo. The fact that some countries were uncompetitive and could not respond by depreciating or devaluing their currencies was a fundamental problem that could not be ignored. Ultimately, there was a limit to how much pain citizens would take.

Broadly speaking this was the dilemma faced by the Greek government in the summer of 2015: was it worth a chaotic period in which an already severe recession would initially get worse, in order to regain control over the big levers of economic policy? The Greeks, in some degree thanks to their failure to make any of the necessary preparations, decided to accept more austerity as the price of staying inside the Eurozone and receiving a third package of financial assistance. The Ditchley discussions suggest, however, that there may be a different answer on the next occasion.

Some participants said the cost of divorce was too high, and that this left policymakers with no choice but to come up with a way of making monetary union work. Others disagreed, with one saying that the euro was poisoning support for integration, and pointing to the way in which Britain was drifting away from other member states as an example of Europe's growing divisions. Another said that attempts to remedy the structural flaws of individual economies were being 'swamped' by economic failure, and efforts to make countries more competitive through wage cuts were proving politically harmful. 'The social capital built up since 1945 was being frittered away, and support for anti-euro parties would rise. Although many market participants had learned that betting against Eurozone leaders could be costly, eurosceptic politicians were doing well, and they would not have the same commitment to the single currency if they came to power.'

Neither of the authors of this book was present for these well-argued and civilized discussions, although it should now be clear which side of the argument we would have supported. The rest of this chapter looks at monetary union through the prism of Ditchley's 'great and good'. Has the euro been a failure? Is it possible to make the euro a success? What would a break-up look like? Would the benefits outweigh the costs? The starting point is the performance of the Eurozone economy.

Going nowhere fast: Repeated stalling in the single-currency bloc

The summer of 2012 represented a new low for the Eurozone. Times had been tough before, most noticeably during the recession of 2008–09. But in the months that followed the collapse of Lehman Brothers the whole of the global economy was struggling, so the euro's deeper-seated woes were disguised by a collective failure. Yet, by 2012, the US had regained all its lost ground and the emerging markets were booming, while the Eurozone was vying with Japan for the unwanted title of the no-growth capital of the world.

American policymakers made no secret of their frustration at the Eurozone's failure to deal decisively with the sovereign debt crisis that had started in Greece but was now threatening Italy and Spain. The message coming out of Washington, from Barack

Obama, his White House staff, and the US Treasury, was simple: Europe was so big that its problems were acting as a brake on the entire global economy. American policymakers were incredulous that their counterparts in Europe had allowed the budgetary laxity of Greece – a country that accounted for less than one-fiftieth of the EU's gross domestic product and which had a population only slightly bigger than that of Los Angeles – to contaminate the entire Eurozone. Nor could they understand why the European Commission, the ECB and Germany were so wedded to the idea of austerity, since to American eyes austerity was counterproductive at a time when the Eurozone was struggling to grow. The results spoke for themselves.

If the US authorities thought they could shame or cajole the Europeans into an economic U-turn, they were mistaken. The Eurozone's economic performance improved after 2012, but only modestly. There was still austerity, just a bit less of it. There was more action from the ECB, but that was only enough to raise growth from the abject to the poor.

The Eurozone crisis did not disappear. Cyprus was an obvious candidate for trouble. It had joined the euro for political reasons rather than because it was economically ready: like Iceland, its banks were many times bigger than its gross domestic product; it had a communist government that made promises to voters it could not really afford; and it was exposed heavily to neighbouring Greece. The bailout of Cyprus in 2013 followed a familiar pattern: an austerity programme in return for financial support, although with two new twists. For the first time, a country was forced by the ECB to make those with bank deposits of more than €100,000 pay for part of the package; and controls were imposed to halt the flight of capital out of the country. This proved to be a case of shutting the stable door after the horse had bolted.

But Cyprus was one of the Eurozone's minnows, and it was assumed in policy circles that it represented merely a coda to the problems in Greece, which had now been resolved. That proved to be as false an assumption as the idea that Europe had rediscovered its lost growth mojo.

In Germany, 2015 was considered something of a vintage year because the economy expanded by 1.7 per cent – one-third of the rate managed year after year by West Germany during the period from 1950 to 1973 known as the *Wirtschaftswunder* ('economic miracle'). Similarly, France's 1.2 per cent growth fell a long way short of the 4–5 per cent increases on average seen during *Les Trente Glorieuses* ('the glorious thirty') from 1945 to 1975. Throughout 2013 and 2014, the Eurozone edged closer and closer to deflation even though the double-dip recession came to an end. Growth of 1.5 per cent in 2015 was sufficient to reduce unemployment but not rapid enough to bring the jobless rate back into single figures. Nor could recovery from 2012's double-dip recession prevent the Eurozone from sliding ever closer to deflation during 2013 and 2014.

Moreover, the growth of the Eurozone was entirely the result of exports to the rest of the world, which in turn required the two big engines of global growth to remain healthy. Between the first half of 2011 and the first half of 2015, the Eurozone economy expanded by 1 per cent – or 0.25 per cent a year on average. Had exports not been rising more quickly than imports, the Eurozone economy would have contracted by 1.3 per cent over the same period, so had it not been for external demand there would have been no recovery at all.

Mario Draghi's task as president of the European Central Bank was complicated by three factors. The first was that the ECB's policy had been too restrictive for too long, and this had allowed long-term unemployment to become engrained and deflationary pressures to build. The second was that every one of his attempts to make ECB policy more stimulative were fought tooth and nail by Germany. Finally, Draghi could only overcome German opposition by agreeing to water down his proposals, which made them less effective.

As a result, it was not until January 2015 – six years later than the US Federal Reserve and the Bank of England – that the ECB announced its own quantitative easing programme, under which the bank agreed to buy bonds in the hope that it would drive down both the level of long-term interest rates and the value of the euro. The move was eventually deemed necessary because by then even Jens Weidmann, the president of the Bundesbank, had to admit that inflation – running at -0.6 per cent – was too low for comfort. In part, the fall in the cost of living had been caused by a collapse in oil prices in the second half of 2014, but so-called core inflation, which does not include fuel and food prices, was also on a downward trend and stood at 0.6 per cent.

Draghi had been preparing the ground for quantitative easing during the course of 2014, first by imposing negative interest rates on commercial banks, and then by admitting that the ECB was 'behind the curve' at a time when debt deflation was happening on the Eurozone's periphery. When the announcement was made in January 2015, it sounded big. The ECB would buy €60 billion of public- and private-sector bonds a month for seventeen months, or a total of €1.1 trillion in all. Critics warned that the bond-buying programme was smaller than that of the Fed or the Bank of England once the respective size of the economies was taken into account, and would have only limited impact on bond yields because they were already very low. As it turned out, the critics were right. There was a small pick-up in growth during 2015, but this was largely caused by the drop in oil prices, since cheaper crude increased the spending power of consumers and reduced the transport and energy costs of business. The main impact of QE in the Eurozone occurred before the programme was announced, but in anticipation of it happening. This was felt through a drop in the exchange rate of the euro, and this provided a boost for countries such as Italy, where there had been a loss of competitiveness since the launch of the single currency.

The effect, however, was only short-lived. The euro rose during the course of 2015 as other countries – most notably Japan – increased the size of their QE programmes, and an expected increase in US interest rates was delayed, putting downward pressure on the dollar. With weaker performance in China and other emerging markets affecting exports, the Eurozone growth rate peaked in the second quarter of 2015 at 0.5 per cent and had tailed off to 0.3 per cent by the end of the year. In early 2016, Draghi signalled that there was a need for further action from the ECB, and when this was announced in March it took the form of a further cut in already negative interest rates and an expansion of both the monthly pace of QE and the types of assets that could be bought.

From the perspective of the Organisation for Economic Co-operation and Development, not much had changed. The OECD, which has thirty-four rich-country members, produces quarterly updates on the state of the world economy and in February 2016 expressed its concern at the absence of a sustained recovery from the recession of 2008–09. It said the sluggishness of the recovery in the Eurozone was still an important factor dragging on the global economy and left the monetary union vulnerable to another worldwide shock. This was despite QE, the beneficial impact of a falling euro on exports, and the drop in commodity prices. The OECD did not pull any punches, stressing that its central concern was of the single-currency area getting stuck in a spiral of low growth and low inflation, with the lack of confidence that things might eventually improve choking off investment, inno-vation and the reallocation of resources into new products and enterprises that might lead to stronger productivity, higher living standards and more jobs. It was also worried that low growth would have a feedback effect on financial institutions, noting that the first few weeks of 2016 had seen sharp declines in equity and bond prices for European banks, with share prices trading at levels close to those seen during the crisis of 2009.[2]

From the outside looking in: Britain's splendid isolation

The day the OECD published its critique of the Eurozone, David Cameron was in Brussels negotiating the terms under which he would agree to support Britain's continued membership of the European Union. One of the assurances sought by the prime minister was that the interests of countries that had no intention of ever joining the single currency should be protected as the members of Eurozone forged closer ties. Despite the warnings of many on the centre-left that Britain would be banishing itself to the economic equivalent of the Gobi Desert if it failed to join the single currency, this part of Cameron's negotiating stance proved entirely uncontroversial at home.

Those who supported Britain's EU membership said the prime minister had achieved the best of all possible outcomes: outside the single currency, inside the single market. Retaining sterling was seen as a masterstroke rather than a strategic blunder by the Yes camp, which had to admit that monetary union had, all things considered, been a bit of a disaster. Leaving the EU itself was the real danger, they warned. Undaunted by their earlier Gobi Desert warnings, the Yes camp again insisted that Britain would need a Lonely Planet guide to the Central Asian steppes if it voted to leave.

Charles Grant, the director of the Centre for European Reform, and John Springford, a senior research fellow at the think tank, wrote a piece analysing what the prime minister had secured in his negotiations, concluding that Britain was better off remaining where it was – inside the EU but definitely not part of monetary union.[3] Writing in the *Observer* over the same weekend, the Irish journalist Fintan O'Toole said Britain should stick with the EU despite the 'grandiosity' that had 'led to the woefully misdesigned euro project, with its blind faith that the mere creation of a single currency as an act of will would sweep aside all doubts about whether there was actually such a thing as a European economy.'[4]

Pride of place, though, went to Peter Mandelson, who in 2003 was cheerleader-in-chief for the 'if Britain doesn't join the single currency it will be find itself so deep in the tundra it will take a latter-day Marco Polo to find it' camp. Four days after Cameron came back from Brussels claiming triumph, Mandelson wrote in the *Guardian*: 'The deal gives full protection to our economy from the operation of Europe's single currency. Nobody is suggesting that we should join this currency, and our businesses should not suffer as a result.'[5]

This was progress, of a sort, even though it was vaguely reminiscent of the way in which Stalin had Trotsky removed from Lenin's side in the photographs taken during the Russian Revolution. Still,

better late than never. It had taken seventeen years, the biggest
boom–bust Western Europe had seen since the early 1920s, a
30 per cent contraction in the Greek economy, and the near break-
up of monetary union, but the question that should have been
asked during the drafting of the Maastricht Treaty was at last being
posed: did the economics of the single currency stack up?

Incurable optimalists: A lesson from the single currency's godfather

Economists have their own way of describing whether the
economics of the single currency will prove workable: it is called
optimum currency area theory. As with a lot of economics, this
sounds a lot more complicated than it is. There are both benefits
and costs if a country gives up the right to issue its own currency
and joins a union with other nations: if the benefits outweigh the
costs it is an optimum currency area; if the costs outweigh the
benefits, it isn't.

The benefits of a monetary union include the lower transaction
costs that arise because individuals and businesses no longer have
to change money from one currency into another when they cross
borders; the elimination of the risk that the exchange rate will move
suddenly up or down; enhanced transparency through the ability
to compare more easily the prices in different countries because
they are using the same currency; and lower prices as a result of this
greater transparency. As far as the architects of the euro were
concerned, monetary union would be the lubricant that would
make the European single market work better. The costs of a monetary union are that countries lose the freedom to decide their own
fate, and losing that flexibility can have serious consequences when
times get tough, as they did in the Eurozone from 2008 onwards.

Optimum currency area theory first surfaced in a paper by
Canadian economist Robert Mundell, published in 1961, just four
years after the signing of the Treaty of Rome. Mundell won a Nobel
Prize for his work, was a supporter of monetary union, and is
sometimes called 'the godfather of the euro', but some economists

believe his seminal paper, 'A Theory of Optimum Currency Areas',[6] paradoxically explains why the single currency was a bad idea.

Mundell said that a common currency made sense for a group of countries that all behaved in the same way at all times. It would work provided, say, all nineteen members of the single currency were growing at the same steady pace or even if they were all in a boom or a slump. In reality, this sort of world is confined to economics textbooks, and even countries that have been currency unions for prolonged periods – the UK and the US – are subject to what economists call asymmetric shocks, changes in fortune that affect only one part of the monetary union. An example of an asymmetric shock in the UK was the collapse of manufacturing industry in the early 1990s, which had a particularly marked effect on the northern regions of England, and on Wales, Scotland and Northern Ireland. In the US, some states, such as Florida and Nevada, were hit especially hard by the subprime mortgage crisis.

Currency unions needed to have strategies to cope with asymmetric shocks, according to Mundell. He suggested that it should be possible to move the factors of production from depressed parts of the union to those that were faring better. Of the three factors of production, land is immovable and there are few curbs on the movement of capital, so Mundell was really focusing on the ability of workers to escape unemployment by finding a job somewhere else. In the case of the UK in the early 1980s, it was possible for those who lost their jobs in steel mills and in car plants to move to the south-east of England where companies were hiring. This happened, but only to a limited extent. There was a brain drain from the depressed regions, where employment rates remained low.

Later economists built on Mundell's theory. Peter Kenen said what really mattered if a currency union was going to work was not labour-market mobility but a common budget big enough to transfer money from rich to poor regions. In the US, states that were especially hard-hit by the sub prime crisis were helped by the central government in Washington. States such as Florida and Nevada paid less into the federal budget because one effect of the property crash was a sharp decline in tax revenues, but at the same time received more in the form of higher welfare payments.

From the outset, there were economists who warned that the euro lacked both a single language that would increase labour mobility and a mechanism for transferring resources. Barry Eichengreen, for example, wrote a paper in 1991 in which he concluded that Europe was more vulnerable to shocks and less capable of dealing with them than the US.[7] America has a single language and a federal budget that has at its disposal 25 per cent of US GDP. The European Union has no single language and a budget worth 1 per cent of EU GDP.

Up until recently, European policymakers were adamant that these discrepancies did not really matter. They convinced themselves that there would be no asymmetric shocks because the existence of the euro, buttressed by the Stability and Growth Pact, would keep every member country on the same virtuous path. Moreover, if problems arose, countries would adjust by making their economies more competitive. This has always seemed the triumph of hope over experience, and so it has proved.

The Eurozone has not been immune to asymmetric shocks. Indeed, the adoption of a one-size-fits-all interest rate that was too low for some countries and too high for others made an asymmetric shock inevitable. Countries on the periphery boomed and then went bust. Before the creation of the euro, the arrival of a recession in Spain or Greece would have led to a sizeable fall in the peseta or drachma, making exports cheaper and having a positive effect on the tourism sectors of the two Mediterranean countries. Inside monetary union, Spain and Greece found that they could not devalue and nor could they expect any budgetary support from other members of the Eurozone. That left only one way to regain competitiveness. Workers in the troubled countries of monetary union have found to their cost the real meaning of labour-market 'flexibility'. Mass unemployment and wage cuts have been the price paid for the loss of exchange-rate flexibility. Belatedly, European policymakers have accepted that the Eurozone is not an optimum currency area and that this is a problem.

Nobody should be surprised by the response. The single currency had been created through an act of will. Another act of will would turn the Eurozone into an optimum currency area.

Economic blueprints and political barriers:
The search for solutions

The mood in Brussels and in the individual Eurozone countries has changed since the financial crisis. Ten days after the collapse of Lehman Brothers in September 2008, Germany's finance minister Peer Steinbrück told his country's parliament: 'The US will lose its status as the superpower of the world's financial system.' No European policymaker, not even one from Germany, would dare say such a thing today. Nor is there likely to be an updated edition of the 2009 paper by Lars Jonung and Eoin Drea mocking US economists for daring to question whether the Eurozone was an optimum currency area. Comedy and economics are not natural bedfellows, but re-reading the thirty-four pages of 'The Euro: It Can't Happen. It's a Bad Idea. It Won't Last: US Economists on the EMU, 1989–2002' is a bit like unearthing a lost script by the Marx Brothers.

The extent to which thinking had changed was underlined by the so-called Five Presidents' Report released in June 2015, just as the Greek crisis was coming to a climax. Defects in monetary union had to be addressed, the five presidents said. Members of the single currency would have to take steps, both individually and collectively, to compensate for the loss of the 'national adjustment tools' ceded on entry. What's more, the report said, individual countries 'must be able to absorb shocks internally through having suitably resilient economies and sufficient fiscal buffers over the economic cycle':

> This is because, with monetary policy set uniformly for the whole euro area, national fiscal policies are vital to stabilise the economy whenever a local shock occurs. And with all countries sharing a single exchange rate, they need flexible economies

that can react quickly to downturns. Otherwise they risk that recessions leave deep and permanent scars.[8]

This is optimum currency area theory writ large. A monetary union involves costs as well as benefits, and these costs will be high if economies are not harmonized but are instead subject to problems that affect some but not all of them. Unless there is a way of coping with these shocks, there will be deep and enduring pain.

The Five Presidents' Report provides a road map not just for the completing of monetary union but for the original goal of ever closer union set by the founding fathers back in the 1950s. It recognizes that this can happen only in stages, with economic harmonization tackled first and the tougher issues, such as a common Eurozone budget, left until later. The process would be crowned by political union.

Just as monetary union was a classic example of Enlightenment thinking, so too was the Five Presidents' Report. They identified a problem; they worked out what the remedy should be; and they explained how and when the cure would be administered. Rousseau, Voltaire or Montesquieu could not have done a better job. An ambitious target was set: the Eurozone would get its new Social Contract in three stages within ten years.

As it happens, the Five Presidents' Report was not quite what it was cracked up to be. In part, that was because it identified the wrong problems and so came up with the wrong remedies, but Jean-Claude Juncker, Mario Draghi, Martin Schulz, Donald Tusk and Jeroem Dijsselbloem also skated over the difficulties of turning the blueprint into action. Europe's political gridlock meant that even the perfect plan – which this was not – would have run into opposition, and this was well illustrated by a report on the future of Europe published by the Swiss bank UBS in January 2016. The UBS authors agree that monetary union is a half-finished project and therefore inherently unstable; they accept the argument made by Mr Juncker and his colleagues that the answer is 'more Europe, not less'; and argue that more Europe means a proper plan rather than a 'patchwork of fixes'.[9]

But the UBS report then details what it would actually take to complete monetary union, at which point it becomes obvious why the Eurozone will, for the time being at least, continue to rely on a patchwork of fixes. After all that has happened since the first bailout of Greece in 2010, no European policymaker would relish the prospect of negotiating a new treaty, since that would require the backing of voters in referenda in some member states, including France. But as the UBS report notes, a new treaty would be needed to address contentious issues such as 'more sovereignty sharing through a central treasury and fiscal ministry, debt mutualization, provisions for government default among members, more authority for the European Parliament and increased power for the high representative for foreign affairs.'

As to when this will all happen, UBS admits that the timing could be tricky in the current circumstances, but envisages the day when Jean Monnet's notion that European Union will be forged as a result of crisis will again come up trumps. 'Until another defining moment triggers another shift in mindset, the EU will probably continue to take arduous piecemeal steps towards greater integration under its current inadequate treaties.'

Many things were considered good ideas in the 1950s and 1960s, including building high-rise flats and encircling city centres with dual carriageways. Not all of them have stood the test of time, and the same goes for Monnet's theory of crises. In 2015, Europe faced the possibility that Greece might leave the Eurozone and the potential break-up of free movement under the passport-free Schengen Agreement. Both were seen as existential threats rather than opportunities to press ahead with Monnet's ever closer union. The risk that Schengen might break down under the weight of mass migration was, if anything, the bigger threat.

As with monetary union, Europe's policymakers discovered that Schengen was a building without a roof. Just as capital could move freely from one part of the Eurozone to another, causing economic and financial instability, so criminal gangs and terrorists could move from one jurisdiction to another, minimizing the chances of being caught. Just as there was no common fiscal policy to moderate the impact of economic shocks, so there was no joint body to police Europe's borders.

In both cases, European policymakers had three options: they could agree collectively to the urgent steps necessary to complete the job; they could decide that their plans lay in ruins and accept the need to try an alternative; or they could muddle through with the current flawed structures in the hope that something would turn up. Greece was a classic case of muddling through and it came at a time when Draghi was using his influence at the ECB to make the central bank more responsive to the needs of the weaker members of the monetary union. The five presidents assumed that the appetite for reform and further integration would be linked to the performance of the Eurozone economy and were grateful to Draghi for cutting interest rates, acting as a lender of last resort and embarking on a quantitative easing programme.

Draghi fended off opposition from Germany and some other Eurozone member states, a process made easier by persistently weak growth and the prospect of deflation. But he was unable either to transform the Eurozone's economic prospects or whip up much enthusiasm for the Five Presidents' Report. One issue was that growth dulled the enthusiasm for the reforms suggested by Juncker et al. Another was the reticence of Germany. The third was migration.

When it came to Schengen, many of the member states of the European Union decided that, with refugees arriving in large numbers in their own countries from the Middle East and North Africa, the Mr Micawber approach of waiting for something to turn up was not really good enough. Germany sought to impress upon its European partners the need for collective action so that the refugees could be absorbed across the EU rather than the burden falling disproportionately on one country. Predictably, given that this was at complete variance with Germany's 'sort out your own problems' approach to the Eurozone crisis, the call for solidarity found little support. Unimpressed by the attempts of Brussels to muddle through, countries imposed their own controls and by the early months of 2016 there was talk of a two-year suspension of Schengen.

Greece recalled its ambassador from Vienna after Austria imposed strict quotas on the number of refugees it would take. With its economy in a desperate state, Greece made it clear that it would not become Europe's Lebanon, the place where refugees from Syria would be quarantined. Alexis Tsipras, Greece's prime minister, said his country was not a 'warehouse for souls'.

The resort to national strategies was inevitable given that the prime responsibility of any state is to secure the safety of its own citizens. But as one commentator, Paul De Grauwe, has noted, there was really no difference between the two supranational systems: 'The Eurozone and the Schengen area have fundamentally weakened national governments while nothing has been put into place at the European level to offset this loss of power of nation states.'[10]

Seen in this light, the reason why there was talk at Ditchley and elsewhere about a possible break-up of the euro started to become clearer. The euro and Schengen both represent pan-European approaches that require the ceding of power by nation states. Both have been found wanting, with Schengen no more an optimum crime-fighting area than the euro is an optimum single-currency area. In one case – Schengen – individual countries have started to repatriate powers. They may soon be tempted to do so in the other.

Where to now? Dilemmas, trilemmas and contradictions

Until recently, the notion that monetary union might not survive has been a taboo subject. In his 2009 account of the euro's creation and its first decade in existence, David Marsh interviewed an array of Europe's great and good, including the former German chancellor Helmut Schmidt, the governor of the Bank of France Christian Noyer and ECB board member Lorenzo Bini Smaghi. All agreed that it would be disastrous for a country to leave the euro. Peer Steinbrück said the consequences of departure would be so terrible that no country would contemplate it.

Voters in Eurozone countries seem to understand how painful break-up would be and support for the single currency remains strong even in those countries with the highest unemployment and the slowest growth. In Greece, the public wanted an end to the austerity imposed by the rest of the Eurozone but was keen to remain in the single currency.

Similarly, there is growing unhappiness about the underperformance of the Eurozone economy but this has not led to a groundswell of support for the sort of reforms laid out in the Five Presidents' Report. On the contrary, it has manifested itself in the growing popularity of parties intent on protecting the rights of individual governments to resist austerity measures. The Eurozone, it is acknowledged, is a currency without a country. The five presidents want eventually to create a country that will make the currency work. But the failure of the currency makes it even less likely that nation states will give up any more powers that would make a United States of Europe a realistic proposition.

The plan for a banking union has illustrated the problem. Europe has a large number of weak banks that lent recklessly in the first half of the 2000s and, because they are still burdened with non-performing debts, are vulnerable to a fresh downturn. If the Eurozone is serious about further integration, banking union should be low-hanging fruit ripe for the picking.

Some progress has been made, with a common supervisor, a Eurozone-wide resolution mechanism and a system for ensuring that bondholders take a share of the losses if an individual bank fails. But a full banking union involves a common system of deposit insurance. If, for example, a bank in Lisbon failed, responsibility for compensating its customers would be the responsibility of all Eurozone states, not just Portugal. Such an arrangement requires the stronger Eurozone countries to stand behind the banks of the weaker states, with a particular onus on Germany. But support for common deposit insurance is weak in Germany, where taxpayers fear they will have to take responsibility for the problems of weak banks in Spain, Greece, Italy and Portugal. Banking union has been blocked and is likely to remain so. The only way to make progress currently would be to press on with banking union and hope to sort out design faults later. This, though, is precisely what happened with monetary union.

Germany would be prepared to talk about fiscal union, but only on its own terms. When the French and Italians talk about fiscal union, they envisage a Keynesian approach, with the use of Eurobonds to fund investment and a relaxation of budgetary rules that would allow, even encourage, countries to raise public spending or cut taxes in order to boost demand during economic downswings. This runs counter to the view of what the Germans think fiscal union should look like, which involves instigating rules that countries would be penalized for breaking. Governments in Paris and Rome have not the slightest intention of ceding this sort of power to Berlin.

The Five Presidents' Report takes Germany's side in this debate. It stresses the need for stronger rules that would result in debt reduction rather than the use of fiscal policy to stimulate demand. Similarly, it supports the idea of co-ordinated structural policies that would seek to make every country in the Eurozone more like Germany. This, though, will only make it harder to convince countries to sign up for a harmonized approach. Governments jealously guard the right to make their own choices over pensions, collective bargaining rules, tax rates and public spending.

Fiscal policy is not simply the 'other side of the coin' from monetary policy, with fiscal union following monetary union as surely as night follows day. Taxing and spending define what a country is in a very intimate sense; monetary policy is considerably more impersonal. Put crudely, the difference between monetary union and fiscal union is the difference between a joint bank account and a common shopping list. There is little sign that the Eurozone countries are ready for the deep fiscal and political federation that the five presidents are proposing; certainly not by 2025 and perhaps not ever. Dani Rodrik has described a trilemma in which it is impossible to have two but not all three of globalization, democracy and national sovereignty, noting that nowhere is the trilemma clearer than in Europe. If European leaders want to maintain democracy, Rodrik argues, they need to make a choice between political union and economic disintegration. 'They must either explicitly renounce economic sovereignty or actively put it to use for the benefit of their citizens.' The first, he said, would involve coming clean with their own voters and building democracy above the level of the nation state. The alternative would mean giving up on monetary union and taking back control of monetary and fiscal policies so that they can pursue longer-term economic recovery.[11]

There have been attempts to solve this trilemma.

De Grauwe argues that it would be easier for countries to renounce economic sovereignty if the strong countries did more to help the weak. At present, the burden of adjustment falls squarely on debtor countries, which are forced to deflate their economies in order to balance their budgets and eliminate trade surpluses. This has encouraged them to jealously guard those economic levers they are still able to pull. De Grauwe has called for economic policies in which the burden of adjustment ceases to fall primarily on deficit countries and for banking union to pave the way for fiscal union.[12] Christian Odendahl states that banking and financial markets should be fully integrated, the ECB should be given a stronger mandate to ensure there is adequate demand across the Eurozone, and that central banks should have the responsibility for ensuring that fiscal policy in their own countries is both 'robustly counter-cyclical and debt sustainable'.[13]

There is, though, the small and unresolved matter of how these suggested reforms would be implemented. De Grauwe says his proposals comprise a number of small steps that signal moves towards greater integration. Odendahl says his proposals would help to solve what he calls a fundamental contradiction at the heart of the Eurozone's troubles:

> On the one hand, the economics of a monetary union requires considerable integration of policies at Eurozone level, and a high degree of economic discipline at national level. On the other hand, most people do not want to be ruled by some 'Eurozone government'. They prefer national democracies – of the sort that struggle to impose sufficient discipline. This contradiction is both intellectually and politically hard to resolve.[14]

Unpicking this modern Gordian knot has so far proved impossible.

Kicking the can down the road – and the alternatives

Thus far, the Eurozone has not really tried to resolve Rodrik's trilemma. Carrying out the reforms deemed necessary to complete monetary union have proved too difficult; breaking up monetary union has remained unthinkable. Policymakers have decided, therefore, to continue kicking the can down the road, the approach followed for the past seventeen years.

To be clear, can-kicking is not the same as doing nothing. The third way between political union and collapse has so far involved a more activist stance by the ECB, a European Stability Mechanism that can provide up to €500 billion in financial help to member states in economic difficulties, and bailouts for four of the Eurozone's hardest-hit economies.

On the other hand, kicking the can is still a deliberate political choice, and it is a choice that has consequences. The best example of this is Greece, which by early 2016 was back in recession and resisting demands from its creditors to implement reforms to its pension system.

This impasse was predictable even before the ink was dry on the deal that gave Greece a third bailout. When the package was announced in August 2015, the International Monetary Fund said it would not work without a considerable write-down of Greece's debts. Learning from the experience of the first two financial rescues, the IMF said that the budgetary targets set for Greece were unrealistic and that the result would be slower growth and unsustainable levels of debt. The IMF said it would not put any of its own funds into the bailout until it could be sure it would not be throwing good money after bad.

Nothing that has happened since has led the IMF to change its mind. Poul Thomsen, the IMF official who was a participant at Ditchley, said in February 2016 that Greece's plan had to 'add up', making it abundantly clear that, as things stood, it did not. No amount of pension reform would make Greece's debt sustainable without debt relief, and no amount of debt relief would make Greece's pension system sustainable without pension reform.

Greece and its European partners, Thomsen said, faced politically tricky decisions and these could not be 'kicked down the road' courtesy of unrealistic assumptions. With an unspoken nod to Rodrik's trilemma, Thomsen said that while there was scope for structural change to make a difference to the efficiency of Greece's economy, the past six years had shown 'that the scope and pace of reforms acceptable to the Greek society is not commensurate with an early improvement of productivity and sustained high growth'.[15] It was not credible to expect Greece to grow its way out of its debt problem by making a rapid transition from the lowest to the highest productivity growth within the Eurozone, and nor could the Greek government realistically claim that they could obviate the need for pension reform by making the rich pay their fair share of tax.

Thomsen stressed that the deeply flawed nature of the Greek plan meant that the crisis would quickly resurface. Forcing the Greek government to impose deep public spending cuts in the belief that this would reduce its debt burden was asking for trouble, because the cuts would harm growth and so make it harder to run the budget surpluses demanded by the rest of the Eurozone:

> The IMF does not want Greece to implement draconian fiscal adjustment in an already severely depressed economy. In fact, we have time and again been the ones arguing for a fiscal adjustment path that is more supportive of recovery in the near term and more realistic in the medium term. We have yet to see a credible plan for how Greece will reach the very ambitious medium-term surplus target that is key to the government's plans for restoring debt sustainability. This emphasis on credibility is crucial for generating the investor confidence that is critical to Greece's revival. A plan built on over-optimistic assumptions will soon cause Grexit fears to resurface once again and stifle the investment climate.[16]

On past form, Thomsen's warning will not be heeded until it is too late. Greece's economy will struggle, it will not hit its budget targets, its debt will become ever more unsustainable, and eventually the choice will be between a fourth bailout and Greece leaving the Eurozone, either willingly or unwillingly. The assumption has tended to be that a country would leave the single currency voluntarily, although the possibility that Greece might be asked to go was raised by Germany's finance minister, Wolfgang Schäuble, during the negotiations in the summer of 2015.

Either way, a Greek exit from the euro would be a costly and painful business. Departure would allow the government to regain competitiveness through devaluation, but that would also mean that the real value of Greece's external debt – which stands at more than €400 billion – would increase. It is hard to see how a debt default could be avoided, and stringent capital controls would be needed to prevent the flight of capital out of the country. The European Commission and the European Central Bank believe that the necessary precautions are in place to prevent a Greek exit infecting the rest of the Eurozone, but there is no way of knowing whether or not there would be contagion effects on some of the other countries deemed by the financial markets to be vulnerable.

An alternative to Greece leaving would be for Germany and a few likeminded countries to peel off to form their own hard currency bloc unencumbered by the weak nations of the southern periphery. Interestingly, this was the one way that David Marsh, in 2009, could envisage the euro breaking up, not least because the costs would be much lower for a country departing from a position of strength. Marsh predicted that Germany could become alarmed at the lack of a 'stability culture' elsewhere in the monetary union, and frustrated at being outvoted at the ECB. Even so, this would require what in 2009 was considered a somewhat unlikely nightmare scenario in which Germany recovered speedily from the global recession but other parts of the single-currency zone remained stuck in a 'substantial and long-lasting economic downturn'.[17]

This has proved eerily prophetic. Germany has been alarmed at the lack of 'stability culture'; it doesn't much like being outvoted in the ECB; and it has recovered more quickly from the global downturn than other members of the Eurozone. But would Angela

Merkel (or any other German leader for that matter) like to go down in history as the politician who smashed up the euro and ended the dream of ever closer union? It seems unlikely.

But nor is any German chancellor going to accept that the answer should be a dose of Euro-Keynesianism, which would be one alternative to kicking the can down the road. A Keynesian solution would be based on three key principles: that the burden of adjustment should fall on the strong as well as the weak; that the time to tackle budget deficits is during a boom rather than a slump; and that there is a role for the state in promoting activity when animal spirits – the willingness of business to invest – are low. Keynes, were he still alive, would insist that the only way for the euro to survive would be for Germany to import more, accept the need for a higher ECB inflation target, agree to the need for Eurozone-wide deposit insurance, and underwrite a greatly enhanced budget. Writing in the 1930s, Keynes believed that the mass unemployment and the poverty of the Depression posed a threat to the capitalist system; he would doubtless say the same about the Eurozone.

For many on the left, Greece in 2015 was the moment they finally realized that this Keynesian vision of a kinder, gentler Europe was never going to happen. Instead, the way in which Greece was bludgeoned into submission was anti-Keynesianism: a policy based around the discredited notion that countries could deflate their way back to prosperity, and which used brute force to subvert the will of the Greek people as expressed in both a general election and a referendum on austerity.

In the short term, it looks probable that the Eurozone will remain in a zombie-like state. Growth will remain weak, unemployment will remain high, banks will live in a netherworld where they don't go bust but are too feeble to fulfil their normal function of lending to businesses and individuals. The ECB will continue to do its best with a series of short-term fixes, but recession, deflation and the next sovereign debt crisis will never be far away. In the longer term, the Eurozone looks ripe for a dose of 'creative destruction' unless it takes heed of the dictum attributed to Einstein:

insanity is doing the same thing over and over again and expecting different results.

The architects of the new Europe had a dream: they would create a new and better version of the United States of America. Europe would have all the good bits about the US – such as the economic dynamism, a large barrier-free market and a single currency – without any of the bad bits: the inequality, the high levels of incarceration, the poverty and the inadequate welfare safety net.

Things have not gone according to plan. Economic policy has been relentlessly deflationary. The interests of bankers have been given a higher priority than those of workers. Greece, Ireland, Portugal, Cyprus and Spain have been the laboratory mice in a continent-wide neoliberal experiment of a sort that would be a US Tea Party Republican's wet dream. The experiment has failed. The Eurozone would not survive a repeat of the 2008–09 global recession, or anything close to it.

As we have outlined in this book, the gap between the US and Europe has widened, not narrowed, since the launch of the single currency. The Eurozone has high levels of unemployment, under-employment and inactivity, and these risk becoming permanent features of the economic landscape. What's more, the US has a clear advantage in higher education, which tends to be the wellspring of the new ideas and products that generate dynamism. In the list of the world's fifty top universities, only one – LMU in Munich – is from a Eurozone country. The US can boast twenty-eight.

The Eurozone's combination of weak growth and semi-permanent crisis has meant that in recent years a different, less flattering comparison has been made. With the economy dipping in and out of recession and the ECB battling to prevent deflation, the idea has been floated that the Eurozone is less like the US and more like Japan: sluggish, ageing and incapable of rousing itself from its torpor. This comparison is valid to the extent that both the Eurozone and Japan have had a prolonged period of economic underperformance, and have failed to sort out the problems of their banks. But

Japan is a culturally homogeneous country with a stable political tradition; it has had the resilience to live with the aftermath of the spectacular collapse of the stock market and property bubbles at the end of the 1980s. It is not a currency without a country.

There are two other historical comparisons that may be relevant. From the end of the First World War, authors have described how the writing was on the wall for the British Raj in India. A series of short-term fixes meant that the rise of nationalism was checked and policymakers in London were able to convince themselves that the British Empire had a long-term future. There was, as Adam Tooze has described in his book, *The Deluge*, a complacency bred of the feeling that Britain had 'weathered the storm' and would always be able to see off the nationalist forces of anti-imperialism.[18] Within a quarter of a century, the British had left India, and within another two decades the rest of the empire had been dismantled. The idea of Britain as a world power did not survive Suez.

Twenty-five years after Suez, another empire was in trouble. This empire was big but failing economically. Its centralized model had proved incapable of raising living standards, although the small elite that made up the governing class did well out of the system. This empire was undemocratic and dismissive of the interests of the nations within its orbit. Only true disciples could conceive that it was pursuing progressive or left-wing goals. Those running it assumed it would go on for ever. That empire was, of course, the Soviet Union in its twilight years under Andropov and Chernenko. The European Union was supposed to be the US without the electric chair; instead, it turned out to be the USSR without the Gulag. Draghi has done his best, but may prove to be monetary union's Gorbachev.

Privately, Eurozone policymakers accept the premise of this chapter. The can has been kicked down the road. Draghi's hyperactive monetary policy reflects the fact that he is trying to do the work of both a central bank governor and a finance minister, but with the tools only to do the former job.

Various remedies have been suggested. Yanis Varoufakis has called for a surplus recycling requirement that would force

Germany to import more and thereby help those Eurozone countries running trade deficits. Varoufakis says that Germany should behave like the US in the decades after the Second World War, a period during which America was willing to expand domestic demand to the benefit of Western Europe and Japan.

There was, however, no obligation on the Americans to behave in this public-spirited fashion. The same argument made by Varoufakis had been made by Keynes at the 1944 Bretton Woods Conference, only to be firmly rejected by the US representative, Harry Dexter White. From the days of the gold standard, there has been a clear pattern: the strong dictate terms to the weak. Germany calls the shots in the monetary union just as the US called the shots at Bretton Woods.

Another possibility, as we have mentioned previously, would be for Germany to set up a 'hard' euro with a number of countries that have shown they can live comfortably with the pace set by Europe's strongest economy. Austria and the Netherlands would be obvious candidates for such a group.

Europe could turn the clock back two decades and return to an ERM or Bretton Woods-style arrangement, with currencies that are fixed but adjustable. This would have some attractions for countries such as Italy, because it would allow them to remain competitive. It would also mean that the currencies of strong countries would appreciate as those of poor countries were depreciating. Exports from Germany would become more expensive as Italy's goods became cheaper.

The final option is full monetary autonomy: a decision by a member state to reinstate its own currency. If it was ever able to break the masochistic mentality detailed in Chapter 3, France might eventually find this a more attractive proposition than struggling (and failing) to keep up with Germany.

All of these options would be costly, especially the demise of the euro. But all break-ups are painful and expensive. It may be time to admit that what looked to the left like a perfect marriage has turned into an abusive relationship, with divorce the only realistic option. It is to this that we turn in the final chapter.

CHAPTER 10

THE END OF THE AFFAIR

Why the left is falling out of love with the euro

'I wish you had never met that young Sergeant Troy, miss,' he sighed.

Bathsheba's steps became faintly spasmodic. 'Why?' she asked.

'He is not good enough for 'ee.'

Thomas Hardy, *Far from the Madding Crowd*

Anyone logging on to the website of the Party of European Socialists (PES) in mid-February 2016 may well have been left with two impressions. One, that it had been not so much a slow news day for the PES as a slow news half-year: the most recent stories on the site were dated 17 February 2016 and 15 September 2015. Two, that the United Kingdom loomed large in the organization's world view: the September item comprised a message of congratulations to Jeremy Corbyn on his election as leader of the British Labour Party, and that from February declared that 'progressive Europe ministers [are] working for a fair solution to keep UK in the EU'.

With regard to this second impression, there is a double irony. First, it is unlikely that one person in 100,000 in the UK has ever heard of the PES. That Britain's Labour Party formed part of the PES would have been news to a good many Labour members, let alone to anybody else. The most prominent recent member of

Labour's front rank to have enthused about the PES was the late Robin Cook in his role as leader of the House of Commons from 2001 to 2003, who wrote of his agreeable get-togethers with PES colleagues in his memoirs.[1] PES is not only a highly influential umbrella grouping for all the major leftist parties within the European Union, including the Social Democratic Party of Germany and France's Socialist Party, but is supposedly a party in its own right, receiving large subsidies from the EU as part of the union's longstanding attempt to create a common political consciousness across Europe, one in which, as with the United States, political figures would stand on reasonably common platforms from one end of the union to another. Other political groupings across the spectrum are similarly subsidized by EU taxpayers.

Britain in 2015–16 – whatever the changes in leadership of its principal centre-left party, and the discussions about the terms of its EU membership – was entirely irrelevant to the real issue. What ought to have been occupying the minds of a supposedly socialist political grouping was the havoc being wrought by the travails of the single currency on the lives of working people across the nineteen-nation Eurozone.

To be fair, the PES did address this, but under the heading 'Our Issues' rather than as something urgent, demanding immediate action and an accompanying news release. The subheading 'Jobs', for example, opened with a sentence with which few could disagree: 'European cooperation must focus on improving the lives of people and supporting the most vulnerable.' This was followed by a paragraph replete with bureaucratic waffle about 'concrete proposals towards a true Social Europe', such proposals being 'regularly discussed with progressive ministers and Prime Ministers, representatives from the member parties, our MEPs, our Commissioners, experts and representatives from civil society in the PES Employment and Social Affairs Ministers' network and the PES Social Europe Network.'

Anyone with the stamina to get through all that would, on reaching the third paragraph, have arrived at the meat of what the 'Jobs' section is actually about – that is, jobs, or rather the lack of them: 'As the European Union faces the consequences of the economic crisis, close to six million young people are without a job and often without hope. Since the beginning of the crisis, unemployment has steadily risen in Europe, affecting particularly young people. In some countries, one out of two people under 25 cannot find a job.'[2]

What is surprising is that these two paragraphs contain only one mention apiece of the economic and financial crisis that struck in 2007 and triggered the Great Recession, generally considered to have lasted globally from 2008 to 2013, although for some major economies the recessionary period was considerably shorter. As a lame man leaning on a stick, the PES seems determined that 'the crisis' shall bear the full weight of its analysis of what is, by any account, an unemployment scandal of colossal dimensions.

As with T.S. Eliot's 'mystery cat', Macavity, the euro's 'not there'. True, after two more stodge-filled paragraphs about proposals for a 'youth guarantee' of a job, further education or training, the PES brought itself to declare: 'the PES will work towards a more balanced macroeconomic coordination of the European Union that seriously takes into account social consequences of economic, fiscal and monetary policies.' And then, off on on another tangent, discussing the need for more public and private investment.

Under the subheading 'Economy and Finance', the PES declared: 'Europe is still facing economic, financial, social and political challenges. The social and economy impact of the austerity-only policies has gone far from what was predicted by the conservatives ... The economy is stagnant, deflation is looming and despite the recommended budgetary discipline and the overhaul on social spending, public debt is still rising.' Here, the shells are at least landing a little more closely to the real target, the single currency, given that the 'austerity-only' policies are a direct consequence of its existence. But again, the euro has managed to slip away; as with Bob Dylan's elusive outlaw the Jack of Hearts, it is the only person on the scene – missing.

Thus the 'Jobs' narrative seeks to pin the blame entirely on the financial crisis and Great Recession. This argument, however, falls apart once comparisons are made between Eurozone unemployment levels and those elsewhere.

The jobless rate in Britain is 5.1 per cent, in the US it is 5.5 per cent and in Japan it is 3.3 per cent. By contrast, the rate for the Eurozone is above 10 per cent. The UK, US, Japan and the Eurozone all suffered badly from the crisis; only one of them adopted a multinational single currency with a single interest rate.

The PES's 'Economy and Finance' section took the alibi one stage beyond the 'crisis', blaming the response to the crisis, the austerity policies, for the Eurozone's employment disaster. Quite what the PES had expected, however, is hard to glean. From the start, the fiscal stance of the Eurozone had rested on a barely modified balanced budget approach, bolstered by a 'no bailout' clause in the Maastricht Treaty. In the absence of the option of devaluing a national currency, the correct course to regain competitiveness was through 'internal devaluation' – wage cuts and reductions in public expenditure in tandem with 'structural reforms' to regulation, product markets and, especially, labour markets, with extensive use of what the Americans call 'give-backs', the surrender of employment conditions won previously.

Perhaps still under the illusion that austerity-driven unemployment had all been a terrible mistake, PES finance ministers gathered in Brussels on 15 January 2016 to 'discuss the economic priorities and challenges for 2016'. In the chair was Rimantas Šadžius, Lithuania's finance minister. He declared: 'Priority now must be given to completing the Banking Union with the implementation of its final pillar, the European Deposit Insurance Scheme for protecting depositors in case of financial shocks. Safeguarding people's savings and ensuring that the financial sector is accountable, viable and contributes its fair share, are fundamental.'

Again, there is little with which any reasonable person could disagree, at least in principle. But should 'completing the Banking Union' really be the top priority for centre-left finance ministers at a time of sluggish growth and chronic unemployment? To be fair, Mr Šadžius did move on to other matters, explaining that the banking union 'complements our continued efforts to relaunch sustainable economic growth via intensified investments'. Then: 'Our goal is to create new and decent jobs, to bridge inequalities and to ensure the durability of our social model.'

Not everybody on the European left was whistling to keep their spirits up. Some had faced the ghastly truth not only that the euro, rather than banking regulation or inadequate job training, lay at the heart of the problem, but also that, after all, there had never been anything especially 'progressive' about the single currency.

Apostates came no grander than Oskar Lafontaine, the former finance minister of Germany's Social Democratic Party, who declared in May 2013 that the single currency should be scrapped. Lafontaine warned: 'The economic situation is worsening from month to month and unemployment has reached a level that puts democratic structures ever more in doubt. The Germans have not yet realised that Southern Europe, including France, will be forced by their current misery to fight back against German hegemony sooner rather than later.'[3]

Lafontaine remained a big figure on the European left nearly fifteen years after his short-lived 1998–99 stint in the cabinet of Chancellor Gerhard Schroeder. 'Red Oskar' departed citing lack of cooperation from colleagues, widely interpreted as meaning that he had lost the argument for Keynesian pro-growth policies.

Two years after Lafontaine's about-turn, leftist disillusion with the euro was spreading far and wide.

On 22 June 2015, Aditya Chakrabortty commented in the *Guardian*:

> Nearly every meeting of the Wise Folk in Brussels and Strasbourg comes up with the same communique for 'reform' of the labour market and social-security entitlements across the continent: a not-so-coded call for attacking ordinary people's living standards. This is what the noble European project is turning into: a grim march to the bottom. This isn't about creating a deeper democracy, but deeper markets – and the two are increasingly incompatible.

He concluded that there was little comfort to be drawn from the fact that 'this entire show is being brought in by agreeable-looking Wise Folk often claiming to be social democratic'. This simply added 'a nasty tang of hypocrisy'.[4]

Nor was the euro the sole focus of such disillusion, as can be seen from the time of Lafontaine's recantation. One commentator located the problem in the whole of what he called Europe's 'economic constitution', taking in the euro and the single market, 'both deeply liberal economic initiatives' that contained an inbuilt structural bias towards free-market policies.[5]

It was a far cry from the excited talk a few short years earlier about Europe's 'social dimension' and the potential of the single currency to fix progressive policy as a permanent pillar in the construction of the post-Cold War Europe. The love match between the left and the euro was in poor shape, as testified by the emergence of new left-wing movements such as Syriza and Podemos, simultaneously creatures of romantic rejection and last-ditch attempts to rekindle the flame that had once burned so brightly.

This chapter looks at the development of this romance, its blossoming and its eventual fading. We look at some of the reasons behind the affair, bearing in mind always that reason may be a poor guide in matters of the heart.

It had been very different as the single-currency project took wing.

At first sight? A fine romance begins

On 1 January 2002, the day the euro notes and coins went into circulation, the centre-left French newspaper *Libération* filled its front page with a euro symbol made up of euro coins. 'The European Union has crossed the Rubicon,' it said. 'No more U-turns are possible on the road to the unification of Europe.'

As we saw in Chapter 2, the irreversibility of the single currency was one of its attractions to the left, because it blocked up the escape hatches through which businesses and government could seek to avoid progressive policies. That begged the question (using the phrase, for once, correctly) of whether the euro would promote or at least safeguard such policies. We have also demonstrated that talk in the late 1980s of Europe's 'social dimension' was deeply attractive to leftists. It goaded Britain's Margaret Thatcher to issue her famous counterblast at the College of Europe in Bruges in September 1988. But it is important to recall that the social dimension had been conceived as a countervailing force to the single *market*, not the single currency. It could hardly have been otherwise, given that the Committee for the Study of Economic and Monetary Union chaired by Delors did not report until the spring following the UK prime minister's address.

The Delors Report, as Chapter 3 explained, makes no mention of such a social dimension, although it was keen on measures to encourage regional development. As the publication date for the report approached, social policy was the topic furthest from the mind of the committee's most influential member, the president of the Bundesbank, Karl Otto Pöhl.

Charles Grant, Delors's biographer, writes that Delors needed to treat Pöhl 'with kid gloves' because the German had appeared to blow hot and cold throughout the negotiations, intransigent on some occasions, cooperative on others.[6] The key effect of this kid-glove treatment was to give Pöhl and his Bundesbank colleagues what they wanted in terms of fiscal discipline. Grant's account has Pöhl insisting on 'binding rules' to control government deficits within the single-currency area. German fears, writes Grant, related not only to the notion that a country such as Italy would be able to go on a 'borrowing binge', pushing up interest rates for the whole European Community (it was then assumed that the EC and the single-currency area would be one and the same thing), but that such a delinquent nation could then try to pressure the future central bank to run a loose monetary policy to ease the interest-rate burden. Writes Grant: 'Delors and his committee agreed, although Delors himself believed the rules would be unenforceable.'[7]

Later in 1989, Delors himself addressed the College of Europe in Bruges in what some saw as a riposte to Margaret Thatcher's speech of the previous autumn. A lengthy address on 17 October encompassed Delors's personal philosophical influences including the doctrine of 'personalism'. This is a school of thought largely unknown in the UK but which attempts to strike a balance between the individual and the community. Even now there was little to link the euro with leftist notions of social justice, but there was at least a mention in the form of a possible debate on the economic and social benefits of a monetary union.

To an extent, of course, the left, having been wooed and won by the social dimension of the single market, perhaps rather assumed that the single currency was part of the package deal. Indeed, the Delors Report is explicit in linking the single currency to the single market: 'The essence of the single market programme hinges to a decisive extent on much closer co-ordination of national economic policies, as well as on more effective Community policies. This implies that in essence a number of the steps towards economic and monetary union will already have to be taken in the course of establishing a single market in Europe.'[8]

Thus, having accepted the single market as the price of the social dimension, the left now learned that a single currency was an integral part of the single market. This may sound rather less like a devoted courtship and rather more like a variation of the old technique of bait-and-switch, in which a customer, believing they are buying one thing, ends up buying something quite different.

Furthermore, there was a ratchet effect in terms of enthusiasm for a united Europe. Labour's manifesto for the 1987 general election was explicit in its desire to 'work constructively with our EEC partners to promote economic expansion and combat unemployment', but, critically, maintained that it would put the interests of Britain first. By the 1992 general election, the position was far more enthusiastic, with the party declaring its determination to ensure that 'Britain will be a leader in the New Europe', with Labour rescuing the UK from the European 'second division' into which it had been relegated by the Tories. Part of this first-division status would involve not merely participating in negotiations on EMU but demanding that the future central bank for the single currency should be based in Britain. This enthusiasm for the single currency was tempered only by two tentative conditions: that the European Union be committed to fighting unemployment and that the central bank be somehow under the supervision of the EU's finance ministers. Come the 1997 ballot, and Labour's pro-European credentials were sufficiently burnished for the party to feel the need to talk tough about standing up for British interests and to pledge a hard-headed assessment of the desirability of joining the single currency.

Elsewhere in the EC/EU, left-wing parties, as a rule, had been more enthusiastic about the single currency *ab initio*. The Party of European Socialists (PES) manifesto for the European Parliament elections of 1999 committed it quite simply to 'ensuring that the single currency is smoothly introduced and provides growth, employment and stability'. Europe's most prominent socialist leader, François Mitterrand, used an address on 25 October 1989 to the European Parliament to propose a new treaty to introduce both economic and monetary union and political union.

For the left, of course, such a union would be desirable only if it could be relied upon to develop in a largely social democratic direction. There would be little support for a euro-bolstered union that proved to be a 'United States of Europe' in every sense of the phrase rather than simply as shorthand for political and economic integration. It was an open secret that Mitterrand wanted EMU to rein in the power of the Bundesbank, anchor of the ERM, in order to loosen monetary policy in Europe. This may plausibly be presented as social democratic, albeit right-of-centre governments having on many an occasion favoured low interest rates, whether to lift the price of assets such as shares and property or to provide cheap consumer credit as an alternative to increases in real take-home pay.

But again, the specifically leftist nature of the single currency remained elusive. The left's dashing suitor was skilled in striking gestures and bold poses, but vague as to the precise nature of 'happily ever after'.

Not everyone was swayed by emotional blandishments. Indeed, in some cases, leftist support for the euro was actually grounded in a view of the technical desirability of a single currency to those of a centre-left persuasion. In a *Guardian* piece on 19 February 1996, Dan Corry, a future adviser to Prime Minister Gordon Brown, hailed the prospect of radical policymakers no longer having 'to look constantly over one's shoulder at how the currency markets are likely to respond'. This, he said, would allow them to break free from the need to tailor their policies to the interests of these markets. Policies trimmed to fit the requirements of the currency-market players, he wrote, would be likely to be weak on jobs, excessively tough on fiscal policy and to show an overemphasis on low taxes and deregulation. The conclusion was obvious: 'This should lead anyone with a progressive agenda to support moves to a single European currency.'

This argument, by suggesting that currency markets are gunning for any sign of a 'progressive agenda', ignores the unquestionable fact that sterling was driven to its lowest point ever against the dollar – just above $1 – in January 1985, midway through Margaret Thatcher's second term, a period the policy priorities of which few would lightly describe as progressive.

But, if the leftish nature of the single currency was not to be found in the mechanics of the foreign currency markets, perhaps it could be located in the essence of the European Community/ European Union itself?

David Clark, former New Labour adviser at the Foreign Office, certainly thought so. Writing in the same newspaper six years later, on 21 May 2002, he enthused at the prospect of British membership of EMU bringing down the curtain on a certain kind of Britain, the Britain of the Tory Party, which, apparently, involved 'post-imperial illusions, cultural insularity and vulgar *laissez-faire* economics'. Joining the euro would take Britain into a club that was 'based on the values of community and social solidarity'.

The circuitous argument on offer seemed to suggest that the euro was a social-democratic project because it helped sustain the European Union, which was itself a social democratic project. Such a view of the EU was, of course, a far cry from that taken by members of the left in Britain and elsewhere in the quite recent past. Writing in 1981, Sam Aaronovitch declared that not only did the British people not need the European Community, 'they need to get out'. The Treaty of Rome, he said, was a charter for the free movement of capital and labour, for cuts to public spending and to industrial subsidies and for unbridled competition. Britain had joined in 1973, he said, in 'an act of political bankruptcy', and 'Leaving it would be a positive advantage.'[9]

Nearly twenty years later, some on the left were still resisting the blandishments of EMU, despite the EC/EU's post-Cold War reinvention of itself from a free-enterprise bastion against communism to a citadel of social democracy. As a general rule, they tended to be the sort of leftists who had never bought into the reinvention of Britain's Labour Party and its fellow movements in European and Commonwealth countries as enthusiasts for free markets. John Pilger is a case in point. He issued a scorching blast in 1998 at the notion that the single currency could have anything much to do with 'the joys of European togetherness or with European notions of democracy and prosperity for all'. In terms that would have delighted many a Tory Eurosceptic, Pilger ripped into Europe as a cartel run by Germany's 'conservative elite' and the Bundesbank, which wanted to bring all the other member countries to heel with stringent economic conditions 'so that the deutschmark can reign all-powerful'. Thundered the veteran campaigning journalist: 'As governments strive to meet these conditions by cost-cutting on jobs, health, welfare, education and transport, economic and social disaster beckons throughout the European Union, especially in the poorer countries.'[10]

For most on the left, however, all this merely comprised 'noises off'. British memories of the left's longstanding opposition to Community membership was forgotten as thoroughly as the humiliation of French socialists in the May 1983 franc crisis and the subsequent policy U-turn demanded by the exigencies of ERM membership. Indeed, as the 1980s, 1990s and early 2000s progressed, it seemed that, as with other forms of political modishness, 'pro-Europeanism' could be seen as a 'positional good', rather like a Rolex watch or a mobile phone. Once others have it, the lustre has gone and a more costly and elaborate version is called for.

In this regard, the European pilgrimage of leading British Labourite Neil Kinnock is instructive, not because it is unusual but because it is not. From campaigning in 1983 along with the rest of his party (but more enthusiastically than many) to leave the Community, he used the early years of his party leadership to modify the policy to one of 'withdrawal as a last resort'. Kinnock's Labour then outflanked the Tories in the late 1980s by supporting ERM membership, and went into the 1992 election more 'positive about Europe', in the phrase *du jour*, than the sitting government. After the second election defeat, Kinnock served as a European commissioner from 1995 to 2004, during which time he naturally supported British membership of the euro. More recently, he has used his seat in the House of Lords to promote a strongly pro-EU position.

This is all perfectly honourable and, indeed, consistent with regards to a man of whom it was said: 'He changed his mind on almost everything, but only once. Having moved from left to right, he never returned.'[11] But it does underline the dynamic nature of 'good Europeanism'. Plenty of senior Labour figures have shrugged off youthful republicanism to gain an appreciation of the constitutional worth of the Crown, just as many French leftists have come to accept and even value the role of the Catholic Church in the life of the nation. Yet no-one expects either of these changes of heart to develop to the point of staunch advocacy of the divine right of kings or the restoration of the papal states.

Going steady: The romance blossoms

All new relationships involve adjustments by both parties. Those who as single people got used to pleasing only themselves need to learn or relearn the habits of companionship – that there is someone else there now to be considered.

Contemporary ideals suggest that the adjustments ought to be shared, with neither party making all the sacrifices. But when one looks at the adjustments the left made in order to accommodate its new amour, the single currency, it is hard to see much by way of a quid pro quo.

Perhaps the first and most obvious relinquishment by the left was on the question of the free movement of capital across national frontiers. Contrary to recent belief, the 1957 Treaty of Rome did not abolish exchange controls entirely within the European Community but rather urged that: 'Member-states shall . . . grant in the most liberal manner possible such exchange authorisations as are still necessary after the date of the entry into force of this Treaty.' Furthermore, members not only retained exchange controls but could actually tighten them during periods of trouble. One example would be France in the early 1980s, when successive franc crises prompted devaluations and a retrenchment of the expansionist economic policies on which the socialist government of François Mitterrand had been elected in May 1981.

As finance minister, Jacques Delors unveiled a number of austerity measures, including a wage freeze and a 1 per cent levy on incomes. He turned also to capital controls. Charles Grant records that in April 1983 Delors introduced the *carnet de change*, a sort of passbook limiting holidaymakers' access to foreign currency. 'He knew the economic impact would be minimal, but hoped the carnet would bring home the gravity of the crisis and show that everybody had to do their bit.'[12]

Britain maintained capital controls for seven years after joining the Community and would doubtless have continued to do so had the Labour government been returned to office in the May 1979 general election. As it was, the abolition of exchange controls in October 1979 was not only controversial but was considered risky by even some who supported the idea. On 11 October 1979, Sir Geoffrey Howe, the chancellor of the exchequer, minuted Margaret Thatcher on the topic, raising concerns about the likely impact on the exchange rate. This may have seemed odd given the pound was in strong demand at that time as a petro-currency, but the horrors of 1976 and 1967 were presumably still fresh in the official mind and the prospect of a huge outflow of funds dragging sterling down in a colossal exchange-rate crisis was a serious cause for concern.

Beyond the currency markets, Howe was concerned also that free capital movements could conflict with the government's signature economic policy of controlling the money supply. Direct physical controls over bank lending, he told Thatcher, would be largely ineffective, because banks could simply take their money and go offshore. However, he concluded, 'In my view, the present is as good a time as we are likely to get.'[13] Furthermore, the Rome Treaty referred only to capital controls within the Community. There was no suggestion that money ought to flow freely to and fro across the 'external border'.

All that changed quite rapidly as the prospect of a single currency moved into view. Perhaps unsurprisingly, rapid capital-account liberalization resulted from an interaction between the wishes of the French and those of the West Germans. France wanted monetary union and Germany wanted free capital movements. In those terms, it was a straightforward quid pro quo.

However, as Rawi Abdelal of the Harvard Business School notes, Germany was not interested solely in removing barriers to capital movements inside the Community – which would have made good logical sense as an aspect of the Common Market – but with everyone else as well, the so-called *erga omnes* ('towards everyone') principle. 'The result was profoundly important, for the European Union ended up with the most liberal rules imaginable ... Europe's rules oblige members to liberate all capital flows, no matter the source or direction.' Germany, he writes, was determined that there would be no 'fortress Europe' in capital-market terms and that financial globalization would be embraced more or less unconditionally.[14]

It is a mark of how far Delors had moved in a few short years that he devoted an early part of his first presidency of the European Commission (1985–88) to an attempt to remove all barriers to the free movement of capital. Abdelal notes that in the early part of 1986, the Commission president was working on plans to oblige member states to liberalize capital movements among themselves and with the outside world. What would once have been a hugely controversial suggestion was agreed in two years, and the June 1988 capital movement directive mandated that there be no obstacles to transfers or transactions of any kind. Abdelal quotes Delors speaking in 2004: 'Although I had concerns, I came to the realization that the free movement of capital was essential to the creation of the internal market.'[15] Indeed, Delors's *carnet* was an early victim of French conversion to the notion of free capital movements, its unpopularity with the French middle class making its extinction politically astute as well as being in conformity with Europe's new orthodoxy of free capital movements.

The abolition of all exchange controls, 'internal' and 'external', exposed the various national currencies of Europe to potentially unlimited, tidal movements of capital, and with these movements the prospect of grand-scale speculation. Such speculative activity, of course, was very much more likely to arise when the speculators were given a target at which to aim, such as the various currency parities within the European Exchange Rate Mechanism, in existence since 1978 but since the 1989 Delors Report and subsequent Maastricht Treaty designated as the 'conveyor belt' that would carry Europe's currencies into an economic and monetary union.

Hardly had capital-account liberalization been completed at the start of the 1990s, barely was the ink dry on the Maastricht Treaty, than sustained speculative attacks effectively broke up the ERM in late 1992 and early 1993. The conspiratorially minded may see in this a deliberate sequence of events, a long chess game, from single market to single capital market to the complete abolition of exchange controls thence on to the gales of speculation that blew away the ERM, also known as the European Monetary System (EMS), leaving just one option on the table capable of reconciling free capital movements with currency stability: the euro. Indeed, this was suggested by a European Commission paper of February 2008, published ahead of the tenth anniversary of the May 1998 decision to proceed with the final stage of Economic and Monetary Union.

It states that several lessons were learned from the twenty-year experience of the Exchange Rate Mechanism, but in reality all these lessons add up to the same thing – that the ERM was incompatible with free capital movements. It is certainly a recipe for tension and worse if inflation rates differ and monetary authorities appear to be pursuing different goals from each other. The notion of 'keeping separate currencies' was identified as the problem here, with a predictable answer: 'A "corner solution", such as monetary union, is seen as a solution to this dilemma.'[16]

But a look at the main players of the time – Germany, the Commission president and France – would suggest that any such long-range conspiracy would have been unlikely. Germany was cool, to say the very least, on the idea of abandoning the mighty Deutschmark for an uncertain European currency, and Delors, a religious man and a straight-shooter by the standards of international officialdom, was more inclined to blurt things out than keep them quiet. Of the trio, France had perhaps the strongest motive for a 'stealth' approach of this sort towards the adoption of a single currency, but initial reluctance by Mitterrand and his officials to embrace the joys of free capital movements (the Socialists' 1981 manifesto had included a specific pledge to defend the franc against speculation) would suggest that realization in Paris of the potential of a barrier-free currency market to provide the pretext for monetary union dawned somewhat late in the day.

If control of capital movements was one treasured objective that had to be abandoned by the left as it embarked on its relationship with the single currency, so too was the notion of controlling trade, especially imports. Germany's Social Democratic Party (SPD) tended to frame any support for trade restrictions in terms of either a pro-European initiative or a policy designed to protect the environment. For historical reasons, the French left could afford to be less bashful about economic protectionism and less inclined to present it as something else, whether a method of bolstering Europe's position on the world stage or of protecting the environment. Indeed, commercial nationalism did not come much more blatant than the policy enacted in November 1982 with regards to the import of video recorders, then the up-and-coming piece of consumer technology.

On 14 January 1983, the *New York Times* reported on extraordinary scenes from Poitiers: 'Since last November, all foreign-made video recorders entering France must be cleared through a nine-man customs depot in this pleasant town in western France – which, not coincidentally, is hundreds of miles from the northern ports where the units are landed.' The recorders, once safely arrived, were then subjected to laborious 'checks' in what amounted to a 'cumbersome procedure' that had throttled the supply of video recorders into France, a development welcome to the government, which had fretted 'about the country's huge trade deficit, particularly with Japan', and the consequent threat to jobs. The Poitiers episode ought perhaps to have caused little surprise, given the 1981 Socialist manifesto had committed the party to protecting those economic sector threatened by American and Japanese competition.

By December 1993, French protectionism had shrivelled to (successfully) attempting to insist that the 'Uruguay Round' trade talks contain a provision allowing for countries to control the number of foreign films aired on their television networks, the so-called 'cultural exception'. No longer, it seemed, did France seek to block imports of audio-visual equipment, preferring merely to restrict imports of the sort of productions that people might watch on them. Hollywood was resolutely unfrightened by this provision. US trade negotiator Mickey Kantor recalled a conversation with Lew Wasserman, the octogenarian head of Music Corporation of America: 'He said: "This [movie] issue doesn't matter. We're going to dominate this business anyway. They can't keep us out of Europe. The technology will make it impossible for them to do that." '[17]

Pascal Lamy, Jacques Delors's former lieutenant from his time at the finance ministry, served as EU trade commissioner from 1999 to 2004. The heady days of May 1981 must have seemed another era as Lamy settled into his role as EU chief negotiator in the trade talks that were intended to result in the striking of a comprehensive global trade deal under the auspices of the newly minted World Trade Organization. These talks failed in Seattle in 1999, were relaunched in 2001 in the Qatari capital Doha, only to fail again in Cancún, on Mexico's Caribbean coast, in 2003.

On 28 October 2003, shortly after the breakdown of the Cancún talks, Mr Lamy rejected accusations that Brussels was largely to blame for the failure of negotiations. 'We [the EU] fed the beast meat in Doha, meat in Cancún and meat in between. It didn't work.

We have not seen much coming from other people's pockets, apart from the US on agriculture,' he said.[18] For the uninitiated, 'the beast' in this context referred to those of the world's poorest countries who had brought down the Cancun talks, being inexplicably reluctant to accept Western assurances that a deal would be in their best interests. Lamy 'jumped the counter' in 2005, becoming director-general of the WTO, in which role he served until 2013.

By the time he stood down, it was clear his French Socialist colleagues had followed him on the long and winding road away from the customs shed at Poitiers to the joys of free trade. On 15 June 2013, the *Financial Times* reported that France's Socialist president François Hollande had dropped objections to an EU–US trade deal, having won, yet again, a 'cultural exemption' covering the country's creative industries. The days when France sought shelter for farmers, steelworkers and those working in car factories were long gone. Now, it seemed, only film directors, music producers and their ilk could expect a protective arm from the socialists in power.

If the left's heady romance with monetary union had required the sacrifice of exchange controls and most protectionist trade measures, the third demand would once have proved a deal-breaker: a de facto prohibition on the creation of new state-owned enterprises, other than in an emergency, and strict rules on how existing publicly owned entities were to be financed.

The EU's tough new regime covering state aid and state-owned industries emerged in the late 1980s and early 1990s under the aegis of Sir Leon Brittan (as he then was), EU competition commissioner from 1989 to 1993 (and later EU trade negotiator). Henceforth, nationalization would be permissible only if the entity in question were treated on an arm's-length commercial basis, and public investment would have to meet the same criteria as private investment. If it were inconceivable that a private-sector investor would have put in the money, then the state was barred from doing so. Furthermore, any advantage derived from state assistance of any kind would have to be 'given back' further down the road. This was to assume special relevance during the financial crisis that erupted in 2008, when bailed-out banks were required, once the storm had passed, to surrender market share and divest themselves of various assets.

Brittan addressed the issue in a speech to the Atlantic Council Round Table in Washington on 16 January 1991. The link between monetary union and a tough line on state involvement in industry was explicit. He opened his remarks by declaring that a single market and single currency went hand in hand, and asked his audience to imagine a US in which each component state issued its own currency. In the single market, said Brittan, some companies were thriving as barriers came down and the bracing winds of competition blew strongly. But others would be feeling the chill, and ought not to be indulged. '[They] are likely to go running to their governments for support. It is crucial that we should control the use of state aids to prop up uncompetitive industries just as we must resist pressures to put up barriers to external trade.'[19]

Brittan did not initially have things entirely his own way. Predictably, perhaps, his new rules clashed with French traditions of public assistance to 'strategic' industries, which some saw as dinosaur enterprises whose lives were being artificially prolonged. On 13 May 1994 the *Spectator* highlighted one particularly glaring case: 'The pterodactyl of European skies is Air France. Grotesquely overstaffed, its losses reached FFr7.5 billion last year. [It] now asks instead for an injection of up to FFr20 billion of state cash, to follow FFr7.5 billion thrown down the hole over the past three years, some of it still "under investigation" in Brussels.' It gave a whole new inverted meaning to the airline's then advertizing slogan: *Demandez-nous le monde.*

To start with, the bailout of stricken lender Crédit Lyonnais seemed to suggest business as usual, regardless of the ministrations of Commissioner Brittan. Nicknamed Debit Lyonnais over the scale of its losses, some of them incurred (ironically, given the cultural sensitivities of French officialdom) in unwise lending to Hollywood studios, the bank was on its knees by the early 1990s. The authorities bailed out the bank in 1993, but the European Commission made stick a series of conditions to meet the criterion of 'giving back' the advantages of state aid, with restrictions on its international activities and disposal of assets.

Meanwhile, one of the severest tests of the strict new state-aid regime emerged not in France but in Germany. The *Land* (regional government) of Saxony had assembled an aid package to support investments in Mosel and Chemnitz by the car giant Volkswagen. On 26 June 1996, the European Commission ordered Saxony to reduce the size of the assistance. Saxony appealed against this to the European Court of Justice. So far, so unexceptional. However, the Saxon government did not wait for the outcome of the appeal and paid the full amount to VW, flagrantly defying the Commission decision, a move that strained relations with the federal government, with other state governments in the old East Germany and, of course, with the Commission. In an account of the affair, Eiko Thielemann of the London School of Economics records that 'a face-saving solution for all sides was found on November 18 1997,' but notes: 'The VW case raised fundamental questions about the legitimacy of the Commission's involvement in member states' internal affairs.'[20]

The sweeping nationalizations of the incoming Mitterrand government seemed like something from another era, as did a summary of economic policymaking in West Germany that stressed the 'key place' given to the state, without an understanding of which it would be impossible to grasp 'the nature of German economic argument'.[21]

Similarly remote was the comfortable world of corporate Italy as described by Wolfgang Achtner in the *Spectator* on 28 August 1992, by which time it was already under threat. Despite high labour costs and quality problems, Achtner said, official measures such as high rates of VAT and import quotas shielded Italian industry from outside competition. He could have added that the Italian public sector invariably purchased the products of Fiat, Olivetti and other domestic producers and would have been astonished at Britain's open tenders for many such contracts. Achtner concluded: 'Italy behaved in its domestic market like a walled mediaeval city state, where foreigners were not allowed to participate.'

But none of these major adjustments – capital controls, trade restrictions, nationalization and state aid – could match the superlative sacrifice being demanded of the left in return for life ever after with the single currency: Europe's 'social model'.

Tug of love: The left's favourite child is torn away

From the start, the potential of the single currency to 'reform' Europe's welfare states and labour markets was discussed quite openly. Indeed, some said such reform was essential if the currency union was to prosper. One was Otmar Issing, member of the executive board of the European Central Bank.

Speaking at a lecture in Frankfurt on 20 September 1999, Issing said that the dangers to a successful monetary union could be easily identified. The most obvious one was lack of labour-market flexibility. Combined with the high levels of unemployment prevailing at the start of EMU, 'this poses an almost lethal threat'. Rigidities in the labour market, he said, joined with 'the misguided incentives provided by the social security and welfare systems' to keep joblessness levels high. Issing acknowledged 'calls for a social union', but only to dismiss them, however well-meaning they may be. Nor did he have any time for the argument that such a union was needed to counterbalance the existing union of bankers and financiers espied by critics. Said Issing: 'If one were to concede to such demands, rising unemployment and mounting tensions between countries and regions would be the consequence.'[22]

In 1997, Maurice Obstfeld – now economic counsellor at the International Monetary Fund, then at the University of California, Berkeley – prefigured Issing's comments by suggesting that dealing with employment-market reforms was a precondition for the successful functioning of the single currency, along with fundamental fiscal reform. 'If Europe's leaders cannot do an end run around domestic opposition in the name of European integration, EMU could prove unstable.'[23]

Anticipation in some financial-market quarters at the prospect of welfare and labour-market 'reform' could be positively indecent. Having warned in our first book, in 1998, that the single currency would act as a severe constraint on social provision and employment, we were a little taken aback to be invited to lunch at an investment bank in London and told how excited were our hosts at the prospect of our warnings coming to pass.

We were not alone in viewing the euro as inimical to traditional social-democratic objectives. In 2013, Dutch academic Anton Hemerijck recalled that the single market and EMU package had been seen by some alarmed fellow academics as 'a Trojan horse' that would bring the forces of neoliberalism into the citadel of European social democracy and put European welfare states to the sword in 'a vicious cycle of deflationary "beggar-thy-neighbour" strategies of internal devaluation through social dumping and competitive wage moderation'.[24]

Amy Verdun, of the University of Victoria in British Columbia, gave a paper to the European Union Studies Association conference in May 1995. Introducing her contribution to the conference, she stated that many saw the single currency as a way of harnessing market forces to the restructuring of over-rigid and over-costly welfare states, a 'necessity' if they were to be able to continue to compete in world markets. In words that ought to have set alarm bells clanging on a deafening scale for the left, she added: 'In the monetary field, the EMU institutionalises and legitimates German monetary policies within a European framework, whilst in the economic and social field the EMU offers political legitimation for restructuring the welfare state.'[25]

In light of all this, it is difficult to see why the left resolutely swallowed one humiliation after another in order to keep in existence its relationship with the single currency. But perhaps the explanation is that these indignities were not the worst of it, that there was an even more unpalatable truth about the left's new love, one that dwarfed its insistence that the left subordinate long-held goals to the doctrines of the single currency. Quite simply, the euro was two-timing the left with the free-market right.

Faithful to you in my fashion: The cheating heart of EMU

Some have long wondered at the supposedly progressive credentials of the single-currency project, and wondered also at the doggedness with which its leftist fan club insists that the euro is, or at least could be, a mighty engine for the achievement of social democratic objectives. The single currency was dreamt up by a committee of central bankers, is managed by a powerful and unaccountable central bank, is designed to give top priority to establishing low or no inflation, is strongly supported by corporate Europe and, as we have seen, is the centrepiece of a European settlement that militates against currency controls, trade restrictions and government intervention in the economy.

Some spotted EMU as being essentially a sound-money, free-market scheme from the very start. One of them was distinguished former Labour cabinet minister Peter Shore, to whose analysis we shall return shortly.

There were those on the free-market right who were equally baffled by the hostility of some of their ideological compatriots to the EU in general. Writing in *Forbes* on 17 March 2014, Dmitry Vasishev declared: 'Although European bureaucrats and leftist pro-EU parties do not realize it, the EU has essentially been a free market project. Conservatism is a political philosophy based on the principles of individual liberty and free markets. The EU has brought major improvements on both of these principles. Therefore, conservatives should support it.' On 2 February 2015, Adair Turner, former director-general of the Confederation of British Industry, reflected on his own past support for the single currency: 'EMU . . . seemed justified as an impeccably free-market project, driving forward completion of the single market and supporting in particular the free flow of capital.'[26]

What was the left doing in such company? What was it thinking? Part of the answer may be that in the post-Cold War era, leftist politicians and commentators had become attracted to the notion of the 'broad tent' in which the class battles of yesteryear were forgotten and within which everyone's interests could be aligned: capital and labour, rich and poor, left and right. In this managerial political culture, as John Laughland noted, 'political systems are . . . unable to manage (let alone encourage) the kind of lively conflict within the law which is at the heart of the liberal order. On the contrary, they prefer to dissipate all conflict away into false bonhomie and social "consensus".'[27]

Talk of 'struggle' was old hat, it seemed. Henceforth, everyone was going to be nice to everyone else. This attitude was to peak during New Labour's first spell in office from 1997 to 2001, not coincidentally the period during which the party's pro-Europeanism was at its height and it was widely expected that Tony Blair would try to use his immense electoral popularity to swing the voters behind a Yes vote in a referendum on joining the euro.

Parts of the European left – in Germany, Scandinavia and the Low Countries – had long felt comfortable seeking common ground with business. By the mid-1980s, those with a fiercer leftist tradition, including sizeable communist parties – in France, for example, and Italy – were settling into the new dispensation.

Beyond this Europeanist consensual all-things-to-everyone approach was another attraction of the euro to the left: it promised to be that rarity, an economic argument that the left could actually win.

By the turn of the century, a settled view was emerging on both sides of the Atlantic that market-based solutions had won the argument in terms of economics, a claim made as early as 20 January 1989 in the inaugural address of President George H.W. Bush: 'For the first time in this century, for the first time in perhaps all history, man does not have to invent a system by which to live.' The liberal-left, however, had won important social arguments in terms of tolerance, diversity and human rights. It was also culturally dominant in the same way the free-market right was economically dominant. Perhaps nobody any longer suggested nationalizing the steel industry or the telephone system, but there were far fewer figures from entertainment and the arts speaking up for Britain's Conservative Party or the Republicans in the United States than had been the case in the past.

UK journalist Andrew Marr put it this way: 'It's almost as if we're now in a situation where the right or free-market conservatives, whatever, have control of the economic levers and have had for a very long time, but the penalty they must pay for it is being mocked by the popular culture and not liked by the satirical popular culture. There seems to be a division of spoils. The left gets the cartoonists and the satire and the right gets the levers.'[28]

Back then, however, the single currency held out the prospect that the left could actually be on the winning side of an economic debate. The euro was 'going to happen', it was 'inevitable' and there was every reason, in the early days, to believe it would be successful. Institutions such as the International Monetary Fund were supportive and grand figures in business and politics chorused that EMU was a wonderful idea. As former Labour Party leader Hugh Gaitskell had said of British supporters of membership of the European Community: ' "We must go in," they say, "not because of the power of logic, of fact and conclusion suggest it is to our advantage; we must go in because the people who really understand it, the top people, all want it." '[29]

The euro was 'doomed to succeed'. Leftists needed only line up behind it in order to be on 'the right side of history'. That there was, as we have seen, nothing especially leftist about the euro was a problem that could be mitigated by left-wing support for The Project. In a circuitous way, the presence of leftists in the euro camp could be taken as proof that the single currency was intrinsically progressive.

This fundamentally weak rationale was helped by the mood music coming from opponents of membership, especially in Britain. Calls to 'save the pound' and defend parliament and national sovereignty came over as tweedy and middle-aged in the late 1990s and early 2000s. When the opposition switched to arguments based on optimal currency areas and internal devaluations, it sounded nerdy. The euro was modern and exciting. Its opponents were anything but, comprising some (but not all) of the Parliamentary Conservative Party, ageing elements in the Labour Party who had never 'got with the programme' in terms of the Blair revolution, some public-sector trade unionists (rightly) fearful of spending cuts were Britain to join and, in a bizarre twist, some Irish nationalists in Northern Ireland whose dislike of the euro exceeded even their aversion to the 'colonial' currency, sterling.

After the love has gone: Recrimination and regrets

'Of *course* it is a political project.' This was a phrase doing the rounds as the euro was readied for launch in 1997 and 1998. It underlined the sophistication and 'in the loop' status of the speaker, given that the official line coming out of Brussels and Frankfurt was that the single currency was simply an economic arrangement, a more durable version of the Bretton Woods currency regime or the Exchange Rate Mechanism. Admission that its inspiration was sited in politics rather than economics identified the speaker – always an advocate of the euro – as someone in the know and furthermore one who was not afraid of grand and ambitious political visions.

In truth, the impulses that led to the birth of the euro went beyond even politics and into the realms of emotional mysticism. It was not so much a currency, more a potent life force that would heal the wounds of Europe and bring prosperity and unity to all. From a leftist point of view, this was especially appealing. National currencies – the lira, the franc, the pound – had been the playthings of speculators and the means by which leftist governments had been forced to abandon their economic programmes at the behest of grim-faced central bankers. The new currency would be quite different: enabling, liberating, energizing.

True, details of just how the management and performance of the euro was to differ from those of its predecessor currencies were sketchy, to say the least. Peter Shore asked how a country was to regain competitiveness once it had surrendered the option of adjusting its exchange rate, interest rate and monetary policy. The answer, to Shore, was only too clear.

The alternatives, he said, were stagnation, rising unemployment and large-scale emigration or, on the other hand, deep cuts in wages and salaries – the internal devaluation that has been visited on the troubled Eurozone economies. 'No-one in their senses would wish to be faced with such an unattractive choice.'[30]

Shore was writing in 2000 and his words were to prove deeply prophetic. But in the emotional dam-burst following the fall of the Iron Curtain and reunification of Germany, few were subjecting to detailed scrutiny the notion that the euro would be a liberator rather than an enslaver. At the end of Europe's tormented twentieth century, scarred by the Great War, the Depression, the Second

World War, the Holocaust and the Cold War, a visible, tangible symbol of the continent's renaissance was at hand. Who with even a scrap of idealism could resist its charms?

One who in the aftermath of the breaching of the Berlin Wall warned against emotional investment in mechanistic entities was the British statesman Denis Healey. He was writing about treaty organizations, but his remarks could apply equally to the single currency: '. . . NATO and the European Community were given an absolute value quite out of character with their real role as instruments of particular policies at particular times'.[31]

Few were listening, and thus the left's heady romance with the euro headed off on its giddy way.

From today's perspective it is clear that the euro was the centrepiece of what amounted to a huge wrong turning for the European Community after the 1989 fall of the Berlin Wall. That the twin conference on not just EMU but political union was held a mere thirteen months later may suggest that a proper stocktaking had not been made. When one considers that the papers for both sets of proposals were circulating at an intergovernmental level as early as March and April 1990, this suggestion becomes a certainty.

Even dating the proposal for monetary (as opposed to political) union from the April 1989 Delors Report, less than two years was devoted to pondering the desirability of creating a single currency.

A proper stocktaking would have listed the assets of the Community, not simply the open market and the ability to strike major trade deals but also the unique habits of cooperation developed in an organization that went beyond conventional alliances or routine diplomatic relationships, habits of potentially great value in the uncertain waters of the post-Cold War world. Such a stocktaking would also have listed the less desirable aspects of the Community's operations – its mania for 'harmonization', its insistence that once an area of activity was moved to the Community level it should stay there for ever – and its peculiar part-political, part-judicial, part-administrative Commission, a body one would have thought ripe for reform, along with its politicized Court of Justice.

Instead, the good things were taken for granted, the bad things left where they were and a twenty-five-year march of folly embarked upon, a journey to gigantism with the euro at its centre. For many on the left, this was the romantic trip of a lifetime. Millions of unemployed and billions of euros in spending cuts and austerity measures later, and the folly of that doomed affair of the heart is plain to see.

Those that were caught up in the spirit of post-Cold War Europe can perhaps be excused. Those on the left who accused opponents of euro membership of xenophobia and worse ought to be ashamed of themselves. Those who warned from the very start that the single currency would prove a disaster for working people can take a certain grim satisfaction in the fact that they – we – were right.

EPILOGUE

Still not working: The view from 2017

Wisdom and Wit are little seen, But Folly's at full length.
Philip Dormer Stanhope, Earl of Chesterfield (1694–1773)

By the time dawn broke on a glorious midsummer day, the result was not in doubt. Voting had closed in the referendum on Britain's membership of the European Union just after sunset on Thursday, 23 June, and for a while, exit polls had suggested that, as expected, voters had chosen to stick with the status quo. But as the ballots were counted, a different picture emerged. In the northern towns of England, places like Sunderland and Hartlepool, there were big majorities in favour of leaving the EU. At 2.30 a.m., the result was still hanging in the balance. By 4 a.m., the TV stations were confident that the UK had voted for Brexit. By 8 a.m., David Cameron was standing outside 10 Downing Street announcing that his failure to do what Harold Wilson had achieved forty-one years earlier – to convince Britain to stay within the political and economic structures of its nearest continental partners – meant he was resigning as prime minister. The financial markets had witnessed a sharp drop in the value of the pound over-night, and Cameron's announcement came as the City's share-dealing was getting started for the day. The prospect of a period of political upheaval coupled with economic uncertainty saw billions of pounds wiped off the value of stock market-quoted companies.

But it was not only the financial markets that were in a state of shock. Liberal Britain had what can only be described as a collective nervous breakdown. There was a sense not just of horror but also of disbelief that the British public had voted for Brexit. Although the polls had been tight throughout the campaign, the consensus had been that there would be a late swing to the Remain side, just as there is usually rising support for the governing party in the last few days before an election. Sterling had risen in the final forty-eight hours before the referendum in anticipation of history repeating itself, but the final result was 52 per cent for Leave and 48 per cent for Remain. Cameron had been able to call on the support of big business, the majority of trade unionists, university vice-chancellors, the Labour Party, the Liberal Democrats, the Greens, the SNP and most of his own parliamentary party. Even so, 17 million people still decided they wanted no more to do with the EU.

The liberal establishment did not take defeat well. For some, shock quickly turned to anger, whilst others said that Britain should follow the example of other countries and have a second referendum so that Leave voters could think again. Remainers took the knee-jerk reaction of the financial markets as evidence that the economy was about to plunge into an immediate and deep recession that would bring on a serious dose of 'buyer's remorse'. Every possible explanation for this political earthquake was canvassed apart from the obvious one: that Europe wasn't working and hadn't been for some time.

The first alternative explanation was that the people who voted for Brexit didn't really understand what they were doing. That voters were suffering from what Marxists call false consciousness is a polite way of putting it; less polite is the intimation that Brexit voters were thick. The point was made that university towns voted strongly in favour of Remain and that Leave voters tended not to have degrees. Taken to its logical conclusion, this line of argument would see a return to the days before 1948 when Oxford and Cambridge had an extra seat in parliament; or it might lead to the repeal of every extension of the franchise since the Great Reform Act of 1832 on the grounds that the lower classes don't really understand what they're voting for. This seems to us patronizing, undemocratic and wrong.

It is wrong because it is reasonable to assume that many of those who voted Leave did so because they considered it to be in their best interests. Just as it made sense for Oxbridge academics to vote Remain because they wanted to retain access to EU funding, so it was logical for those in less well-off areas to be concerned about the impact of free movement of labour on wages, housing shortages and the quality of public services. Britain was one of only three countries that decided against having transitional measures to control immigration from eight countries in Eastern Europe when they joined the European Union in 2008; at the time, because the economy was growing strongly, it didn't seem to matter. After 2008, a period that has seen strong employment growth but falling real wages, it clearly did.

A second explanation was that the defeat for Remain came down to avoidable political miscalculation. Just as Hillary Clinton appeared to think she was entitled to beat Donald Trump in the 2016 US presidential election by virtue of her years of public service, so Cameron was convinced that he could rely on the deference of voters to sway a tight vote. We will explore the consequences of the then prime minister's misplaced arrogance later in this epilogue, but it was surprising that the Remain camp had nothing up its sleeve to offer in the last two weeks of the campaign, especially since this was an approach that had worked in the Scottish referendum in 2014.

Cameron's lack of a Plan B was all the more surprising given the weakness of Plan A, the remorselessly negative tone of the Remain campaign. As such, the third explanation for Britain's EU exit was that voters were turned off by what became known as 'Project Fear', the increasingly lurid warnings of what would happen in the event of a victory for the Leave side. The Treasury, for example, warned that the cost of Brexit would be £4,000 per household by 2030 and that the economy would shrink by 1 per cent in the year following a Leave vote. The then chancellor, George Osborne, announced that he would have to introduce an emergency budget that would cut spending or raise taxes by £30 billion. What's more, Osborne was able to rustle up some heavyweight support for his argument. The OECD said a Leave vote would be the equivalent of a self-imposed tax increase, while the International Monetary Fund helpfully produced some blood-curdling forecasts five days before the referendum took place. Mark Carney, the governor of the Bank of England, said a recession in the six months after the referendum would be a distinct possibility if Leave won.

Project Fear had worked for Cameron in the Scottish referendum, and it had also delivered the goods in the 2015 general election – so it is not hard to see why it was the strategy for the EU referendum too. That it didn't work this time was in part because the newspapers that had been Project Fear's 2014 and 2015 cheerleaders were on the other side in 2016, and rubbished the claims made by the Treasury, the OECD, the IMF and the Bank of England. Another reason was that voters smelled a rat as the weeks wore on and Project Fear turned into Project Overkill. They sensed that the last thing the government would do if the economy went into recession after the referendum would be to announce a £30 billion punishment budget. That might have been a credible threat from Philip Snowden in 1931; from Osborne it simply sounded desperate.

As it happens, voters were right to take the warnings of immediate economic armageddon with a very large pinch of salt, because the economy grew by 0.6 per cent in the third quarter of 2016 and by 0.7 per cent in the fourth quarter – faster than the Office for Budget Responsibility had forecast in March when it had assumed a vote for Remain. There was no recession and no buyer's remorse either. Within days of the referendum, members of the public were getting on with their lives, and opinion polls taken since 23 June do not suggest a second referendum would achieve a different result. Presumably, Leave voters thought one of three things: that Project Fear was nonsense; that it was not nonsense but that other things mattered more to them than the state of the economy in 2030; or that they thought their lives could not get much worse than they already were.

This leads to the fourth explanation for the vote to leave: the impact of the Great Recession of 2008–09. As we argued in our recent co-authored books, the events of 2008, when the collapse of Lehman Brothers brought the global financial system to the brink of collapse, were as profound an economic shock as the oil crisis of 1973–74. While the crisis of the mid-1970s led to deep structural change, the response to the crisis of 2008 was business as usual.

The counter-revolution launched in the mid-1970s was an attempt to bring about a purer form of capitalism unencumbered by all the restrictions and obstacles put in place by Keynes and his followers in the middle of the last century. The time was ripe in 2008 for reformers to do what Milton Friedman and Friedrich Hayek did in the mid-1970s – mount a challenge to the prevailing orthodoxy.

It didn't happen. Instead, policymakers played for time by cutting interest rates to record low levels. They boosted asset prices through quantitative easing, a money-creation process that involves central banks buying bonds in exchange for cash. They bailed out the banks. They briefly borrowed more to cushion the blow of the recession but then embarked on public spending cuts that hit the poor hardest. Across the developed world, a rift opened up between those for whom the political system delivered and those who considered themselves left behind. To our minds, though, Brexit was more than a protest vote.

Europe's woes, we argued earlier, resulted from a huge wrong turning taken after the fall of the Berlin Wall in 1989, a turn towards gigantism and centralization typified by, but not confined to, the creation of the euro. The events of 2017 have done nothing to undermine our thesis; on the contrary, they have served only to confirm it.

Wherever you looked in the European Union and the Eurozone, dysfunction was the order of the day. There was the jubilation as Eurozone growth finally showed some signs of life after an enormous stimulus from the European Central Bank. There was the relief that the Dutch far right was seen off by a 'moderate' rival who had adopted much of its anti-immigrant tone. In France, the presidential election victory of Emmanuel Macron, a Gallic Tony Blair with similarly little by way of ideology, was thunderously applauded in Brussels and elsewhere, giving the lie to his self-image as some sort of insurgent.

In April 2017, Guglielmo Verdirame, a professor at King's College London, wrote:

> According to the Pew Research Centre, in all major European countries there is a clear majority supporting the repatriation of powers from Brussels. Yet, in the latest high-profile initiative – the appeal for a 'March for Europe' in Rome to coincide with the 60th anniversary of the Treaty of Rome – 300 European intellectuals and academics are demanding the exact opposite: the transformation of the European Commission 'into a fully-fledged government'.[1]

And Europhiles complain whenever it is said that 'Europe' is an elitist project.

Then there was the European response to the UK referendum result and the subsequent triggering of Article 50 of the Lisbon Treaty, beginning the withdrawal process. Ahead of the departure talks, all the rival power centres in Brussels – the European Council (representing the twenty-seven remaining member countries), the European Commission and the European Parliament, each with its own 'president' – outlined their positions. Briefing and counter-briefing suggested the talks would be amicable, that Britain would be punished for its temerity, that an enormous 'divorce settlement' from Britain to the EU was non-negotiable, that nobody really wanted to punish Britain . . . and so on.

Much has happened in the EU since this book was first published, but nothing has yet come close to the seismic significance of the UK decision to leave. It is to that event and its ramifications that we turn first.

'I can win this': The road to Brexit

As is now a commonplace observation, the first step on the road to Brexit was taken on 23 January 2013, when David Cameron, prime minister in a Conservative–Liberal Democrat coalition, addressed the vexed issue of the UK's relationship with the EU in a speech at the offices of the Bloomberg news and information service in London. Having enumerated British discontentment with the manner in which the EU had developed over the years, Cameron announced: 'That is why I am in favour of a referendum. I believe in confronting this issue – shaping it, leading the debate. Not simply hoping a difficult situation will go away.'[2] Reading the speech as a whole from the perspective of today, it is very tempting to be wise after the event. But it may be more useful to address just two aspects that seem especially pertinent in the light of the result of that pledged referendum.

The first is that, from the very start, it seems fairly clear that Cameron, whatever he said, was never remotely likely to recommend a Leave vote, regardless of the EU deal offered during renegotiations. Remain sentiments infuse the speech:

> Of course, Britain could make her own way in the world, outside the EU, if we chose to do so . . . But the question we will have to ask ourselves is this: is that the very best future for our country?
>
> Alone, we would be free to take our own decisions, just as we would be freed of our solemn obligation to defend our allies if we left NATO. But we don't leave NATO because it is in our national interest to stay.
>
> Even if we pulled out completely, decisions made in the EU would continue to have a profound effect on our country. But we would have lost all our remaining vetoes and our voice in those decisions.
>
> Continued access to the Single Market is vital for British businesses and British jobs.
>
> We would have to think carefully, too, about the impact on our influence at the top table of international affairs. There is no doubt that we are more powerful in Washington, in Beijing, in Delhi because we are a powerful player in the European Union.

With a few name-changes, this is boilerplate 1975 referendum material, full of top tables and the supposedly illusory advantages of going it alone, pulling up assorted drawbridges and turning our many and various backs on the world. In effect, the Remain campaign started on that day and continued right up to 23 June 2016.

The second aspect worth attending to is this remark from the then prime minister: 'Those who refuse to contemplate consulting the British people, would in my view make more likely our eventual exit.' Well, quite. Cameron, after his surprise general election victory in 2015, did keep his pledge and consult the people. But the powers that be in Europe – both the big nations like Germany, and the key institutions such as the European Commission – saw no concomitant need to listen to the British PM, or to try in any meaningful way to accede to his requests for a changed UK–EU relationship. With Europe having refused to properly consult with the British people (via their elected leader), the British did indeed respond by voting to exit. It will be of little comfort to David Cameron to have been proven entirely right on that score.

But if 23 January 2013 marked the beginning of the 'road to Brexit', the 'road to Bloomberg' started an awful lot earlier. David Cameron's in/out referendum pledge did not arrive out of the blue but resulted from the development of two distinct but intertwined types of British disillusionment with EU membership.

The first concerned the progressive tarnishing of the EU's superior economic performance, both among the 'core' countries and later joiners such as Spain and Ireland which had enthusiastically embraced all things *Bruxellesian*. The second was a growing and ultimately irreversible feeling that the constitutional and legal arrangements of the EU were unsuited to British traditions, the British temperament and the British way of doing things.

This was a slow-motion, grand-scale reversal of the position that had obtained from the late 1960s until roughly the signature of the Maastricht Treaty in 1992. During that period, continental economic success was proof positive of the triumph of the EC/EU pudding, which meant Britain had no choice but to grab an apron and get stirring with the rest of them in the Brussels kitchen.

France, Italy and, above all, West Germany had enjoyed 'economic miracles'. Britain had not.

As late as 1976, Chancellor of the Exchequer Denis Healey was on television assuring a youthful David Dimbleby that 'Britain's miracle' was finally in prospect. Shortly afterwards, Healey and his colleagues were nearly overwhelmed by an enormous sterling crisis. But for the Labour government, in which Healey served, the answer was at hand – as laid out in the party's 1979 election manifesto, *The Labour Way is the Better Way*: 'each year there will be three-way talks between ministers, management and unions to consider the best way forward for our country's economy. Germany's Social Democratic Government under Willy Brandt and Helmut Schmidt has proved that this is a good way to reach agreement on how to expand output, incomes and living standards.' But even then, when other European countries were taking the first tentative steps towards monetary union, Britain was reluctant to join them. It was to be more than a decade – two recessions and one inflationary boom later – until Britain finally submitted to German monetary discipline by joining the Exchange Rate Mechanism. It was a short-lived and unhappy experiment that ended two years later with the pound being ejected from the ERM by a group of speculators led by George Soros, on Black Wednesday, 16 September 1992.

ERM membership, and its accompanying return to recession, was to prove the high point of Britain's (or at least its establishment's) conviction of the superiority of all things continental. But it is interesting that even given what amounted to more than a quarter of a century of a British inferiority complex when confronted with the marvels performed by its rivals across the Channel, the constitutional arrangements of the EC/EU aroused remarkably little interest in the UK. The reason for this was, in part, the initially dominant role of the Common Agricultural Policy (CAP), which ensured time-consuming discussions in Brussels on subjects such as the 'sheep-meat regime' and the 'butter mountain', all of which were guaranteed to turn off British voters.

Furthermore, the public had been assured during the 1975 referendum on EC membership that 'No important new policy can be decided in Brussels or anywhere else without the consent of a British Minister answerable to a British Government and a British Parliament.'[3] Such debate as existed focused on two fairly narrow matters: the supposedly unfair financial contribution Britain was required to make for the privilege of belonging to the club, and the question of whether 'the housewife' was being rooked by the 'Common Market' on her grocery bills. That changed somewhat after the Single European Act 1986 brought in wide-ranging majority voting, robbing each country of its veto in many areas. But even in late 1980s Britain, the constitutional implications of EU governance were of interest largely to political figures whose time had gone or had never arrived in the first place: they included Enoch Powell and Nicholas Budgen on the Tory side, Tony Benn and Peter Shore for Labour.

John Major's handling of the Maastricht negotiations, under which the UK reserved the right not to join the euro, initially seemed likely to keep the lid firmly on this potential can of worms, but even without the shock Danish No vote in June 1992, it is likely that the issue simply could not be avoided forever. As more power was ceded to the centre – giving the lie to repeated British establishment promises that 'the debate in Europe is coming our way' and 'the high-tide of federalism has been passed' – so increasingly the link between 'positive engagement with Europe' and economic success was seen to weaken. Sitting out the first, or even the second, wave of euro membership gave the British people a chance to assess the results.

By the time of Tony Blair's third election victory, in 2005, it had become clear that the predictions of disaster following Britain's failure to sign up for economic and monetary union had been wide of the mark. What had in fact happened was the conventional opening up of an exchange-rate differential between sterling and the euro. Trade and investment had taken place across that exchange rate, in the normal way. The City had not decamped to Frankfurt. The big motor companies that had moved into the UK in recent years, such as Nissan and Toyota, had not upped sticks for the single currency bloc. Britain's place on the world stage had not been hopelessly compromised by its miserable failure to get with the programme in Brussels.

Meanwhile, Eurozone growth remained sluggish at best, and it was increasingly obvious that the supposedly galvanizing effects of, in essence, adopting a jury-rigged Deutschmark for the entire single currency bloc, complete with a single interest rate, existed only in the sense of stimulating hopelessly unsustainable boom conditions in the weaker 'peripheral' economies.

Come the latter part of the 2000s, an articulate breed of younger politicians and commentators – Tory MEP Daniel Hannan and journalist Allister Heath come to mind – were making the case that there was no mystery as to the coincidence of ever-greater EU/ Eurozone centralization and poor economic performance. They were two sides of the same (euro) coin.

At the same time, interest in the constitutional arrangements of the EU had grown and, for a large section of the British population, it seemed that the more they found out, the less they liked them. In part, this interest had been prompted by debate about a series of treaties signed after that of Maastricht – which had supposedly been the last word in centralization – which transferred more authority to the EU institutions. There was the Amsterdam Treaty of 1997 and the Nice Treaty of 2001. But most notorious was the Lisbon Treaty of 2007, which created an EU foreign minister, a president for the European Council and an EU diplomatic service, and which took other steps towards political integration.

This document did not start life as a treaty at all, but as a constitution for the EU. Signed by all EU governments in October 2004, it was to be subject to referendums in a number of countries, including Britain. However, before the UK could hold its own vote, electors in France and the Netherlands rejected it in May and June 2005 respectively. With two founder members having thrown it out, the constitution was pronounced dead. But, this being the EU, what that meant in practice was that most of it re-emerged as a treaty that did not have to be ratified in this way, handily bypassing the voters.

In Britain, the New Labour government, now headed by Gordon Brown, gratefully seized on the chance to slide out of the referendum commitment. David Cameron, leader of the Conservative opposition, gave his own 'cast-iron guarantee' that Britain would get its vote on the Lisbon Treaty should he be elected. Duly returned to office in 2010, Cameron went back on this pledge.

Whether they knew it or not, the UK's mainstream political leaders, specifically Blair, Brown and Cameron, had, as a result of such a cavalier attitude to the voters, heaped up large piles of combustible electoral material on the whole question of Britain and Europe. This first blazed into life in spectacular fashion in the 2014 elections to the European Parliament, in which the UK Independence Party took the largest share of the vote.

UKIP had come a long way from its somewhat hapless 2010 campaign, the most memorable moment of which was the election-day crash of a light aircraft pulling a UKIP banner which injured the party's once and future leader, Nigel Farage. UKIP was picking up votes not only from those enraged by Cameron's failure to deliver his 'cast-iron guarantee', but also from voters who disliked (or worse) the prime minister for reasons unconnected with the EU, whether his support for same-sex marriage and wind farms, or his apparent indifference, in the eyes of some Labour defectors to UKIP, to the difficulties of those less privileged than himself. Heading off UKIP had been pretty much the whole point of Cameron's Bloomberg speech. That the 2014 elections suggested the opposite of a cowed UKIP ought to have been a portent. There is little sign that it was seen as such.

True, the Conservative Party's 2015 election manifesto included a commitment to an in/out referendum – as foreshadowed in the Bloomberg speech – but this pledge did not appear until page 29, well after assorted 'retail offers' to the voters on everything from apprenticeships to mobile phone coverage. By page 72, the tempo had increased a little, with the assertion that 'membership of the European Union depends on the consent of the British people – and in recent years that consent has worn wafer-thin'. Powers would be reclaimed from Brussels, said Cameron's Tories, and 'a new settlement' negotiated for the UK within the EU. Then the public would have its say.

It has become the conventional wisdom that Cameron never expected to win a majority and thus would not need to deliver on the referendum pledge. Whatever the truth of that assertion, his surprise victory on the night of 7/8 May 2015 ensured he would need to come up with something.

Cameron's actions during the fateful thirteen months that followed suggested that this 'something' would be the bare minimum needed to get a Remain vote in a referendum to be held as soon as possible. In this endeavour, there seemed little doubt that he saw the successful manoeuvrings of his Labour predecessor Harold Wilson in 1974–75 as something of a template.

On such a reading, a few simple rules had to be followed.

First, the 'renegotiation' should be completed as swiftly as decently possible while public expectations of what could be achieved were managed downwards.

Second, whatever meagre concessions could be obtained should be presented as marking a changed UK–Brussels relationship. Wilson called it 'Britain's New Deal in Europe'; Cameron referred to the UK now enjoying a 'special status' in the EU (an expression used, as far as we can tell, by precisely none of his opposite numbers in either the EU institutions or other member states).

Finally, once the voters had endorsed this 'new' relationship, the focus should be briskly moved as far away from matters European as possible.

At the time, this must have seemed a strategy with every chance of success. After all, if Cameron's 'special status', unveiled in February 2016, fell far short of what many in his party and beyond were demanding, it was at least more substantial than anything Wilson had obtained – not difficult, as the Labour leader had gained virtually nothing. But even without the huge constitutional and economic changes that had occurred between 1975 and 2016, Cameron would have been fighting on far less favourable terrain than had Wilson. Community membership was still something of a novelty in 1975, not even three years on from British accession. No-one could say the same in 2016 of EU membership. The British media was less raucous in 1975 and more respectful of diplomatic communiques and the like, and even its rowdier elements were almost entirely pro-Europe.

Furthermore, Wilson had a ready-made issue onto which the political focus could be switched once Yes had won, namely the need to hose down an inflationary bushfire which saw prices rising annually at more than 25 per cent. No sooner had British households discarded the referendum pamphlet *Britain's New Deal in Europe* (with an introduction by Wilson, complete with serious monochrome byline photo) than another official booklet was hitting the doormat, *Attack on Inflation: A Policy for Survival* (ditto). Cameron, by contrast, planned to move on to a 'progressive' social agenda which, while undoubtedly worthy, would have stood little chance of healing the divisions within his own party over what many on the Leave side considered underhand tactics – imposing purdah on Leave-supporting ministers until the start of the official campaign, for instance, while Cameron and his allies were free to talk up the joys of remaining in the EU on the grounds that they were merely stating government policy.

That said, the prime minister had few doubts. With the outline of a deal sketched out, and fresh from an unexpected general election victory, Cameron was brimming with confidence. 'I am a winner. I can win this,' he reportedly told fellow European leaders at a meeting in December 2015.[4]

HM Government's *The Best of Both Worlds: The United Kingdom's Special Status in a Reformed European Union* was published in February 2016. It was always going to get a rough ride from certain sections of the Parliamentary Conservative Party and from the Eurosceptic media. But apparently even Cameron was taken aback by the ferocity of the reaction to the fruits of his renegotiation.

'The UK set out to fix four key problems with the EU and we delivered,' declared the document. The first was 'permanent protection for the pound and our right to keep it', which was a little puzzling as such protection had supposedly formed part of John Major's negotiating triumph at Maastricht twenty-four years earlier. True, there were some additional guarantees regarding Eurozone bailouts and non-discrimination against British businesses, but many had assumed that these had formed part of the original 1992 opt-out. The second problem referred to 'commitments from the EU to cut red tape' and other liberalizing measures. This was good for a hollow laugh from those who had heard it all many times before – i.e. everybody. Point 3 covered a 'formal agreement that the Treaties will be changed in the future so that the UK is carved out of "ever closer union" and we will have new powers to block or remove unwanted European laws'. Depending on how it worked in practice – for example, can future EU treaty negotiations really be bound by such an agreement? – this may have been the most substantive of the four points. The final 'key problem' concerned immigration from within the EU and Britain's 'new powers' to pull an 'emergency brake' when migration levels were deemed too high, and to prevent new arrivals from claiming full benefits for up to four years. In any event this latter point would have been under-whelming, given it raised the migration subject and then failed to deal with it convincingly. But in light of fact that the 'emergency brake' law would need approval from the European Parliament and any use of the brake would need agreement from the other EU governments before it could be activated, this was not so much underwhelming as a near-total non-event.

Cameron was widely scorned by pro-Leave media as a weakling who had achieved nothing, and who had caved in to his interlocutors on the continent. Cartoons depicted him as a large child sat on the lap of German Chancellor Angela Merkel, or as an embarrassed waiter whipping the lid off a huge silver salver to reveal a minuscule portion of food. As the starting gun was fired for the 23 June vote, early good news for Cameron in the form of the support of Eurosceptic minis-ters including Foreign Secretary Philip Hammond and Defence Secretary Michael Fallon was balanced by the loss to Leave of Justice Secretary Michael Gove and five other cabinet members, to be joined by former London Mayor Boris Johnson, whose decision, against expectations, to throw in his lot with Leave electrified the campaign. Meanwhile, papers such as the *Daily Mail*, the *Sun* and the *Daily Telegraph* exuberantly promoted the Leave cause.

But despite this, the auguries were good for Cameron and the Remain campaign. As Hywel Williams had written in 1998 on Tory Euroscepticism: 'European institutions had been so indelibly grafted upon the old British stock that paradoxically the anti-European cry of keeping Britain's institutions "sovereign and independent" appeared to be a revolutionary one – and England is not a land fit for revolutionaries.'[5] This, surely, was a correct reading of the situation. The 'respectable' people, however defined in the twenty-first century – perhaps encompassing senior clerical, supervisory, technical and managerial types through to the caring and teaching professions and the much-discussed (however inaccurately) 'liberal metropolitan elite' – would vote to stay in the European Union. The fish knives and the net curtains may have gone, but the yearning for social acceptance had not. Talk of the 'decline of deference' in British society was surely overstated?

Had anyone sought a portent for an alternative outcome, they may have alighted on the special edition of the BBC television programme *Question Time* during the 2015 election campaign, broadcast from Leeds, Yorkshire, on the evening of 30 April. All three party leaders appeared, separately, in front of a studio audience, an audience whose members proceeded repeatedly to accuse said leaders, one by one, of being liars.

To those of us who learned the journalist's craft in the days of nervous adherence to the laws against either publishing or broadcasting a libel, this was an extraordinary programme. The anger and contempt of the audience suggested a public mood that could be described as mutinous were it not for the fact that a mutiny requires a legitimate power to be defied, and there was no sign then or later that large numbers of British voters recognised any such authority.

We make no apology for devoting so much space to the Brexit vote. It is, at the time of writing, the starkest illustration of the dysfunction of the European Union. At the end of this epilogue we shall return briefly to Brexit developments since the referendum result. But first, it is time to catch up on happenings in the Eurozone.

'Each European day is a new beginning'

Pierre Moscovici, European Commissioner for Economic and Monetary Affairs, was full of the joys of spring. It was 11 May 2017 and the latest economic forecast for the EU apparently made for cheery reading. Europe, declared Moscovici, was entering its fifth year of growth and 'the high uncertainty that has characterised the past 12 months may be starting to ease'. The EU and, in particular, the nineteen members that use the single currency had weathered the storms. Better still, the picture was gloomier for the UK, and Brexit was to blame. 'Measures of investment intentions from recent surveys are soft and businesses are expected to defer investments in the face of uncertainty relating to the negotiations regarding the UK's withdrawal from the EU,' according to the forecast.

Look closer, however, and the Eurozone's Maytime appears a little less sunny. Growth for 2017 was forecast at 1.7 per cent for the year, as against 1.8 per cent in the supposedly ailing UK. True, for the following year the respective forecasts for expansion were 1.8 per cent in the Eurozone and 1.3 per cent in Britain, the falling off there caused by a squeeze on consumption triggered by a decline in real disposable income. True, also, Moscovici did mention job creation as a 'key challenge' for the Eurozone, as well he might. In April, the International Monetary Fund's latest World Economic Outlook forecast Eurozone unemployment at 9.4 per cent of the workforce in 2017 and 9.1 per cent in 2018. In contrast, the respective figures for the UK were 4.9 per cent and 5.1 per cent.

But the generally self-satisfied nature of Moscovici's remarks was of a piece with a new mood of complacency in the Eurozone in the first half of 2017. The old year, the year of the Brexit vote, had ended with a less seismic but still significant defeat for Europe's political class when Italy's electorate voted No in a referendum called by Prime Minister Matteo Renzi on changes to the country's constitution. Nearly 60 per cent of those who voted rejected the proposed reforms, and Renzi resigned. But by the middle of 2017, the Italian vote was, from the Brussels perspective, looking less like a harbinger of more populist uprisings to come – Italy's Five Star

Movement led by former comedian Beppe Grillo had campaigned for a No vote – and more like the last whirl of a *danse macabre* that was thankfully now slipping out of history's rear-view mirror.

The first proclaimed sign that the tide of anger against Europe's political elites was ebbing was the result of the 17 March general election in the Netherlands, in which sitting Prime Minister Mark Rutte led his People's Party for Freedom and Democracy (VVD) to victory over the second-placed Party for Freedom (PVV), the anti-immigration and anti-EU movement led by the charismatic Geert Wilders. Resonant of the future reaction to the result of the French presidential election in May, Europe's great and good were exultant. European Commission President Jean-Claude Juncker said it was a victory for 'free and tolerant societies in a prosperous Europe', while Chancellor Merkel described it as a 'very pro-European result' and a 'good day for democracy'. Later in March, Merkel's Christian Democrats easily won a state election in Saarland, a good omen ahead of the country's general election in September. It seemed a long time ago that some had been talking up the threat to Merkel from the anti-immigration Alternative für Deutschland (AfD).

Come May, and the run-off ballot for the French presidency, and joy was unconfined at the victory for Emmanuel Macron, an apolitical former banker who had campaigned on a pro-EU and pro-globalization platform, defeating Wilders's Gallic equivalent, the former leader of the right-wing Front National, Marine Le Pen. (She temporarily stood down as leader during the later stages of campaigning in order to present a more unifying image.) According to the BBC, Juncker tweeted, 'Happy that the French chose a European future', while Merkel described the Macron triumph as 'a victory for a strong united Europe'. Outgoing president François Hollande congratulated Monsieur Macron and said the result showed that the French people wanted to unite around the 'values of the republic'. On 14 May, Merkel was again celebrating a win at the polls, having seized control of North Rhine-Westphalia, Germany's most populous state.

The traumas of 2016 had, it seemed, been cauterized, albeit Donald Trump remained in the White House and Britain had triggered the Article 50 process for leaving the EU. Perhaps a better analogy would be to say that the infection had been quarantined and that the danger of a populist uprising on the continent was contained. Juncker's somewhat flowery remarks at an official dinner on 16 February were starting to seem prescient: 'Anybody who thinks the day will come in Europe when we can say that the job is done is mistaken. Each day is a new day, but each European day is a new beginning. If you think about it, each European day also brings the magic of a new beginning, every single day.'

Leaving aside the Italian vote, the ongoing defiance of Brussels by Hungary's Prime Minister Viktor Orban, and the fact that Poland, the EU's sixth-largest economy, was governed by the some-what Eurosceptic and conservative Law and Justice Party, let's revisit the above-mentioned victories for the European consensus and try to work out if they were all that they were supposed to be.

Mark Rutte did indeed win the Dutch election. But his election-eering did not always seem to have much to do with the 'free and tolerant societies' that Juncker felt his victory epitomized. On 23 January, the *Guardian* reported that 'The Dutch Prime Minister, Mark Rutte, has published an open letter to the country's citizens ahead of elections in March, telling anyone who cannot respect its customs to leave.' The paper went on: 'People who "refuse to adapt, and criticise our values" should "behave normally, or go away", Rutte said in a full-page newspaper message seen as a bid to win over voters drawn to Geert Wilders's anti-immigration, anti-Muslim Freedom Party.' Quoting further, it added: 'He said the Dutch were "increasingly uncomfortable" with those who abused the freedoms they enjoyed after coming to the Netherlands, who "harass gays, or whistle at women in short skirts, or brand ordinary Dutch people racists".'

Nor was this a one-off. On 24 February, the *Daily Express* reported some more of Mr Rutte's *obiter dicta* concerning Muslims:

Mr Rutte – who faces voters next month in the Netherlands' parliamentary elections – was being interviewed for Holland's Christian radio station, Evangelical Broadcast Service. He was asked about an earlier statement, when he had called the Muslim call to prayer song 'whiny music'.

The song – played from mosque minarets – has become commonplace across the Netherlands.

But when Rutte was asked to confirm what he had said, he told show host Tijs van den Brink: 'Yes, I find it horrific.'

Elsewhere in the interview, Mr Rutte warned Muslims not to abuse their freedom of worship in order to upset non-believers.

Despite all this, Wilders and his PVV came in second place, having gained five seats while Rutte's VVD lost eight. At some future point, it may be that the Dutch will prefer to elect a party that has always been hostile to Muslims as opposed to one that is striking a pose for political advantage.

Angela Merkel's Saarland victory did not see off the AfD – far from it. As the BBC reported on 26 March, the party 'which has played on dis-satisfaction with Mrs Merkel's policy on immigration, did succeed in winning seats in the Saarland legislature with 6.2 per cent of the vote'.

Macronmania in May threw up wildly exaggerated claims that the political novice had reunited France and would proceed to perform the same feat with the rest of the EU. Such a Panglossian view was made possible only by ignoring the fact that a third of those who voted backed Le Pen, that one in four voters abstained (the highest level since 1969), and that 12 per cent went to the trouble of turning up to vote in order to spoil their ballot papers. Not much sign there of a nation uniting around the 'values of the republic', in Mr Hollande's words.

We devoted separate chapters to France, Italy, Greece and Germany earlier in this book. By the summer of 2017, it was clear that these countries' problems were no closer to being resolved. France still confronted the dilemma it had faced since the early 1980s: the impossibility of importing Germany's hard-currency regime without suffering slow growth and high unemployment. Italy continued to suffer from slow growth as a result of its inability to compete with its more productive partners. Greece, meanwhile, had slipped back into recession during the winter of 2016–17 and, enmeshed in its own *Groundhog Day*, had just completed negotiations with its creditors over the austerity measures required for a fresh package of financial support. Germany had a different problem: it was being criticized by the IMF and by Donald Trump's administration for exporting too much and running too high a current account deficit. To US Treasury Secretary Steven Mnuchin, the answer was at hand: 'Germany, the largest economy within the euro area, should take policy steps – particularly greater use of fiscal policy – to encourage stronger domestic demand growth, which would place upward pressure on the euro's nominal and real effective exchange rates and help reduce its large external imbalances.'[6] There may be some mordant amusement to be gleaned from the fact that Germany, jointly with France, the architect of the euro, was being landed with the blame for the dysfunctional single-currency bloc. What few within the Eurozone seemed prepared to admit was that Germany's alleged mercantilism was an inevitable by-product of the fact that the euro simply did not work. Had the Germans retained their own currency, the country's export boom would have been damped down as that currency rose on foreign exchanges.

Within the euro, there was no such mechanism. Emmanuel Macron, elected France's new president in May 2017, arrived in office with a plan that would result in Germany running down its current account surplus and importing more. This involved a deal whereby France would agree to a range of structural reforms of its labour market long deemed necessary by Berlin, in return for moves towards greater integration of the Eurozone, including the creation of a single Treasury and a finance minister accountable to a Eurozone parliament. This had echoes of France's original enthusiasm for the single currency in the late 1980s, seen then as a way of influencing German economic policy. The response in Germany to Macron's overture was cool. Having been taken in once, German politicians insisted that they wanted to see the French reforms before making any commitments that would dilute Berlin's power.

Going separate ways: Brexit and the Eurozone

Britain's departure from the EU was to some degree an accident. Cameron called the referendum to prevent UKIP from capturing Conservative votes rather than because there was a great clamour from the public to have a say about the EU. Indeed, opinion polls taken at the time of the 2015 general election show that Europe came well down the list of issues concerning voters, after jobs, living standards, education and the NHS.

But once the referendum was called it became clear that support for the EU was not nearly as widespread or as strong as Cameron had believed. Remain's strongholds were the richer parts of Britain, London and the south-east, and the university towns. This was perhaps understandable, given that the economic geography of the single market had meant that countries tended to specialize in what they did best. The UK's speciality was the provision of financial services and, as a result, the City of London became Europe's financial centre. To the extent that Britain had an industrial strategy, it was to bolster, protect and expand the financial services sector. Britain's exit from the European Union will potentially make it more difficult, although not impossible, for the City to continue in this role; hence the support for Remain in London and the commuter towns of the home counties.

During the recession and its aftermath, workers in Britain effectively sacrificed income in order to avoid being laid off, with the result that the typical employee is earning around £3,000 a year less than he or she would be getting had the modest pre-recession upward trend in earnings continued. Britain's old industrial areas bore the brunt of both the free-market revolution of the mid-1970s and the austerity that followed the crash of 2008. Those were the parts of the UK that saw the biggest increases in unemployment in the 1980s, the biggest increases in the number of people on incapacity benefits as attempts were made to bring the jobless total down, the heaviest reliance on tax credits to top up low pay, and the deepest welfare cuts in the years since 2010. As one study put it: 'In effect, communities in older industrial Britain are being meted out punishment in the form of welfare cuts for the destruction to their industrial base.[7] These were the parts of the UK that voted heavily for Leave. Brexit happened because no mainstream remedy was posited for an economic system that had ceased to deliver for too many people. The EU was part of that dysfunctional system.

As we noted earlier in this book, the age of globalization began on the day the Berlin Wall came down. From that moment in 1989, the trends evident in the late 1970s and throughout the 1980s accelerated: the free movement of capital, people and goods; trickle-down economics; a much-diminished role for nation states; and a belief that market forces, now unleashed, were unstoppable.

There has been pushback against globalization over the years. The violent protests seen in Seattle during the World Trade Organization meeting in December 1999 were the first sign that not everyone saw the move towards untrammelled freedom in a positive light. One conclusion from the 9/11 attacks on New York and Washington in September 2001 was that it was not only trade and financial markets that had gone global. The collapse of Lehman Brothers put paid to the idea that the best thing governments could do when confronted with the power of global capital was to get out of the way and let the banks supervise themselves.

In this context, Britain's rejection of the EU was more than a protest against the career opportunities that never come knocking and the affordable homes that never get built. It was a protest against the economic model that had been in place for the past three decades.

To be sure, not all Britain's problems are the result of its EU membership. It is not the European Commission's fault that productivity is so weak or that the trains don't run on time. The deep-seated failings that were there when Britain voted in the referendum on 23 June are still there as we write a year later.

In another sense, however, the EU is culpable. In the shiny new post-Cold War world when former communist countries were integrated into the global model, Europe was supposed to be big and powerful enough to protect its citizens against the worst excesses of the market. Nation states had previously been the guarantor of full employment and welfare. The controls they imposed on the free movement of capital and people ensured that trade unions could bargain for higher pay without the threat of work being offshored, or cheaper labour being brought into the country. In the age of globalization, the idea was that a more integrated Europe would collectively serve as the bulwark that nation states could no longer provide. Britain, France, Germany or Italy could not individually resist the power of transnational capital, but the EU potentially could. The way forward was clear: move on from a single market to a single currency, a single banking system, a single budget and eventually a single political entity.

That dream is now over. As Charles Grant, the director of the Centre for European Reform think tank put it, 'Brexit is a momentous event in the history of Europe and from now on the narrative will be one of disintegration not integration.'[8]

The reason is obvious. Europe has failed to fulfil the historic role allocated to it. Jobs, living standards and welfare states were all better protected in the heyday of nation states in the 1950s and 1960s than they have been in the age of globalization. Unemployment across the Eurozone is more than 10 per cent. Italy's economy is barely any bigger now than it was when the euro was created. Greece's economy has shrunk by almost a third. Austerity has eroded welfare provision. Labour market protections have been stripped away.

Inevitably, there has been a backlash, manifested in the rise of populist parties on the left and right. An increasing number of voters believe there is not much on offer from the current system. They think globalization has benefited a small privileged elite, but not them. They think it is unfair that they should pay the price for bankers' failings. They hanker after a return to the security that the nation state provided, even if that means curbs on the core freedoms that underpin globalization, including the free movement of people.

This has caused great difficulties for Europe's mainstream parties, but especially those of the centre-left, which have been perfectly happy to countenance the idea of curbs on capital movements such as a financial transaction tax, and have no problems with imposing tariffs to prevent the dumping of Chinese steel, but feel uncomfortable with the idea that there should be limits on the free movement of people.

The risk is that if the mainstream parties don't respond to the demands of their traditional supporters, they will be replaced by populist parties that will. The 2017 French presidential election demonstrated that the Socialist Party has lost most of its old blue-collar working-class base to the hard left and the hard right. In the UK, Labour is trying to pull off a balancing act in which it keeps the support of its white-collar metropolitan supporters who backed Remain as well as that of many of its traditional blue-collar voters in the Midlands and the north who thought tighter control on immigration could best be achieved outside the EU.

There are those who argue that globalization is now like the weather, something we can moan about but not alter. This is a false comparison. The global market economy was created by a set of political decisions in the past and it can be shaped by political decisions taken in the future.

Torsten Bell, the director of the Resolution Foundation think tank, analysed the voting patterns in the referendum and found that those parts of Britain with the strongest support for Brexit were those that had been poor for a long time. The result was affected by 'deeply entrenched national geographical inequality', he said. There has been much lazy thinking in the past quarter of a century about globalization. As Bell notes, it is time to rethink the assumption that a 'flexible, globalised economy can generate prosperity that is widely shared'.[9] Self-evidently, large numbers of people across Europe do not believe a flexible, globalized economy is working for them. One response to the Brexit vote from the rest of Europe has been that a tough line should be taken with Britain to show other countries that dissent has consequences. This would only make matters worse. Voters have legitimate grievances about an economic system that has failed them. Punishing Britain will not safeguard the EU. It will hasten its dissolution.

For those who had supported the successful Leave campaign, the immediate euphoria of the morning of 24 June was soon replaced by a gnawing anxiety that 'the establishment', however defined, would somehow overturn the result of the referendum. Reasons to be fearful were not hard to find. The High Court ruled that Parliament – both houses of which had a majority of Remain supporters – would have to consent to the triggering of the two-year Article 50 process that would see Britain leave the EU.

The Court of Appeal, to no-one's great surprise, agreed. Meanwhile, suggestions abounded that the vote had been only advisory, or even a very expensive opinion poll, and could be disregarded. And, as Britain's new prime minister Theresa May ploughed on with her 'Brexit means Brexit' agenda, diehard Remainers dug into a last ditch: the 'second referendum', which would give the public a vote on the departure terms. For a while, the Remainers seemed quite chipper. 'Brexiteers, stop twitching!' bellowed the former deputy prime minister Nick Clegg in the *Evening Standard* on 8 November 2016. 'The Government has a mandate to pull the UK out of the EU. It has no mandate on how to do so. Parliament has every right to be involved at the outset – and the people have a right to have their say at the end.'

What Mr Clegg didn't quite say, but which was his party's policy, was that the people's 'say' would include an option to remain in the EU. To overturn the first vote, in other words. Those who think as Clegg does may retort that the final shape of Brexit is uncertain. Indeed it is: it was at the time of the referendum, and remains so today. But similarly uncertain would have been the outcome of David Cameron's negotiations, given it had to be approved by MEPs, would have been adjudicated by the European Court of Justice, and that a key part of it would have been entirely dependent on future treaty negotiations that were not even on the horizon. It is possible, of course, that in the event of a Remain outcome at the referendum Mr Clegg would have nevertheless insisted that the British people be given a second vote to make sure they approved whatever would have ultimately emerged from Cameron's negotiations. But we think it unlikely.

In the face of legal and parliamentary opposition, Theresa May met her deadline of triggering Article 50 by the end of March, and shortly thereafter called a general election, victory in which would strengthen her negotiating hand during the Brexit negotiations. The Liberal Democrats sought to appeal to Remain voters by pledging to hold a second referendum before the UK actually left the EU so that public judgement could be passed on the deal struck. Somewhat surprisingly, this was not the secret weapon the Liberal Democrats had been seeking since their near wipeout in the 2015 elections. Opinion polls showed that half of those who had voted Remain accepted the result and thought the UK should get on with seeking to make a success of Brexit.

By the time May called the 2017 general election, it was taken as a given that Britain was leaving the EU. Even the strongest Brexit supporters accepted that the uncertainty caused by the divorce proceedings would hurt the economy in the short term. Indeed, there was evidence of this in the first few months of 2017 when the post-referendum fall in the value of sterling led to dearer imports and weaker consumer spending. Yet, for years if not decades, Britain has struggled to cope with the impact of an overvalued pound, leading to an economy that consumed too much and produced too little. The boost to UK manufacturing from a more competitive pound was proof that whilst leaving the EU would be a shock, there were reasons to envisage Britain working out a way to thrive.

The election outcome itself would have been considered inconceivable at the start of the five weeks of campaigning that followed the dissolution of parliament on 3 May. With Theresa May and her Conservatives enjoying enormous opinion-poll leads over Jeremy Corbyn's Labour Party, the scene seemed to be set for a repeat of Margaret Thatcher's 1983 landslide victory when Labour was similarly led by a left-leaning figure, Michael Foot. Indeed, given Foot had been a cabinet minister whereas Corbyn had never held any government position, it was entirely possible that the Tories could outshine their electoral achievement of thirty-four years earlier.

Even as the prime minister proved both a poor campaigner 'on the stump' and an inept strategist, in effect having to ditch a key policy on the funding of social care after it appeared in the manifesto, a comfortable, even impressive win was still thought likely. Now the comparison was not with 1983 but 1987, when Thatcher had defied sometimes-adverse opinion polls and a general view that the Conservative Party's campaign was less slick and professional than that of Labour to bag a majority of 102 seats.

In the event, 8 June proved to be neither 1983 nor 1987 but February 1974, the last time the voters returned a hung parliament and a prime minister had to govern from a minority position. Corbyn's Labour Party had performed surprisingly well, picking up thirty-four seats, although still going down in its third defeat in a row.

Had Labour campaigned against Brexit, the Tories, even with the working majority achieved by a pact with the ten MPs of the Democratic Unionist Party, could have faced serious difficulties implementing the result of 23 June 2016. But Labour, too, had campaigned on a Brexit-supporting platform, albeit somewhat more nuanced. Thus, out of a total of 650 MPs, the new House of Commons comprised at least 580 who had been elected on party programmes in favour of Brexit. Of course, many on the Labour side, and some Conservatives, resented having been conscripted to the Brexit cause. But it is worth remembering that the three parties demanding a second referendum on EU membership – the Liberal Democrats, the Scottish National Party and the Greens – did not fare well on election day.

Paradoxically, however, this overwhelmingly pro-Brexit legislature was more likely than not to modify the so-called 'hard Brexit' position taken by May and her colleagues. Whether this simply means a longer-than-expected transition period as the UK departs, or involves more substantial concessions, such as a continuing financial contribution to the EU in return for a trade deal or some oversight role for the EU in relation to such a deal, remains, at the time of writing, to be seen.

What we do know is that UK withdrawal can be a new beginning, a chance to start thinking afresh.

Far from being the trigger for national economic armageddon, Brexit provides an opportunity to deal with some of Britain's long-

standing economic problems. There is no guarantee that this opportunity will be taken, and Britain's recent economic history is littered
with missed chances and wrong turnings. But for good or ill, Brexit
will result in change. It is still early days but some of the initial signs
have been relatively promising. The government eased the pace of
austerity in favour of a more realistic and growth-friendly deficit-
reduction plan. May announced a new industrial strategy to ensure
that growth was more evenly spread across the UK.

So, after a period of adjustment, we expect Brexit to turn out
well. In part, that's because Britain's relationship with the EU has
become more uneasy. In part, it is because there is no realistic prospect of the EU getting its act together in the way that Macron hopes.
But in another way, it's because there is now an opportunity to do
all sorts of things that hitherto have not been possible: to rebalance
the economy; to reduce food bills by scrapping the Common
Agricultural Policy; to provide more help for infant industries
through more generous state aid; to take advantage of the freedom
to change VAT rates.

As we said in the first chapter of this book, there is a profound
difference between the Anglo-Saxon model of capitalism and the
continental model. The continental model is top-down and elite-
led; technocrats come up with a blueprint and insist it can be made
to work even when the evidence suggests otherwise. The Anglo-
Saxon model tends to be more bottom-up, a matter of trial and
error.

On 23 June 2016, 52 per cent of British voters – more than 17
million – decided that forty-three years was a long enough trial and
that membership of the EU was an error. They decided that Europe
didn't work.

ENDNOTES

1 The real thing

1. Barry Eichengreen, *The European Economy Since 1945: Coordinated Capitalism and Beyond,* Princeton University Press, 2006, 3.
2. John Palmer, 'The Case for Joining', in M. Kettle et al., *The Single Currency: Should Britain Join?*, Vintage, 1997, 15.
3. Tony Judt, *Postwar: A History of Europe Since 1945*, Heinemann, 2005, 799.
4. Mark Leonard, *Why Europe Will Run the 21st Century*, Fourth Estate, 2005, 11–12.
5. Larry Elliott and Dan Atkinson, *The Age of Insecurity*, Verso, 1998.
6. Paul Ormerod, *Why Most Things Fail: Evolution, Extinction and Economics*, Faber & Faber, 2005.
7. Steven Bach, *Final Cut: Dreams and Disaster in the Making of* Heaven's Gate, Cape, 1985.
8. Kathleen McNamara, 'This is What Economists Don't Understand About the Euro Crisis – or the U.S. Dollar', *Washington Post*, 21 July 2015.
9. Jean Monnet, *Memoirs,* Collins, 1978, 293.
10. Tommaso Padoa-Schioppa, *The Euro and its Central Bank: Getting United After the Union,* MIT Press, 2004, 14.
11. Romano Prodi, interview with the *Financial Times*, 4 December 2001.
12. European Commission, 'The Five Presidents' Report: Completing Europe's Economic and Monetary Union', 22 June 2015, available at: https://ec.europa.eu/priorities/sites/beta-political/files/5-presidents-report_en.pdf
13. Ibid., 4.
14. Enrico Spolaore, 'Monnet's Chain reaction and the Future of Europe', VoxEU.org, 25 July 2015, available at: www.voxeu.org/article/monnet-s-chain-reaction-and-future-europe
15. Tony Benn, *Against the Tide: Diaries 1973–76*, Hutchinson, 1989, 341.
16. Ibid., 346.

17. Luigi Guiso, Paola Sapienza and Luigi Zingales, 'Monnet's Error?', paper presented at the Brookings Panel on Economic Activity, 11–12 September 2014, 32.
18. Lars Jonung and Eoin Drea, 'The Euro: It Can't Happen. It's a Bad Idea. It Won't Last: US Economists on the EMU, 1989–2002', European Commission Economic Papers 395 (December 2009), available at: http://ec.europa.eu/economy_finance/publications/publication16345_en.pdf
19. European Commission, 'Quarterly Report on the Euro Area', 12:4 (2013), available at: https://issuu.com/iosonoconsapevole/docs/qrea4_en
20. Ibid., 9.
21. Ibid., 14.
22. Ibid.
23. Ibid., 15.
24. Roger Bootle, *The Trouble with Europe: Why the EU Isn't Working, How it Can Be Reformed, What Could Take its Place*, Nicholas Brealey Publishing, 2015.
25. Stephen King, 'The Euro and the Three Musketeers', HSBC, September 2014.
26. Wolfgang Streeck, 'Why the Euro Divides Europe', *New Left Review* 95 (September–October 2015), available at: https://newleftreview.org/II/95/wolfgang-streeck-why-the-euro-divides-europe

2 'A burning building with no exits'

1. *Observer*, 23 August 2015.
2. *Daily Telegraph*, 7 July 2015.
3. Washington Report, 'Delors and the Euro', *Journal of Commerce*, 12 May 1996, available at: www.joc.com/washington-report-delors-and-euro_19960512.html
4. Bernard Connolly, *The Rotten Heart of Europe,* Faber & Faber, 1995.
5. *Nikkei Asian Review*, 15 September 2014, available at: http://asia.nikkei.com/Features/Jean-Claude-Trichet/Jean-Claude-Trichet-15-Sleepless-nights-and-the-defense-of-the-franc
6. *Guardian*, 19 August 1995.
7. Doug Henwood, *Wall Street: How It Works and For Whom,* Verso, 1997.
8. John Laughland, *The Tainted Source: The Undemocratic Origins of the European Idea*, Little, Brown, 1997.
9. *Guardian*, 11 February 1991.
10. Laughland, *Tainted Source*.
11. 'European Social Dialogue: 30 Years of Experience and Progress, But What Does the Future Hold?', Notre Europe Policy Paper 124, 26 January 2015, available at: www.institutdelors.eu/media/europeansocialdialogue-lapeyre-jdi-jan15.pdf?pdf=ok
12. Charles Grant, *Delors: Inside the House that Jacques Built,* Nicholas Brealey Publishing, 1994, 154.
13. Douglas Hurd, *An End to Promises: Sketch of a Government 1970–74*, Collins, 1979.
14. Grant, *Delors*, 156.
15. Cynthia A. Beltz, 'Lessons from the Cutting Edge: The HDTV Experience', *Cato Review of Business and Government* 16:4 (1993), 32.

16. Ibid., 33.
17. John Gillingham, *European Integration, 1958–2003: Superstate or New Market Economy?*, Cambridge University Press, 2003, 246.
18. Hansard, 25 November 1987.
19. Bruce Millan, address to the European Parliament, 26 March 1992, available at: http://europa.eu/rapid/press-release_IP-92-227_en.htm
20. Jacques Delors, presentation of the Commission's Programme, *Bulletin of the European Communities*, 1985.
21. Margaret Thatcher, interview in *The Times*, 26 October 1988.
22. Margaret Thatcher, statement in the House of Commons, 6 December 1988, available at: http://hansard.millbanksystems.com/commons/1988/dec/06/european-council-rhodes#S6CV0143P0_19881206_HOC_182
23. Gian Paolo Manzella and Carlos Mendez, 'The Turning Points of EU Cohesion Policy', European Commission Report Working Paper, 2009, available at: http://ec.europa.eu/regional_policy/archive/policy/future/pdf/8_manzella_final-formatted.pdf
24. Marjorie Jouen, 'The "Cohesion Pact": Weathering the Crisis', Notre Europe Policy Paper 52, 12 April 2012, 8, available at: www.institutdelors.eu/media/cohesionpolicy_m.jouen_notreeurope_april2012.pdf?pdf=ok
25. 'Report on Economic and Monetary Union in the European Community', 17 April 1989, 7, available at: http://aei.pitt.edu/1007/1/monetary_delors.pdf
26. Ibid., 14.
27. Robert Harvey, *Global Disorder: The New Architecture of Global Security*, Constable, 2003.
28. Connolly, *Rotten Heart*, 9.
29. Ibid.
30. Laughland, *Tainted Source*.

3 The French vice

1. Charles de Gaulle, press conference, Élysée Palace, 4 February 1965, quoted in Peter L. Bernstein, *The Power of Gold: The History of an Obsession*, John Wiley & Sons, Inc., 2000, 329.
2. Ibid., 330.
3. Ibid., 174.
4. 'Gold Demand Trends: Full Year 2014', World Gold Council, February 2015, available at: www.gold.org/download/file/3691/GDT_Q4_2014.pdf
5. John Laughland, *The Tainted Source: The Undemocratic Origins of the European Idea*, Little, Brown, 1997.
6. David Sinclair, *The Pound: A Biography – The Story of the Currency That Ruled the World and Lasted a Thousand Years*, Century, 2000.
7. Bill Bonner and Addison Wiggin, *Empire of Debt: The Rise of an Epic Financial Crisis*, John Wiley & Sons, Inc., 2005.
8. Sumit Roy, 'Gold Has Held Its Value Over The Last 2,500 Years: Fact Or Fiction?', etf.com, available at: www.etf.com/sections/features-and-news/4690-gold-has-held-its-value-over-the-last-2500-years-fact-or-fiction?nopaging=1
9. Niall Ferguson, *The Cash Nexus: Money and Power in the Modern World, 1700–2000*, Allen Lane, 2001, 323.

10. Bernstein, *Power of Gold*, 239.
11. Ferguson, *Cash Nexus*, 330.
12. David Kynaston, *City of London: The History*, Chatto & Windus, 2011, 207.
13. Ferguson, *Cash Nexus*, 325–6.
14. Douglas Jay, *Sterling: Its Use and Misuse: A Plea for Moderation*, Sidgwick & Jackson, 1985, 79.
15. Laughland, *Tainted Source*.
16. Bernstein, *Power of Gold*, 297.
17. Ibid.
18. Kynaston, *City of London*, 313.
19. Ibid., 366.
20. Bernstein, *Power of Gold*, 323.
21. Robert Skidelsky, *John Maynard Keynes 1883–1946*, Pan Books, 2004, 676.
22. Bernstein, *Power of Gold*, 329.
23. Ibid., 330.
24. World Gold Council, 'Gold Demand', available at: www.gold.org/supply-and-demand/demand
25. Laughland, *Tainted Source*.
26. 'The European Monetary System', European Commission, available at: http://ec.europa.eu/economy_finance/euro/emu/road/ems_en.htm
27. Bernard Connolly, *The Rotten Heart of Europe*, Faber & Faber, 1995, 5.
28. Harold Wilson, *Final Term: The Labour Government 1974–1976*, Weidenfeld & Nicolson/Michael Joseph, 1979, 3.
29. Connolly, *Rotten Heart*, 19.
30. Ibid.
31. Charles Grant, *Delors: Inside the House that Jacques Built*, Nicholas Brealey Publishing, 1994, 59.
32. 'Report on Economic and Monetary Union in the European Community', 17 April 1989, emphasis in original, available at: http://aei.pitt.edu/1007/1/monetary_delors.pdf
33. Ibid., 32.
34. Ibid., 22.
35. Connolly, *Rotten Heart*, 254.
36. Ferguson, *Cash Nexus*, 105–6.
37. Consolidated Version of the Treaty on the Functioning of the European Union, Part 5, The Union's External Action, Title V, International Agreements, Article 219, available at: http://eur-lex.europa.eu/legal-content/EN/TXT/?uri=CELEX:12012E219
38. Ann Pettifor, 'Why the Euro is the Gold Standard Writ Large – and Like the Gold Standard, Will Fail', PRIME (July 2015), available at: www.primeeconomics.org/publications/why-the-euro-is-the-gold-standard-writ-large-and-like-the-gold-standard-will-fail
39. Anthony Annett and Albert Jaeger, 'Europe's Quest for Fiscal Discipline', *Finance and Development* 41:2 (June 2004), available at: www.imf.org/external/pubs/ft/fandd/2004/06/pdf/annett.pdf
40. Pettifor, 'Why the Euro is the Gold Standard Writ Large', 8.
41. Quoted in Bernstein, *Power of Gold*, 363–4.

4 No end of a lesson

1. David Marsh, *The Euro: The Politics of the New Global Currency*, Yale University Press, 2009, 211.
2. Ibid., 193.
3. Francesco M. Bongiovanni, *The Decline and Fall of Europe*, Palgrave Macmillan, 2012, 116.
4. Ibid., 117.
5. Heiner Flassbeck and Costas Lapavitsas, 'The Systemic Crisis of the Euro – True Causes and Effective Therapies', *Studien* (2013), 7, available at: www.rosalux.de/fileadmin/rls_uploads/pdfs/Studien/Studien_The_systemic_crisis_web.pdf
6. George Soros with Gregor Peter Schmitz, *The Tragedy of the European Union: Disintegration or Revival?*, PublicAffairs, 2014.
7. Paul De Grauwe and Cláudia Costa Storti, 'Is Monetary Policy in the Eurozone Less Effective than in the US?', CESifo Working Paper 1606 (2005), available at: https://ideas.repec.org/p/ces/ceswps/_1606.html
8. Stephen Nickell, 'Comments on "The Effects of EMU on Structural Reforms in Labour and Product Markets" by Romain Duval and Jørgen Elemskov', Bank of England speech, 17 June 2005, available at: www.bankofengland.co.uk/archive/Documents/historicpubs/speeches/2005/speech249.pdf
9. Ibid., 3.
10. Tom Krebs and Martin Scheffel, 'German Labour Reforms: Unpopular Success?', Vox, 20 September 2013, available at: www.voxeu.org/article/german-labour-reforms-unpopular-success
11. Timothy Edmonds, 'The Euro-zone: Early Years and UK Convergence', House of Commons Library Research Paper 02/45 (2002), available at: http://researchbriefings.parliament.uk/ResearchBriefing/Summary/RP02-45
12. Adair Turner, *Between Debt and the Devil: Money, Credit, and Fixing Global Finance*, Princeton University Press, 2015, 156.
13. Romano Prodi, interview with Alan Little, BBC News, 2012, available at: http://www.bbc.co.uk/news/world-europe-16761087
14. 'Euro Area Policies: 2007 Article IV Consultation', IMF Country Report 07/260 (July 2007), available at: www.imf.org/external/pubs/ft/scr/2007/cr07260.pdf
15. 'IMF Multi-Country Report: German-Central European Supply Chain – Cluster Report', IMF Country Report 13/263 (August 2013), available at: https://www.imf.org/external/pubs/ft/scr/2013/cr13263.pdf
16. Matthew Klein, 'The Euro is Pointless', *Financial Times*, 11 November 2015.
17. Marsh, *The Euro*.
18. Flassbeck and Lapavitsas, 'Systemic Crisis'.

5 Ire and ice

1. *OECD Economic Surveys: Iceland*, vol. 2009/16, OECD Publishing, 2009.
2. Richard West, 'Iceland: The Viking Tradition', *Spectator*, 13 February 1982.
3. Max Hastings, *All Hell Let Loose: The World at War 1939–1945*, Harper, 2011, 398.
4. 'The Cod Wars', available at: http://britishseafishing.co.uk/the-cod-wars/
5. 'The Cod Wars', available at: https://guidetoiceland.is/history-culture/the-cod-wars

6. Joe Haines, *The Politics of Power*, Cape, 1977.

7. West, 'Iceland'.

8. 'In Ireland, A Host of Problems', *New York Times*, 4 June 1984.

9. Winston Churchill, *Great Contemporaries*, Odhams, 1947.

10. Michael Booth, *The Almost Nearly Perfect People: The Truth Behind the Nordic Miracle*, Cape, 2014.

11. Richard Douthwaite, *The Growth Illusion: How Economic Growth Has Enriched the Few, Impoverished the Many and Endangered the Planet*, Green Books, 1992, 281, 282.

12. Ibid.

13. Charles Haughey obituary, *The Economist*, 22 June 2006.

14. Dermot McAleese, 'The Celtic Tiger: Origins and Prospects', *Options Politiques* (July–August 2000), 47, available at: http://www.tcd.ie/ Economics/staff/dmcleese/Web/mcaleese.pdf

15. Ibid.

16. Ibid., 48.

17. Ibid., 46.

18. Cormac Lucey, *Plan B: How Leaving the Euro Can Save Ireland*, Gill & Macmillan Ltd, 2014.

19. McAleese, 'Celtic Tiger', 49.

20. Robert H. Wade and Silla Sigurgeirsdóttir, 'Iceland's Rise, Fall, Stabilisation and Beyond', *Cambridge Journal of Economics* 36:1 (2011), 131, available at: http://cje.oxfordjournals.org/content/36/1/127.full.pdf+html

21. Ibid.

22. Martin Hart-Landsberg, 'Lessons from Iceland: Capitalism, Crisis, and Resistance', *Monthly Review* 65:5 (October 2013), available at: http:// monthlyreview.org/2013/10/01/lessons-iceland/

23. Wade and Sigurgeirsdóttir, 'Iceland's Rise', 135.

24. Magnús Sveinn Helgason, 'The "Corporate Vikings" ', *Reykjavik Grapevine*, 21 July 2010, available at: http://grapevine.is/mag/articles/2010/07/21/ the-corporate-vikings/

25. Ibid.

26. Wade and Sigurgeirsdóttir, 'Iceland's Rise', 129.

27. Ibid., 130.

28. Arwin G. Zeissler, Daisuke Ikeda and Andrew Metrick, 'Ireland and Iceland in Crisis: Similarities and Differences', Yale Program on Financial Stability Case Study 2014-4D-V1 (December 2014), available at: http:// papers.ssrn.com/sol3/papers.cfm?abstract_id=2579081

29. Ibid.

30. Ibid.

31. Ibid.

32. 'Iceland: An Example for Greece to Follow?', European Economics Update, 13 May 2015.

33. Zeissler, Ikeda and Metrick, 'Ireland and Iceland in Crisis'.

34. Hart-Landsberg, 'Lessons from Iceland'.

35. Zeissler, Ikeda and Metrick, 'Ireland and Iceland in Crisis'.

36. Paul Krugman, 'Peaks, Troughs, and Crisis', *New York Times*, 3 July 2012.

37. David Howden, 'Iceland Versus Ireland: Lessons from the Banking Crisis', Institute of Economic Affairs, 25 October 2013, available at: www.iea.org. uk/blog/iceland-versus-ireland-lessons-from-the-banking-crisis

38. Ibid.

39. 'Iceland: An Example'.
40. John Maynard Keynes, 'National Self-Sufficiency', 1933, available at: www.panarchy.org/keynes/national.1933.html

6 A bullet dodged

1. Peter Mandelson, *The Third Man: Life at the Heart of New Labour*, HarperPress, 2010, 329.
2. Anthony Seldon, *Blair Unbound*, Simon & Schuster, 2007, 32.
3. 'The Rise and Fall of Tony Blair', two-part television series, Channel 4, broadcast June 2007.
4. 'John Monks' New Year Message', available at: www.tuc.org.uk/about-tuc/john-monks-new-years-message-8
5. Andrew Rawnsley, column in the *Observer*, 31 January 1999.
6. *UK Membership of the Single Currency: An Assessment of the Five Economic Tests*, HM Treasury Report CM 5776, TSO, 2003, available at: http://news.bbc.co.uk/1/shared/spl/hi/europe/03/euro/pdf/final_assessment/03_1100.pdf
7. Will Hutton, 'If Only Britain Had Joined the Euro', *Guardian*, 13 June 2013.
8. Simon Wren-Lewis, 'How Knowledge Transmission Should Work', Mainly Macro blogpost, June 2013, available at: http://mainlymacro.blogspot.co.uk/2013/07/how-knowledge-transmission-should-work.html
9. Seldon, *Blair Unbound*, 213.
10. Maurice Obstfeld, 'Finance at Center Stage: Some Lessons of the Euro Crisis', European Economy Economic Papers 493 (April 2013), 7, available at: http://ec.europa.eu/economy_finance/publications/economic_paper/2013/pdf/ecp493_en.pdf
11. Paul Krugman, 'Rationality and the Euro', *New York Times*, 6 July 2013.
12. *World Economic Outlook October 2012: Coping with High Debt and Sluggish Growth*, International Monetary Fund Publication Services, 2012.
13. Tony Benn, *Against the Tide: Diaries 1973–76*, Hutchinson, 1989, 343.
14. Ed Balls, *Euro-Monetarism: Why Britain Was Ensnared and How It Should Escape*, Fabian Society, 1992.
15. Ed Balls, 2002 Cairncross Lecture, 4 December 2002, available at: www.edballs.co.uk/blog/speeches-articles/why-the-five-economic-tests-my-2002-cairncross-lecture-4th-december-2002/
16. Robert Peston, *Brown's Britain: How Gordon Runs the Show*, Short Books, 2005, 228.
17. Hugo Young, 'A Tight Treasury Fist Still Grips Our European Future', *Guardian*, 10 June 2003.
18. Sir David Ramsden, 'The Euro: 10th Anniversary of the Assessment of the Five Economic Tests', Mile End Group lecture MEG98, June 2013.
19. Ibid.
20. Wren-Lewis, 'How Knowledge Transmission'.
21. Seldon, *Blair Unbound*, 204.

7 The Sisyphus effect

1. Gerry Rice, press briefing, 14 January 2016, available at: www.imf.org/external/np/tr/2016/tr011416.htm

2. Jeremy Warner, 'IMF Heads Must Roll Over Shameful Greek Failings', *Daily Telegraph*, 27 June 2015.

3. www.cityam.com/232418/greece-accepts-imf-role-in-bailout-programme-as-eurogroup-takes-stock-of-progress

4. Eirini Karamouzi, 'The Argument That Greece Was Granted EEC Accession Prematurely Ignores the Historical Context in Which the Decision Was Made', available at: http://blogs.lse.ac.uk/europpblog/2014/11/25/the-argument-that-greece-was-granted-eec-accession-prematurely-ignores-the-historical-context-in-which-the-decision-was-made/

5. *Foreign Relations of the United States, 1969–1976*, vol. XXX, *Greece; Cyprus; Turkey, 1973–1976*, 2007, available at: https://history.state.gov/historicaldocuments/frus1969-76v30

6. *Der Spiegel*, 10 September 2002.

7. Karamouzi, 'The Argument'.

8. *Foreign Relations of the United States: Greece; Cyprus; Turkey.*

9. *Foreign Relations of the United States, 1977–1980*, vol. XXI, *Cyprus; Turkey; Greece*, 2014, available at: https://s3.amazonaws.com/static.history.state.gov/frus/frus1977-80v21/pdf/frus1977-80v21.pdf

10. Barry Bosworth and Tryphon Kollintzas, 'Economic Growth in Greece: Past Performance and Future Prospects', CEPR Discussion Paper 2852 (March 2001), an updated version of a paper first delivered at a conference in Athens organized by the Bank of Greece and the Brookings Institution, 7–8 December 2000, available at: http://EconPapers.repec.org/RePEc:fth:athebu:134

11. Christos Lyrintzis, 'Greek Politics in the Era of Economic Crisis: Reassessing Causes and Effects', Hellenic Observatory Papers on Greece and Southeast Europe, GreeSE Paper 45 (2011), available at: http://eprints.lse.ac.uk/33826/

12. Bosworth and Kollintzas, 'Economic Growth in Greece'.

13. GDP Statistics from the World Bank, available at: http://knoema.com/mhrzolg/gdp-statistics-from-the-world-bank

14. Bosworth and Kollintzas, 'Economic Growth in Greece'.

15. Bernhard Herz and Angelos Kotios, 'Coming Home to Europe: Greece and the Euro', *Intereconomics* 35:4 (July/August 2000), available at http://50years.intereconomics.eu/coming-home-to-europe-greece-and-the-euro.html. The quotation they include is by Loukas Tsoukalis.

16. http://news.bbc.co.uk/1/hi/business/4012869.stm

17. Lyrintzis, 'Greek Politics', 8.

18. Matt Phillips, The Complete History of the Greek Debt Drama in Charts', Quartz, 30 June 2015, available at: http://qz.com/440058/the-complete-history-of-the-greek-debt-drama-in-charts/

19. 'Greece – 2004 Article IV Consultation: Concluding Statement of the Mission', International Monetary Fund, 14 September 2004, available at: www.imf.org/external/np/ms/2004/091404.htm

20. Lyrintzis, 'Greek Politics', 9.

21. Ibid.

22. Matthew Karnitschnig and Nektaria Stamouli, 'Greece Struggles to Get Citizens to Pay Their Taxes', *Wall Street Journal*, 25 February 2015, available at: www.wsj.com/articles/greece-struggles-to-get-citizens-to-pay-their-taxes-1424867495

23. Manos Matsaganis, Chrysa Leventi and Maria Flevotomou, 'The Crisis and Tax Evasion in Greece: What Are the Distributional Implications?', CESifo Forum 2 (February 2012).
24. Lyrintzis, 'Greek Politics', 10.
25. Matsaganis, Leventi and Flevotomou, 'The Crisis and Tax Evasion'.
26. Lyrintzis, 'Greek Politics', 11.
27. Chris Blackhurst, 'A Greek Tragedy to Send a Shiver Down British Spines', *Evening Standard*, 6 May 2010.
28. Mihalis Panayiotakis, ' "National Unity" in Greece', *Greek Left Review*, 12 November 2011, available at: https://greekleftreview.wordpress.com/2011/11/12/national-unity-in-greece/
29. Lyrintzis, 'Greek Politics', 11.
30. *Bild*, 6 March 2010.
31. Bosworth and Kollintzas, 'Economic Growth in Greece'.
32. www.primeminister.gov.gr/english/2015/07/13/prime-minister-alexis-tsipras-statement-following-the-conclusion-of-the-eurozone-summit/
33. Costas Lapavitsas, 'One Year On, Syriza Has Sold Its Soul For Power', *Guardian*, 25 January 2016.
34. www.secondworldwarhistory.com/world-war-2-statistics.asp
35. Lapavitsas, 'One Year On'.

8 The Italian job

1. House of the Oireachtas, 'Report of the Joint Committee of Inquiry into the Banking Crisis', January 2016, available at: https://inquiries.oireachtas.ie/banking/
2. Perry Anderson, *The New Old World*, Verso, 2009, 330.
3. Ibid., 328.
4. Tommaso Padoa-Schioppa, 'Capital Mobility: Why is the Treaty Not Implemented?', June 1982 address to the Second Symposium of European Banks, Milan.
5. Francesco Giavazzi and Marco Pagano, 'Can Severe Fiscal Contractions be Expansionary? Tales of Two Small European Countries', National Bureau of Economic Research Working Paper 3372 (May 1990), available at: http://www.nber.org/papers/w3372
6. Alberto F. Alesina and Silvia Ardagna, 'Large Changes in Fiscal Policy: Taxes Versus Spending', National Bureau of Economic Research Working Paper 15438 (October 2009), available at: http://www.nber.org/papers/w15438
7. Mark Blyth, *Austerity*, Oxford University Press, 2013.
8. There are good accounts of this by Thomas Fazi (in *The Battle for Europe: How an Elite Hijacked a Continent – and How we Can Take it Back*, Pluto Press, 2014) and Mark Weisbrot (in *Failed: What the 'Experts' Got Wrong About the Global Economy*, Oxford University Press, 2015).
9. Stephen Foley, 'What Price the New Democracy? Goldman Sachs Conquers Europe', *Independent*, 18 November 2011.
10. Yves Smith, 'The ECB's Balance Sheet and Draghi's Confidence Game', Naked Capitalism, available at: www.nakedcapitalism.com/2014/12/ecbs-balance-sheet-draghis-confidence-game.html
11. Foreword by Olivier Blanchard, *World Economic Outlook, September 2011: Slowing Growth, Rising Risks*, International Monetary Fund, September 2011, xiii.

12. Foreword by Olivier Blanchard, *World Economic Outlook, April 2012: Growth Resuming, Dangers Remain*, International Monetary Fund, April 2012, xiii.
13. Matthias Sobolewski and Dina Kyriakidou, 'S&P Downgrades Nine Euro Zone Countries', Reuters, 14 January 2012, available at: http://uk.reuters.com/article/uk-eurozone-sp-idUKTRE80C11V20120114
14. Weisbrot, *Failed*, 34.
15. www.ecb.europa.eu/press/key/date/2012/html/sp120726.en.html

9 Kicking the can

1. 'Conference Report: Has the Euro been a Failure?', Centre for European Reform, 6–7 November 2015, available at: www.cer.org.uk/sites/default/files/Ditchleyreport_11Jan16.pdf
2. OECD Interim Economic Forecasts, February 2016, available at: www.oecd.org/economy/elusive-global-growth-outlook-requires-urgent-policy-response.htm
3. Charles Grant and John Springford, 'Deal Done: Now for the Hard Work', Centre for European Reform, 20 February 2016, available at: www.cer.org.uk/insights/deal-done-now-hard-work
4. Fintan O'Toole, 'Only When it is in Peril is the Idea of Europe So Inspiring' *Observer*, 21 February 2016.
5. Peter Mandelson, 'Cameron's Deal is a Chance to Make the EU Work. Seize It', *Guardian*, 23 February 2016.
6. Robert Mundell, 'A Theory of Optimum Currency Areas', *American Economic Review* 51:4 (September 1961), 657–65.
7. Barry Eichengreen, 'Is Europe an Optimum Currency Area?', NBER Working Paper 3579, available at: www.nber.org/papers/w3579.pdf
8. European Commission, 'The Five Presidents' Report: Completing Europe's Economic and Monetary Union', 4, 22 June 2015, available at: https://ec.europa.eu/priorities/sites/beta-political/files/5-presidents-report_en.pdf
9. UBS, 'The Future of Europe', 13 January 2016, available at: www.fundresearch.de/sites/default/files/partnercenter/UBS/News/news_2016/European%20economy_en_1217027.pdf
10. Paul De Grauwe, 'The Euro and Schengen: Common Flaws and Common Solutions', Ivory Tower blog, 23 November 2015, available at: http://escoriallaan.blogspot.co.uk/2015/11/the-euro-and-schengen-common-flaws-and.html
11. Dani Rodrik, 'The Future of European Democracy', Institute of Advanced Studies, December 2014, available at: www.sss.ias.edu/files/pdfs/Rodrik/Commentary/Future-of-Democracy-in-Europe.pdf
12. Paul De Grauwe, 'Design Flaws in the Eurozone: Can They Be Fixed?', LSE 'Europe in Question' Discussion Paper Series 57/2013 (February 2013), available at: www.lse.ac.uk/europeanInstitute/LEQS%20Discussion%20Paper%20Series/LEQSPaper57.pdf
13. Christian Odendahl, 'We Don't Need No Federation: What a Devolved Euro-Zone Should Look Like', Centre for European Reform, December 2015, available at: www.cer.org.uk/sites/default/files/rp_eurozone_co_2dec15.pdf
14. De Grauwe, 'Design Flaws'.

15. Poul M. Thomsen, 'Greece: Toward a Workable Program', IMF Direct, 11 February 2016, available at: https://blog-imfdirect.imf.org/2016/02/11/greece-toward-a-workable-program/

16. Ibid.

17. David Marsh, *The Euro: The Politics of the New Global Currency*, Yale University Press, 2009, 255.

18. Adam Tooze, *The Deluge: The Great War, America and the Remaking of the Global Order, 1916–1931*, Allen Lane, 2014.

10 The end of the affair

1. Robin Cook, *The Point of Departure: Why One of Britain's Leading Politicians Resigned over Tony Blair's Decision to Go to War in Iraq*, Simon & Schuster, 2003.

2. www.pes.eu/jobs#middle

3. Ambrose Evans-Pritchard, 'German Euro Founder Calls For "Catastrophic" Currency To Be Broken Up', *Daily Telegraph*, 5 May 2013.

4. Aditya Chakrabortty, 'Greece is a Sideshow. The Eurozone has Failed, and Germans are its Victims Too', *Guardian*, 22 June 2015.

5. Bojan Bugarič, 'Europe Against the Left? On Legal Limits to Progressive Politics', London School of Economics 'Europe in Question' Discussion Paper Series 61/2013 (May 2013), available at: www.lse.ac.uk/europeanInstitute/LEQS%20Discussion%20Paper%20Series/LEQSPaper61.pdf

6. Charles Grant, *Delors: Inside the House that Jacques Built*, Nicholas Brealey Publishing, 1994.

7. Ibid., 127.

8. Committee for the Study of Economics and Monetary Union, 'Report on Economic and Monetary Union in the Eropean Community', presented 17 April 1989, 11.

9. Sam Aaronovitch, *The Road from Thatcherism: The Alternative Economic Strategy*, Lawrence & Wishart, 1981.

10. John Pilger, *Hidden Agendas*, Vintage, 1998, 520.

11. Andy McSmith, *Faces of Labour: The Inside Story*, Verso, 1996, 102.

12. Grant, *Delors*, 59.

13. 'Monetary Policy: Chancellor of the Exchequer minute to MT ("Exchange Control")', 11 October 1979, available at: www.margaretthatcher.org/document/128061

14. Rawi Abdelal, 'Writing the Rules of Global Finance: France, Europe, and Capital Liberalization', *Review of International Political Economy* 13:1 (February 2006), 7.

15. Ibid., 11.

16. Francesco Paolo Mongelli, 'European Economic and Monetary Integration and the Optimum Currency Area Theory', European Economy Economic Papers 302 (February 2008), available at: http://ec.europa.eu/economy_finance/publications/publication12081_en.pdf

17. Paul Blustein, *Misadventures of the Most Favored Nations: Clashing Egos, Inflated Ambitions, and the Great Shambles of the World Trade System*, Perseus Books, 2009, 35.

18. 'Lamy Hits Back at Critics', *Guardian*, 29 October 2003.

19. http://europa.eu/rapid/press-release_SPEECH-91-5_en.htm

20. Eiko Thielemann, 'Driving a Wedge between Europe and the Regions? EC State-Aid Control Meets German Federalism', Regional and Industrial Policy Research Papers, No.30, EPRC, Glasgow.
21. William E. Paterson and Gordon Smith, eds, *The West German Model: Perspectives on a Stable State*, Frank Cass & Company, 1981.
22. Otmar Issing, FAZ lecture, 20 September 1999, available at: https://www.ecb.europa.eu/press/key/date/1999/html/sp990920_content.en.html
23. Maurice Obstfeld, *Europe's Gamble*, Brookings Papers on Economic Activity 2:1997, available at: www.brookings.edu/~/media/Projects/BPEA/1997-2/1997b_bpea_obstfeld_alesina_cooper.PDF
24. Anton Hemerijck, *Changing Welfare States*, Oxford University Press, 2013, 131.
25. Amy Verdun, 'Economic and Monetary Integration in the European Union: The Role of Experts in Creating an "Asymmetrical EMU"', delivered at the ECSA Conference, Charleston, South Carolina, May 1995, available at: http://aei.pitt.edu/7309/1/002988_1.pdf
26. Adair Turner, 'Hubris, Realism and the European Project', *CER Bulletin* 100 (February/March 2015), available at: www.cer.org.uk/sites/default/files/publications/attachments/pdf/2015/bulletin_100_at_article3-10514.pdf
27. John Laughland, *The Tainted Source: The Undemocratic Origins of the European Idea*, Little, Brown, 1997.
28. Andrew Marr, 'Start the Week', BBC Radio 4, 2 April 2012.
29. Hugh Gaitskell, speech at the Labour Party Conference, Brighton, 3 October 1962.
30. Peter Shore, *Separate Ways: Britain and Europe*, Gerald Duckworth & Co., 2000.
31. Denis Healey, *When Shrimps Learn to Whistle*, Penguin, 1990.

Epilogue: Still not working: The view from 2017

1. Guglielmo Verdirame, 'How the EU Elite Paved the Way for Populism', *Standpoint*, April 2017.
2. www.theguardian.com/politics/2013/jan/22/eu-referendum-2017-david-cameron
3. *Britain's New Deal in Europe* (HMSO, 1975).
4. www.huffingtonpost.co.uk/2016/06/25/the-waugh-zone-june-25-20_0_n_10668590.html
5. Hywel Williams, *Guilty Men: Conservative Decline and Fall 1992–1997*, Aurum Press, 1998.
6. US Department of the Treasury, Office of International Affairs, 'Report to Congress: Foreign Exchange Policies of Major Trading Partners of the United States' (14 April 2017), available at: www.treasury.gov/resource-center/international/exchange-rate-policies/Documents/2017-04-14-Spring-2017-FX-Report-FINAL.PDF
7. Christina Beatty and Steve Fothergill, 'Jobs, Welfare and Austerity: How the Destruction of Industrial Britain Casts a Shadow Over Present-day Public Finances', Sheffield Hallam University, Centre for Regional Economic and Social Research, November 2016, available at: www4.shu.ac.uk/research/cresr/sites/shu.ac.uk/files/cresr30th-jobs-welfare-austerity.pdf

8. www.theguardian.com/business/2016/jun/26/brexit-is-the-rejection-of-globalisation
9. Torsten Bell, 'The Referendum, Living Standards and Inequality', Resolution Foundation, 24 June 2016, available at: www.resolutionfoundation.org/media/blog/the-referendum-living-standards-and-inequality/

INDEX